We wish you a

Merry Xmas

We wish you a...

and a happy New Year!

Merry Xmas Rob

Lea   Lorisha Luiano*

* blow it out ...

Beppe Severgnini in BUR

English Books

An Italian in America

America reveals itself in the little things. And to discover them,
you need the inquisitiveness of a new arrival and the patience
of a beachcomber, one of those mildly inappropriate individuals
who roam the shores in search of small treasures. The seashore
is America. The mildly inappropriate individual is me.

Saggi - Pages 288 - ISBN 1712553

✧

An Italian in Italy

Ten days, thirty places. From north to south. From food to politics.
From saintliness to sexuality. This ironic, methodical, and sentimental
examination will help you understand why Italy – as Beppe says –
"can have you fuming and then purring in the space
of a hundred meters or ten minutes".

Saggi - Pages 320 - ISBN 1701734

Beppe Severgnini

AN ITALIAN IN BRITAIN

Translated by Kerry Milis

SAGGI

Originally published in Italy as *Inglesi*
by RCS Rizzoli Libri S.p.A., Milan, in 1990
First published in Pocket Edition in 1992
First published in English by RCS Libri S.p.A., Milan, in March 2003
Fourth edition published in September 2008

ISBN 978-88-17-10043-4

Printed in Italy

FOREWORD

I couldn't touch *An Italian in Britain.* It was my first book and I am fond of it. I wrote it between 1988 and 1989, and it was published by Rizzoli in 1990. It was brought up to date only once, in 1992, after the Hodder & Stoughton edition of the previous year, which carried the original title (*Inglesi*), and – much to my surprise – became a bestseller in Britain. In Italy, the book has been reprinted twenty-five times. Now it has been re-translated by Kerry Milis, an American who lived in Britain for many years, to whom I am very grateful.

An Italian in Britain describes the country of Margaret Thatcher as it tried to shake itself out of its post-imperial lethargy. Several years on, I am pleased to see that I sensed its underlying strength – in those days everyone talked about "the British disease" – and predicted a brilliant future (I shouldn't boast but how often does a writer get to say he was right?).

Since my book came out, I've gone back to Britain often. I continue to hang out in Notting Hill and the Reform Club, I occasionally appear on TV and speak on the radio, and I can get any dinner party going by bringing up European monetary union. In 1993, while doing a stint at *The Economist* in London (I've been their Italian correspondent since 1996), I was able to move back into my former house in Kensington. Recently, I went back to London for a short stay and wrote a few more pages about the city. The British still fascinate me, even when I find them hard to understand. I can't tear myself away from them and wouldn't want to.

I have continued to write about them, too. So I thought I might put together a few of these pieces to explain what has changed (Blair has come and Diana has gone, Spice Girls marry football players, the class system is finally showing cracks and in London you eat a lot better). I divided my postscript into two parts. In part one, I offer some thoughts about the "new British", taken mostly from *Corriere della Sera* and *The Economist.* In part two, I have compiled five descriptions of London (from 1993 to 2003) that I hope you will find useful on a visit.

As for everything else – for the eternal Britain, the one that will discover the bidet around 2220 (maybe) – I refer you to the original text. Certain British things fortunately never change.

PREFACE

Beppe Severgnini was a young man not much over twenty scribbling away for a small Crema newspaper when a mutual friend brought him to my attention. I read his pieces and liked them so I phoned their author who was studying for a notary's exam at the time and signed him up at Il Giornale. After a few months of work, he came to me to say he was going back home to resume his studies. A few months later he asked me to take him back. I did, and to get him out of temptation's way, I sent him off to be the London correspondent. I received a lot of criticism for the decision, some of it warranted: to be a correspondent, especially in a capital city like London, you needed experience and Severgnini had none. But I spotted his natural talent and won the argument. Even before he understood the language, the little provincial Severgnini understood the country, its grandeur, its misery, its quirks and vices.

Severgnini stayed in England for four years, and this book is one result. I want to say right away that this is not a rehash of his articles, an operation I've always considered something of a cheat on the reader. This reader may have come across some of the ideas and starting points hidden in Severgnini's articles. But the book is a complete rewriting of his experience and I know few who penetrated so far below the surface. I approached the manuscript with some trepidation because there has already been

11

so much written about England and the English that it is hard to find anything new or original.

Yet Severgnini pulled it off, thanks perhaps to that very lack of experience that allowed him to see a complex country with fresh eyes. One feels that he got inside it and the portrait he paints will probably even please the English who will find in it all those eccentricities and contradictions they play up to underline their diversity.

Something of it stuck to him too, as if it were fated to happen. I don't know of anyone who stays in England very long who isn't affected by the country, especially if they go there when they are young. Many end up apeing the English, something the English loathe. But this didn't happen to Severgnini, who took from them what they all should but few do: the use of understatement and that low-key sense of humour which Italians are in such need of.

INDRO MONTANELLI

Milan, autumn 1989

To Ortensia who accompanied me.

BEYOND MUSEUMS

I spent four years in England and I know the importance of visits from Italy. Experience has taught me that these visits can be divided into pleasurable visits and less pleasurable visits, long visits and short visits, the most demanding visits and relaxed visits. Among the least pleasant, busy and often seemingly interminable visits are the ones paid by the so-called Expert, who arrives equipped with very precise theories and very little experience. As he drags his suitcase through the arrivals hall at Heathrow, he is already explaining England to the natives. This type is living proof of something I've always suspected: the problem with London – one of the few problems – is that Italians think they know it well. It's not only London they think they know. They also think they know the English language, the English, England, and Britain.

I remember a visit like this a while back from a particularly formidable Expert. This chap not only had detailed ideas about post-imperial British decadence and the urban development of London's beltway, but he came armed with a deadly weapon, a Touring Club Italiano guidebook circa 1969. It was a grey hardback from the "Great Cities of the World" series and its title was "Here's London". In 1969 and the years immediately following, the guidebook presented no problems. The researchers at the Touring Club, besides being scrupulous, were also gentlemen. They had no intention of providing the public with a means of torturing Italians living abroad. But by the time my guest withdrew it from his suitcase, his fifteen-year old edition of "Here's London" had become dangerous. Here's why: the Expert was determined to see everything mentioned in the book, even though some of it hadn't existed for more than fifteen years.

A trip down the Thames to Greenwich was particularly enlightening. The Expert, leading us on with guidebook in hand, insisted he wanted to see the "the unvarying multitudes of audacious river-boats, ferries and barges" in the docks of London (page 19) and was irritated when he was told that he would have been able to see the multitudes of boats had they still existed and they would still exist if the docks still existed, but both had disappeared in the seventies, the docks replaced by luxury flats in Docklands inhabited by wealthy architects who passed the time staring out the window through binoculars at Italian tourists passing by with the 1969 Touring Club guide to London in hand. That's when it hit me: maybe the time had come to update the book.

At this point the great American journalist, John Gunther, came to my aid. Many years ago, he suggested a way to write effectively about another country. Write as if it were for a man from Mars, who would want to know the most basic things: How do people live? What do they talk about? How do they have fun? Who's in charge? In other words, don't take anything for granted. This is especially apt for a country like England. Foreigners often arrive full of preconceived ideas: the English are reserved, they love tradition, they like to read, they hate to bathe. Over the course of a few days they discover that everything they thought is true. This discovery generates such euphoria that they go no further. Yet present day Britain should be approached with care. It is still a mysterious island and should be explored as one explores America, with eyes wide open, taking nothing for granted.

To begin with you must remember that no country in the world can be reduced to a city. Britain is not London. Even the things we think we know, from the black cabs to the royal family, change constantly. Many aspects of Britain are fascinating and yet overlooked, like the spectacular pyramid of the class system; the melancholy seaside; the bizarre behaviour of "young fogies", old by choice at twenty; dog races; and the charms of "the season" (Wimbledon, Ascot, and the picnics and opera at Glyndebourne) when the British pretend it's summer.

We can assure the explorer that his efforts will be rewarded. Sixty years ago the English author of one of the innumerable travel books on Italy, E.R.P. Vincent, proved himself a perspicacious visitor with this simple remark: "Italia is not Italy". He was referring to the unchanging country of Botticellis and pergolas that generations of misty-eyed English travellers had described before him. "Italia" he went on, "has a future, Italy does not, it only has a scant present and an immense past. Italia has bitter icy winds, Italy basks in perennial sunshine. Italia is a strange, hard, throbbing land, Italy is accessible, straightforward and very dead." We can turn this around and observe that the Great Britain of parks, red double-decker buses and bobbies does exist.

But there is another Britain, full of silent suburbs and restless minorities, of *nouveaux riches* and old habits. It too is worth study.

Describing this Britain isn't the same as writing a tourist guide. It does mean providing honest information about what has befallen Britain over the last ten years as it come to grips with an onerous past and two prime ministers that no one anticipated. It also means recognising that Britain knows that it can no longer live on its laurels. It must now join the rest of Europe and become a normal European nation. In some cases, it means not taking the British too seriously, any more than they have taken the rest of the world seriously over the centuries.

Like all authors, I have one small hope: that for those of you who keep crossing the Channel to work, to study or to buy a sweater and have finally decided to skip the museums, this book will prove useful. And, who knows, perhaps the British themselves, looking at their image in this book, will discover that they are more interesting than they ever suspected.

WHERE IS BRITAIN HEADING?

For Britain, the eighties were the Margaret Thatcher years, just as the sixties were the Beatles years. The comparison isn't meant to show disrespect either to Beatles fans or to admirers of Mrs Thatcher. The lady, like the lads from Liverpool, left an indelible mark on the country and the British remember her with a mixture of horror and admiration. One thing is certain: she's not likely to be forgotten soon.

At the time of the leadership contest between John Major, Michael Heseltine and Douglas Hurd in November 1990, shortly after Mrs Thatcher's resignation, a class of nine-year-old school children wrote to a newspaper to ask, "Can a man be prime minister?". The answer, as it turned out, was yes. Admittedly John Major, son of an acrobat, has not made much of a mark. Other former prime ministers have already been happily forgotten – James Callaghan, for example, is famous mostly for having made cat's eyes obligatory in the middle of the road.

Not so Margaret Hilda Thatcher. Like Churchill and Elizabeth I before her, she belongs in the category of great leaders. Heroic as the statesman and tempestuous as the queen, she left an indelible mark on post-war Britain. This is not just a result of the length of time she spent in office but of her style of governing. There was no "Wilsonism" after six years of Harold Wilson, just a bit more chaos. After four years of Edward Heath, no one spoke of "Heathism", only of a last ditch effort by the Conservatives to prop up a collapsing country. Yet after only three months of Margaret Thatcher, the term "Thatcherism" was in use. And still is today.

The lady took Britain by storm in 1979 and for the next eleven years she treated the nation with similar delicacy. During the 1980-82 recession, she came up with a revolutionary plan. Instead of stimulating demand, as prevailing economic wisdom dictated, she concentrated on cutting public spending and controlling inflation, and simply ignored the numbers of unemployed, calling them a necessary but passing evil. She argued that you had to produce wealth before you could distribute it and that task was up to the individual. The State had to stand aside and leave the responsibility and decision-making to him.

In Italy, where we were used to prime ministers whose ambition was to get through the summer, we were unnerved by a leader whose ambition was to get into the history books. In Britain, Thatcher's adversaries suffered wounds from which they are only now beginning to recover. To its horror, the Labour Party realised that the lady was not going to be satisfied simply with defeating it at the elections; she meant to convert its followers. Many Conservatives hadn't understood what kind of leader they had nominated and began to invoke Disraeli and his vision of a more compassionate society. The electorate on the other hand picked her three times (1979, 1983 and 1987) and – keep this in mind – never fired her.

Please note that it was her own party that expelled her from Downing Street. Whether they did the right thing, only time will tell. It may be true that Thatcher was authoritarian and ruthless, and that she defended Britain's interests against the rest of the world with an embarrassing vehemence, but it is also true that she alone had the courage to tell the nation to its face what no other prime minister had dared: that Britain may have won the war, but it was behaving as if it had lost. In 1945, poor and exhausted, the country ceased to be a great power and at that point should have begun to transform itself into something else. With her election in 1979, Mrs Thatcher started to badger the country, nanny-like, into facing up to this new reality. She told Britain, one of the greatest imperial powers in history, that there was no shame in competing with the likes of South Korea over the production of cutlery; she told workers that, contrary to what Labour was telling them, not only was it no crime to want to own their own homes, it actually made sense; and she told the public that it was ridiculous to have defeated the Nazis only to be brought down by your own trade unions.

The results of eleven years of Thatcherism can be seen everywhere. Today's Britain is a modern nation, moderately rich, reasonably quiet. It may have left its empire behind but it hasn't abandoned it. Leaders of myriad small countries around the world, members of the Commonwealth, can still have their photos taken in front of Buckingham Palace. Britain's new role was not forced upon it; it was a role Britain itself chose. (The Argentine generals didn't recognise this shift in position in time; as a result of their error they were soundly thrashed in the icy waters of the Falkland Islands.) The turning point for the country came during the winter of discontent in 1978-79 when strikes prevented the dead from being buried and electricity was rationed. Exploiting the changing public mood, Margaret Thatcher seized the opportunity and declared that her values – individual economic initiative, national pride, order and respect for the law – were the values of the middle class and middle class values would be the country's values. She was convincing. The lady had already revealed a quality rare in a politician: she said what she believed. As it turned out, what she believed, three times running, was also what her electorate believed.

Warnings of the approaching storm (for those who knew how to listen) had already sounded in 1975 when Margaret Thatcher was elected leader of the Conservative Party at a time when the Conservatives were in opposition. A few days after her nomination, one of her opponents described the first meeting of the shadow government this way: "As she touched up her hair and hooked her bag on the back of the chair, we were filled with a foreboding of impending calamity". Their foreboding was not unfounded. The Conservative Party of Macmillan and Heath was destined to disappear. Over the next fifteen years Margaret Thatcher completely changed the rules and the goal became one of seducing and winning over the lower-middle classes, from whence she had come, bypassing the traditional elite who claimed to detest her (actually they were rather fond of her, much as the nobility of the past was fond of their stewards: they may not have been likable, but they were still useful and necessary).

Today, the three largest political parties believe they have moved beyond the class system. This, however, is not true. The Labour Party still fishes mainly in working class waters and attracts young people who worry about social justice as they wait to earn a good salary. The Liberal Democrats attract mainly eccentrics, dissatisfied intellectuals, and the young. Only the Conservatives, moulded by the grocer's daughter, then turned over to the son of a trapeze artist, have branched out decisively. Aware that they have only limited support among the upper classes, they have looked for votes wherever they can be found.

Examples of the phenomenon abound. While the central office of the Conservative Party in London's Smith Square may still be full of well-groomed, well-dressed and bejewelled workers looking like they have just come from a party, things are different in other parts of Britain. Take Ealing, a suburb on the outskirts of London. Harry Greenway, the Conservative candidate in a recent campaign, looked like a used car salesman and he talked like a used car salesman. Many of his supporters probably bought used cars. But they were also tenants who had bought their own council houses, thanks to a law passed by the Conservatives, and they were old-age pensioners, convinced that the Labour Party had lost all respect for the police, and they were Pakistani grocers who particularly liked Margaret Thatcher's injunction: make money and your bank account will make you equal.

In Liverpool a group of loyal supporters opened a tearoom called Thatcher's where customers could celebrate that very British ritual under a portrait of the ex-prime minister. The idea enjoyed a modicum of success and showed –

according to the ladies who ran it – two things. One, that the sight of Margaret Thatcher does not turn everyone's stomach and two, that private initiative pays off everywhere, no matter what the opposition says. Neither the proprietors of the tearoom nor its customers were members of the landed gentry. They represented a middle class that has learned to adapt, one that is not convinced that all the troubles suffered in the north of England are the fault of the government.

In the City of London, far from the misery of Liverpool, hymns of thanksgiving were sung daily to the Conservative government in power. That this should have happened in the City was perhaps less surprising than when it happened in Liverpool, but this gratitude did not come just from bond traders hoping to see their earnings grow. After 1979, the year of the first Labour defeat, capital controls were abolished, taxes reduced, trade unions weakened, inflation kept in check and the value of the pound remained stable. The City hopes that with the European Union, Europe will become an enormous supermarket for British financial services. It is no coincidence that the City loves Europe as much as it loves the Conservative Party.

However, even the British who admired Margaret Thatcher most for having turned the nation around, felt little affection for her. The lady didn't seem to have the peccadilloes of the average Englishman or woman and this made the public uneasy. That wasn't all. Mrs Thatcher, unlike milder-mannered John Major, liked to be thought of as uncompromising and ruthless even when she was not (take her cuts in public spending: when all the accounts were added up and settled, they did not turn out to be drastic after all). "After years of self-indulgence, the country needs rigorous and harsh treatment: I will see to it." Over the years this attitude brought her numerous detractors and a slew of poisonous nicknames: the Westminster Ripper, She Who Must Be Obeyed, TBW (That Bloody Woman) and Bossette, this last attributed to Lord Carrington, ex-Secretary General of Nato. "TINA" is another interesting epithet. It is an acronym for There Is No Alternative, a phrase the lady used frequently when she wanted to cut short a conversation about her projects.

The grocer's daughter was of course aware of the feelings she provoked but she could have cared less. Convinced of the rightness of her cause, she simply carried on, going her own sweet way, heedless of the rumbling around her. She refused to consort with the aristocracy, whom she considered out of date. She didn't try to woo the academic establishment. And she shamelessly used the honours list to reward her friends. Each repaid her in kind. The aristocracy admired, detested and feared her. Her *alma mater*, Oxford University, publicly denied her an honorary degree. Her newly be-knighted friends – journalists, industrialists and the occasional trade unionist – are still absolutely devoted to her.

Like France after De Gaulle, Britain after Thatcher will never be the same. Margaret Thatcher terrorised the British, and deep in their hearts, the British admire people who scare them a little. Thanks to her harsh measures, millions of British citizens have rediscovered at least a modicum of the confidence they had lost in the seventies – a time of shabby clothing and poor food – and a commitment to take on history and (possibly) Europe. Even voters who felt a cordial dislike of Margaret Thatcher (and never had the satisfaction of chasing her out of Downing Street) are probably convinced she was a great personage. Of course, they will never admit it. Winston Churchill, when he was thrown out of office at the end of a war won largely by him, said, "A great country has not only the right but the duty to be ungrateful". And Britain, without a doubt, is a great country.

TOO SOON FOR EUROPE?

Even those who loathed her from her first day in office, when she appeared on the steps of No. 10 Downing Street and quoted Saint Francis, admit it: Nanny Thatcher did her utmost to change the country. And she was mostly successful. However, there are still many British who are not persuaded that the country was on the road to ruin in the seventies and don't believe the prime minister's harsh medicine was completely necessary. Even if they won't say it, many people are convinced that being the oldest democracy in the world and having once had the world's largest empire gives Britain a certain superiority. And superior people, they reckon, can dig themselves out of any hole.

In this case they would be wrong. Thatcherism was a blast in the ears of those sound asleep in their cabins as the ship was sinking (though maybe gratitude is too much to expect when you've been woken up in that manner). Pre-Thatcher Britain was not a nation, it was a church. Every tradition and every institution – industry, the trade unions, universities, the civil service – was sacred and untouchable. This was the mentality the lady pitted herself against when she took over as leader of the Conservative Party on February 11th, 1975 and she never let up until she handed the queen her resignation on November 22nd, 1990. If she made mistakes, it was by displaying bad manners and occasionally going too far. The majority of the British were able to digest privatisation, but they didn't want to see every public service privatised. The London Underground – old, crowded and dangerous – is a prime example.

A rejection of some of the hardships under Thatcher, however, shouldn't be used to justify a return to the past. And yet the temptation must be there. The English, who have always had a horror of novelty, are quite capable of returning to their old habits. A deeply conservative people, they don't want to change the things that work, like the radio, television, the mail, or the civil service. They are right. These are indeed excellent institutions and could serve as examples for the rest of Europe. But whether from laziness or arrogance, the English don't want to change the things that do need changing either. The belief that they have had the best and been the best is hard to overcome.

Thus, the country is full of workers who work reluctantly and incompetently (the British Journal of Industrial Relations makes this claim and anyone who has had to deal with a plumber in London can put it to the test). Britain is a country full of houses with old bathrooms without windows or showers but with sinks that have separate hot and cold water taps. Its old schools spew out the worst prepared students in Europe – something even the British themselves will admit, from the Ministry of Education on down. Pubs, which have been allowed to stay open all day since 1988, are often forced to go back to their old closing times because their customers refuse to cross their thresholds during the extra opening hours.

In their resistance to change, old school Conservatives often found themselves siding with the Labour Party. The Conservatives feared that Thatcher's innovations would force them to change and they were also afraid of the money and style displayed by the new rich. The Labour Party was terrified that the working class would turn away from ideology and instead begin to buy little houses in droves. As it turned out, that fear was justified. The number of Labour voters who crossed over to the Conservative Party, especially the C2 band consisting of skilled workers and artisans, led to Thatcher's domination of the eighties and won John Major the election in 1992.

However, if the new prime minister does not have the resolve of Thatcher, her reforms could even now be reversed. Certainly the two biggest parties – Conservative and Labour – might be tempted to recreate the comfortable world in which they previously co-existed, taking it in turn to govern the country (the same temptation with the same motivation exists in Italy between certain Christian Democrats and certain ex-Communists). Little Englanders, isolationist and fearful of change, are ready for the attack. With their 1910 mindset, their 1940's rhetoric and their 1970's clothes, they believe the post-Thatcher era is their last chance to return to the England of yore. I met up with some of these people at the end of 1990 during a television program in Birmingham. I asked them if this love for tradition might possibly be a bit exaggerated. One of them stood up and in an impeccable accent, said "But the Englishman is God!". And so, please, no criticism.

Such conservatism, which is in the blood, would be a blessing if it were contained and controlled.

The British, for example, have a sense of tradition and a respect for institutions which is the envy of all sensible Italians. The trouble starts when the love for everything old and familiar becomes a fear of all that is new and unknown. One sometimes feels that the class system, target number one of the Thatcher revolution, survives simply because it always has. The writer Martin Amis redeems his overwrought novel *London Fields* with an acute observation: "Not even a nuclear holocaust can change the class system". He may be right. Recently a judge of the High Court in London, following an appeal filed by the Duke of Westminster, the owner of Grosvenor Estates, was required to rule on whether the working class still exists. Not surprisingly, he concluded that it was alive and well.

The class system, as we will see, continues because everyone seems content with things the way they are. The upper class is pleased with its eccentricities, real or imagined. The middle class is happy with its manicured gardens. The working class is content watching football on television and looking at photos of half-naked girls in the tabloids. No one wants change. If a working class Italian spotted a beautiful car he'd say, "I'd like one like that". The English worker would simply mutter, "Rich man's car". The middle class Italian would be delighted with an invitation to a wedding full of important people; it would be the subject of conversation for weeks. His English counterpart would suffer through the ceremony, longing to escape to a pub with his wife. In Italy people are stressed, but they work, they have arguments, they are active. In Britain too many are quiet and complacent, content with things the way they are and the way they have always been.

There is little doubt that *the past* in Britain is turning into an obsession. Every week a new museum opens. This must be a world record and it's not necessarily a good one. While other countries produce goods, the United Kingdom serves up tradition. Many have criticised this tendency to mummify the country but they're ignored. As we said before, Margaret Thatcher often came up against this resistance to change. Each time it was necessary to introduce something new, the country rose up in protest. It happened when the pound coin replaced the banknote; it happened when new yellow phone boxes replaced the old red ones; it happened when the new burgundy-coloured passport replaced the old dark blue one, with its hard cover and little window.

The British feel ambivalent about union with Europe for the same reason – because it is *new* and, as we have seen, the British are allergic to new things. It is not impossible that the former resident of 10 Downing Street correctly interpreted the mood of the country when she railed against monetary union and the creeping socialism of Brussels bureaucrats. More liberal British commentators tend to reject that hypothesis. They insist that the British electorate has always been more pro-Europe than its leaders. These commentators talk about Britain's obligation to be a presence in Europe in order to help Italy strike a balance against France and Germany, and they remind listeners of what happened after the Labour Party's 1983 electoral manifesto proposing withdrawal from the Common Market: the Labour Party was soundly trounced in the next elections. Today the manifesto is remembered as "the longest suicide note in history". What people forget is that historically Britain has always detested the idea of the continent united under one flag and has not been shy about taking up arms to defend that view.

Liberal British commentators – and other like-minded intellectuals, from academics to rock musicians – fear that if Britain is kept out of Europe it will go the way of Portugal (Lisbon once had a great empire too). Unfortunately, the man in the street (or the man on the Clapham omnibus, as they used to say in London), adores his "Frogs", "Huns" and "Spaghetti-eaters". He is sceptical of the Channel tunnel and genuinely believes that the European community is full of conmen out to swindle the honest British. When a tabloid reported that the French set fire to lorry-loads of English lambs to prevent them being imported into France, it set off a hysterical Franco-phobic reaction. Opinion polls confirm this ambivalence towards Europe. Within the Community, 65% of the population is in favour of abandoning their national currency for the European euro and only 35% are against. In Great Britain the figures are reversed: 65% want to keep the pound and only 35% are in favour of the euro.

Insulting the president of the European Commission in Trafalgar Square (Up Yours Delors!) may not be as popular of late, but the tabloid *The Sun*, staunch supporter of such protests, still attracts twelve million readers and its editor has been knighted. Even many of the British who would consider themselves "pro-European" believe that British leaders during European summits are hopelessly put upon by what *The Guardian* called a bunch of "useless, vainglorious, spaghetti-eating no-hopers" (a reference, as you may guess, to us Italians). Many people, otherwise well-educated and informed, genuinely believe that the new Europe is a trap for old England. We can only hope that when they invoke the spirit of Dunkirk in their stand against European integration, they are not serious. Standing alone against the enemy in the forties was brave. Standing alone among friends in the nineties frankly is ludicrous.

THE CLASSES

HAPPILY DIVIDED

Take the napkin ring. Forty years ago, someone wrote a treatise arguing that this object was a powerful social indicator. The relationship a person had with a napkin ring revealed his real class origins and his place in the class system. The upper classes, for example, weren't aware of its existence. Their napkins were changed for them each day and so they had no need of an object to indicate where each person had previously wiped his mouth. A duke, ceremonially presented with two exquisite silver napkin rings by the mayor of a village in the north, had to be told what they were before he could begin his thank you speech.

The working class was equally ignorant of the existence of the napkin ring for one simple reason: they didn't use napkins. That's what sleeves were for. Only the middle class, who did use napkins but didn't change them every day, was familiar with the napkin ring. Today, many would argue that all the rules have changed now that *Debrett's Etiquette and Modern Manners*, the bible of the upper class, has allowed the use of paper napkins. This is only partially true: in Britain, napkins still divide the nation in two. The upper class calls them "napkins";

everyone else calls them "serviettes". Social climbers *think* the word "serviette", but they force themselves to *say* "napkin". The effort that takes makes them irredeemably middle class.

No matter what you've been told or what you may have read on the subject, the class system is still a great British obsession. Changes occur, of course, but always within the system. The middle class, marching behind Margaret Thatcher's banner, has grown much larger, while the working class has grown smaller – adding to the despondency of the Labour Party, left with ever fewer workers for its revolution. The upper class has undergone drastic changes of its own. An interesting phenomenon, recently the focus of an entire study (*The English Gentleman* by Philip Mason), is the decline of the gentleman who these days would rather holiday on a Mediterranean island than go off in "pursuit of moral excellence".

Any Italian banker, diplomatic, or indeed journalist who has visited London and voluntarily tried to integrate himself into British society can confirm that not only does the class system exist, but it is extremely complicated. There is an historical explanation for this baffling system. Since the French revolution, the British upper class has been forced onto the defensive and from that position it has achieved great things such as leading a united country right up to the first world war and maintaining an empire with the minimum use of force. To carry this out while continuing to set an example for the rest of the country, the upper class has had to keep a careful distance from the middle class. For example, in Victorian and Edwardian Britain, the middle class tried desperately to copy the subtle nuances of dress and etiquette of the upper class.

The elite, to remain elite, responded by changing the rules.

Today the big change taking place is that the upper class, exhausted after two centuries of pursuit, is finally letting the middle class catch up with it. And the middle class, grown rich through business and the professions, is finally learning what to do: it must send its children to the right schools (Eton, Harrow and Westminster); sew four buttons on the sleeves of their jackets (not two, not three. Four); and say "lavatory" (the middle class says "loo", the working class – *quelle horror* – "toilet"). The upwardly mobile, instead of transforming what George Orwell called "the most class-infested nation under the sun", have simply made the model more sophisticated. The British, especially the ones who deny it the loudest, are ever more devoted to this religion. The Italian journalist ever more despairing.

People still live in stratified compartments. They eat, sleep and spend their time according to the rules of the class to which they belong. Take the house. The true upper class likes things used, like old leather armchairs, and will quite happily put six different chairs from four different centuries around their dining table. If the chairs are falling to bits, so much the better. The Duchess of Devonshire flaunted the holes in her carpets at Chatsworth House in a recent article for the weekly magazine *The Spectator*. On the other hand, Michael Heseltine, the ex-Minister of Defence and eternal candidate for leader of the Conservative Party, and his family have been treated with disdain since they admitted they actually *bought* all the furniture for their house in Oxfordshire. The middle class is proud of its designer cabinets and dishwashers, while that same appliance is looked upon with suspicion by the upper class. If she has a dishwasher, the upper class housewife keeps it hidden away and elevates its status by calling it a "washing-up machine".

Language, understood as the choice of vocabulary, pronunciation and accent, also creates insurmountable barriers. George Bernard Shaw an Irishman who knew the British well, wrote, "It is impossible for an Englishman to open his mouth, without making some other Englishman despise him". There is a world of difference between the greengrocer in Hackney and Princess Diana in their pronunciation, even when they are saying nothing more than the word *actually*. If the greengrocer were to say *actually* like Princess Diana, with a sort of sneeze between the letters "c" and "t", her friends in the East End would fall about laughing. Margaret Thatcher, the daughter of a grocer and prototypical product of the middle class, was given lessons in how to speak like the daughters of the upper class. She didn't learn them to perfection though: she elongates her "a"s like a princess – *salt* comes out more like *soult* – but then she exaggerates, drawling her "o" in the same way so that *involve* turns into *invoulve*.

Even the British government has an opinion on the subject. The Registrar General divides the population into five classes by occupation. In Class 1 are professions like doctors and lawyers, in Class 2 are the semi-professionals, such as journalists (sic), farmers and members of parliament. And so it goes, up to Class 5 which covers "unskilled manual labourers", like the ticket-takers on the Underground. The system, it must be noted, falls apart when it has had to place someone like Viscount Linley, son of Princess Margaret who, for reasons of his own, chose to become a furniture maker.

A detailed study of the British social structure was carried out recently by Oxford University (the Oxford Mobility Survey) with interesting results. One out of every five babies born to working class parents will move into the middle class at some point in his or her life. The middle class has virtually doubled since the end of the war. Hugh Montgomery-Massingberd, co-author of the work *British Aristocracy*, however, takes issue with these generalisations. He thinks one must be careful not to abuse the term "middle class". "Nowadays everyone is middle class with the exception of nine hundred Peers of the Realm and their close relatives, not many in a nation of sixty million inhabitants." A better breakdown according to Montgomery-Massingberd would be to divide British society into 10 classes: 1. the upper-upper class; 2. the lower-upper class; 3. the upper-middle class; 4. the lower-upper middle class; 5. the middle class; 6. the upper-lower middle class; 7. the lower-middle class; 8. the lower-lower middle class; 9. the upper-working class; 10. the lower-working class. "But just as in modern trains" he continues, "these compartments are connected and one is always being pushed about by the crowds going up and down." In spite of this, he assures us, they make great entertainment.

THE UPPER CLASS: THE OLD RICH, THE NEW POOR

The writer Anthony Burgess, in an essay entitled "On being English", claims that the perception foreigners have of Britain is based on certain stereotypes. In ads on French televisions, he writes, there is always an English aristocrat in evening dress sipping a cup of tea while his house is falling to pieces around him. Burgess may be right that people base their ideas on stereotypes, but there is usually an element of truth in the stereotype. The English minor aristocracy is fighting a brave but losing battle against inheritance taxes, the desertion of its butlers, and the collapse of the very roofs over its head. Trained for generations to take the blows of fortune with head held high, the upper class may be faltering, but it is doing it with style. In other words, sipping tea in evening dress as their houses fall down around them.

It should be made clear here that we are not talking about the aristocracy. As far as it is known, none of Britain's twenty-six dukes has problems of this nature. This is in large part thanks to a 1976 law that exempted the most stately homes, considered to be national treasures, from certain taxes. In these national treasures live dukes, not minor aristocracy with dependent family members. Cries of pain from the minor aristocracy can be heard from time to time in letters to the editor of the *Daily Telegraph*. A landowner in Kent not long ago wrote one reminiscing nostalgically about a time when his father employed eight servants. The letter writer had to be content with two Philippinos who had already been in jail eleven times because they kept getting into fights in the basement flat.

Since the British like to document things, even their own misery, someone has theorised that the decline of a class can be measured by the number of times a telephone rings in a country house before someone picks it up. At one time, there would have been a butler stationed in the pantry ready to pick up the phone immediately. Today, it takes about thirteen rings before someone answers it. Sir Marcus Worsly maintains that the same problem exists with the front door bell: at Hovingham Hall, his country home in Yorkshire, there are exactly one hundred steps to the front door. "People go away thinking I'm not in while actually I'm racing like a horse."

Sir Charles Mott-Radclyffe who lives in Barningham Hall in Norfolk has found his own solution to the lack of servants. Every day he sets two tables for himself in the same room. He declares he can't bear the idea of clearing the table twice a day. Lord Cawdor, who owns fifty-six thousand acres near Inverness, is convinced that the disappearance of the serving class has brought about a decline in the culinary arts. Before going to friends' homes for dinner, Lord and Lady Cawdor take bets on the menu, "Our *betes noires*" he maintains, "are meat loaf and steak as tough as an old crocodile".

Another complaint of the minor aristocracy – who whinge a lot but still manage to survive, a sure sign that things are not as bad as they say – is the inheritance tax. In order to leave their country houses to their heirs, the minor aristocracy has had to resort lately to a series of expediencies. The most common one is to transfer their entire property while they are still alive to a son, young and in good health. Two deaths in the family in the wrong order, however, and the entire patrimony can come down like a house of cards. Less tragic but equally insidious for the owners of these mansions are local preservation and protection groups like the RSPCA and English Heritage. As one in every five foxhunts is interrupted by indignant animal rights protesters, marquises and viscounts turn up in court with a certain regularity. Among the most recent to appear, Lord Hertford was obliged to pay £15,000 in court costs and fines. Ploughing his land in

Alcester, he had dug up a good part of a third century Roman settlement. He was turned in by his friend Lord Montague of Beaulieu, the president of English Heritage.

The great strength of the upper class – the one that made it possible for them to put down any revolution – is a serene acceptance of change. When faced with the costs of maintenance, the minor aristocracy simply raised the white flag and moved to the city. There they began a new life, that of the new poor, or as the afflicted like to call themselves in the hopes of confusing everyone else, the *nouveaux pauvres*. Nicholas Monson and Debra Scott, the authors of a dissertation on the subject, maintain that the minor aristocracy is "running an aristocratic lifestyle on a tradesman's budget" and are therefore deserving of our respect. Their symbol is the family silver permanently ready for auction and their tricks to avoid admitting they are broke are legendary. Their Rubicon is the Thames: a member of the minor aristocracy enters the class of the new poor the minute he moves south of the river. Referring to Clapham, just south of the river, one of P.G. Wodehouse's great characters Psmith was in the habit of saying "I have heard of it, but is its existence really proven?". In Battersea, also south of the Thames, one can easily run into "sonlies", a label which is derived from the phrase they often repeat to justify their new address: "It's only five minutes from Sloane Square" (the high street of the highly desirable neighbourhood of Chelsea – north of the river, of course).

The gap between the aristocracy and the vast, mysterious and impoverished minor aristocracy has also been widened by the law. While the latter have to do battle with the various editions of the Rent

Act, the aristocracy cedes and renews the leases of its properties in the centre of London at exorbitant prices. Not long ago, the young Duke of Westminster, the owner of most of Belgravia and Mayfair, turned to the European court of human rights in Strasbourg for help. He felt that the law that forced him to allow some of his tenants to buy the leases to the property he owned constituted a violation of his fundamental human rights. The court decided against him. Since the patrimony of the duke was estimated at around £2.5 billion, his judicial upset left the majority of the public somewhat indifferent.

The problems of the minor aristocracy have speeded up their absorption downwards into the upper-middle class. Not by chance, the term "upper class" today is often applied interchangeably to both. This tacit understanding between the two classes often heralds more concrete agreements, from buying and selling a flat in London to marrying off a daughter. It is not uncommon for a young man from the City to marry a daughter of the minor aristocracy: he has the money, she the name. His table manners are not likely to drive her to tears since the two have almost always gone to the same public schools, and will have common friends and similar accents. They will probably live together quite amicably. England's minor aristocracy has accepted its lot with a stiff upper lip. Given that a couple with two children and two houses, one in London and one in the country, must have an income of at least £80,000 a year in order to "do all the right things", it is clear a helping hand was needed.

The new relationships of strength within the upper class are confirmed by a series of studies and statistics. According to the Royal Commission on the distribution of wealth and income, in 1911 one percent of the population controlled 60% of the wealth. Now that same one percent controls 20%. Today, among the ten richest men in the United Kingdom, only the Duke of Westminster belongs to the aristocracy. New families, like the Sainsburys (supermarkets) have become millionaires while keeping a safe distance from manufacturing industry. The University of Essex conducted a study on the "very rich" and concluded that after the top ten richest, there are a thousand people with incomes over £4 million sterling. The category "garden-variety millionaires" comes next, containing another twenty thousand people with incomes over £1 million. As for where this money comes from, one of the British television stations recently commissioned a study by an Australian sociologist, professor Bill Rubinstein from Deaking University. Looking at the incomes of everyone who died in 1985 and left their heirs at least £1 million, he discovered that 42% of the millionaires were the children of millionaire fathers, while another 29% were the children of professionals or businessmen. "In other words," he concluded, "you need money to make money." Why British television had to call in an Australian expert to figure this out is not clear.

THE LEGIONS OF THE MIDDLE CLASS

Not long ago an Italian guest returned from an afternoon of shopping with a proud discovery: it takes four thank you's to buy a bus ticket in Britain. When the bus conductor approaches with his ticket machine, he announces his presence with thank you number one (translation: "here I am"). The passenger pays him, saying "thank you" back ("I can see that you are here, here is the money for the ticket"). The bus conductor hands him the ticket with a "thank you" ("the sum is correct, the contract concluded, here is the document that proves it"). The passenger takes the ticket and of course says "thank you" (in this case he means it). If there is any change to hand back, the thank you's go up to six. The ceremony amuses Italians who, if forced to buy a ticket, do it with a grunt, and unnerves Americans, who often carry out the whole transaction in total silence.

The British have hundreds of little rituals like this. They are inoffensive customs whose aim is not, contrary to opinion, to make the rest of the world feel rude and vulgar, but to transform the rules of communal living into small everyday pleasures. If foreigners don't find these small pleasures pleasurable, say the British, well, that's their problem.

From time to time, the upper class and the lower class are distracted and forget the rules. Let's go back to the bus. The football hooligan, if he's with his mates and feeling safe, will try to avoid buying a ticket. The elderly gentleman, after an afternoon of gin and tonics, may neglect to make his presence known to the bus conductor. If he is caught out, he will pay, murmuring, "So sorry". The middle class masses, 80% of the population, pay without batting an eye. Or rather they pay with four thank you's.

It is the middle class that dominates Britain today and is its representative abroad. If class war no longer exists, it is because the middle class won it handily some time ago. The legions of the middle class have everything they need for a winning army: a sense of patriotism, a sense of duty, and from 1979 to 1990, an incomparable leader in Margaret Thatcher. The lady, as we have said, decided that her personal values were the same as the values of the middle class and that the values of the middle class would be the values of Britain. People have always had a desire to make money, for example, but it was never considered something one talked about. The working class would have liked to make money, but couldn't quite get its act together. The upper class also wanted to, but was embarrassed to admit it. Margaret Thatcher tried to convince the public that one should be proud of a little healthy greed. She was moderately successful: the British are beginning to discover the joys of an underground economy. Not long ago on BBC radio, a minister explained with alarm that this sector represented 8% of the gross national product and the Treasury was out £5 million in unpaid taxes.

The methods that Margaret Thatcher used to bring new blood into the middle class were myriad and many were brilliant. We will mention only a few. One was to make it possible for tenants to buy their council houses. Labour quickly cried "foul", not because they found this initiative illegal, but because they were afraid their own party faithful would lose their revolutionary zeal once they became small property owners – and, of course, they were right. The Conservative vote increased in proportion to property sales. Today 70% of families are homeowners. A second strategic move was the invention of the term "popular capitalism" to describe the social system that Margaret Thatcher had in mind for Britain. Her government introduced the Personal Equity Plan (PEP) that offered tax breaks to anyone who invested £2500 in shares in the stock market. The success of this plan among low-income workers left the opposition seething with rage once again.

A third demonstration that Margaret Thatcher was a woman able to sell her robust vision occurred in spring 1988 when the then prime minister explained the religious justification of her political beliefs. The occasion was the Synod of the Church of Scotland where first she quoted St Paul in his letter to the Thessalonians and then the Old Testament book of Exodus, saying that creating wealth was profoundly moral. Idleness and the worship of money were sinful, but not work and industry, said she, thereby also winning over the middle class in the north – who up till then had not been able to reconcile religion and Thatcher's politics.

Some preferred to see the movement of the top rung of the working class into the middle class as historically inevitable, and that all Margaret Thatcher did was speed up the process. The observation is correct as long as it is recognised that the lady speeded it up considerably. The Conservative Party, which until the middle of the seventies had been a paternalistic and caring party, was shaken to its core. Of the three hundred and ninety-six conservative MPs that Margaret Thatcher brought to Westminster in 1983 only thirty had gone to Eton, the establishment school. The lady was completely uninterested in what class her staff came from and she was so fond of self-made men that she promoted Norman Tebbit and Cecil Parkinson – men who would have gone fox hunting carrying rifles – to the highest positions in the government and the Party. Men like the Marquis of Lothian's heir, MP for Edinburgh South, and the Count of Kilmorey, MP for Wiltshire North, wisely became known simply as Mr Michael Ancram and Mr Richard Needham.

The middle class has triumphed in all sorts of places. Even the legendary Foreign Office was criticised in an official report for being "too middle class" (and if you look at the attire of British diplomats all over the world, you must admit the criticism was justified). This same middle class safeguards not only the values dearest to Margaret Thatcher but also all the little quirks, habits and eccentricities that attract so many tourists to London. An example of this is their mad passion for gardening, epitomised by *Gardeners' Question Time*, the most popular program on BBC radio. The broadcast, which goes out on Sunday afternoons, is so popular that local garden associations have to wait for years for the chance to pose their questions live. The Orpington Horticultural Society in Kent, which recently hosted the one thousand six hundred and fortieth transmission, had sent their questions in on September 21st 1960. Other obsessions include weather reports, red double-decker buses, black cabs, the countryside, Sunday papers, Sundays spent reading the Sunday papers, Remembrance Day, red telephone boxes and blue passports with the royal seal and the little window, which for years the British refused to exchange for the new claret-coloured European passport, notwithstanding pleas from Brussels bureaucrats.

The middle class is so enamoured of its usages and customs that, it feels an unspoken affection even for its traditional forms of juvenile delinquency, as long as they are traditional: punks, teddy boys, skinheads and mods are considered almost part of the landscape. Here's another example: the middle class remains extremely fond of the London fog, even though it hasn't existed for more than thirty years. It was eliminated shortly after burning coal was forbidden in the city with the Clean Air Act of 1956, prompted by the great fog of 1952 that caused four thousand deaths. The British know this but when they arrive in London with the eyes of the devoted they continue to see the fog of Dickens' novels.

When it comes to new social habits, however, this otherwise triumphant middle class is slow to take the initiative. It is usually the upper class that takes up new habits. The middle class follows, but many years later and with due caution. An interesting example is the kiss. The social kiss, French-style, has always been a nightmare for the English middle class at international meetings. The British public, profoundly rational, has traditionally considered this exercise a health risk and an utter waste of time. A few years ago, however, the British upper class adopted this custom. Now you often see well-borne British children, stiff as carrots, trying to kiss perfect strangers on the cheek at a party. The day that the middle class follows suit though is still far off.

Another characteristic that leaves foreigners perplexed and is almost a trademark of the middle class, is its extraordinary ability to pretend to feelings it doesn't have. A superficial observation of middle class rituals would suggest that Britain is a country of great actors. George Bernard Shaw in *Pygmalion* writes that the English like to hang on to the class system precisely because its rituals appeal to their latent acting talent. Even today, saying goodbye at the end of a party becomes a piece of theatre. The guest, as a kind of thank you, says affably "You must come round to us for a drink sometime," when in fact he has no desire to have anyone underfoot with drink in hand. The host smiles broadly and says, "I'll ring you," though he has no intention of phoning. The guest then asks,

"Do you want my number?" secretly fearing a positive response. The host closes the conversation with another broad smile saying "I'm sure you're in the book", knowing full well that he will never open it to look up the number of the guest who is departing, partly because he has already forgotten his name.

More examples. Telephone operators do not answer Italian-style with a brusque "Tell me," but rather with a smooth "How can I help you," drawling out the "you". The guest is greeted warmly (often with port and cigars) and despatched with courtesy. But if you make the mistake of reappearing too soon, you'll be frozen with a glance. A meeting between two colleagues invariably concludes with a solemn promise of "We must have lunch sometime". If one of the two then replies with "Yes, let's. When?" the surprise of the other is genuine. For an Italian, "*viene, vede, smarrisce*". (He comes, he sees, he's confused.)

WHERE ARE ALL THE FISH AND CHIPS?

If the working class ever chooses an anthem, everyone knows what it will be. The music can't be reproduced here, but the following is the full and complete text:

"Here we go, here we go, here we go (pause).
Here we go, here we go, here we go-o (pause).
Here we go, here we go, here we go (pause).
Here we go-o, here we go!"

Readers who are football fans will recognise in this sophisticated set of lyrics the favourite song of British football fans, exported to football stadiums all over Europe along with other less inoffensive behaviour.

The British working class adores football. Or rather, it adores football, beer, darts, high heels, black suspenders, video games, and holidays in Spain. These generalisations, which might seem risky coming from a foreigner, are confirmed with alacrity by the British. In particular – and proudly – they are confirmed by the working class themselves. This should give you a clue as to how the class system has managed to hang on for so long. There is a curious sense of belonging and an obvious pleasure in being working class, no different from the pleasure of being middle or upper class. Each group possesses its own series of rituals and small pleasures and does not envy those of the other classes. A member of the working class enjoys drinking his fill in a pub, a member of the middle class happily potters around in his postage-stamp-sized garden while the upper class wallows in its own refinement, real or presumed.

Until the appearance of Margaret Thatcher there was a clear political divide in the three-tiered society. The upper class voted Conservative, the working class Labour. The side that managed to get the ever-increasing middle class votes won the election. Then the lady arrived and began hunting in Labour's back garden. Her exceptional manoeuvre created an exceptional situation. Margaret Thatcher won three elections in a row. John Major, thanks to her, won a fourth.

The Conservatives were no doubt helped in their efforts to penetrate the working class by tabloid newspapers. Their power is hard to comprehend for anyone who has not lived in Britain. Let's try, using some statistics. The Census recently published a report on "social tendencies", which said that every day eleven million seven hundred and fifty thousand readers buy *The Sun*, the best-selling daily paper. Thirteen million people read the Sunday edition of *The Sun*, which is called *The News of the World*. Both in their time were ardent supporters of "Maggie", the leader, and "Maggie" was grateful. Appearing among photos of breasts and bottoms and advice to readers ("What could you do with a million pounds? Buy four thousand miles of panty elastic and throw it from London to Nicosia and back"), were articles written and signed by that same Mrs Thatcher and her ministers. If this embarrassed the lady, no doubt there were stronger concerns out there than embarrassment.

The popular press manages to make itself completely understood by its crudeness. The editorials underline phrases so that the dimmest reader gets the point and begins his sentences with "*The Sun says...*". What *The Sun* says, often and unashamedly, are things that make your hair stand on end. Not long ago an editorial referred to Spain as "a country of bloodthirsty butchers". "We must not spend our money in that wretched country. Let's leave the Spaniards to their acid wine and their turgid (sic) food." Another editorial commenting on a public speech given by the Duke of Edinburgh, ended by saying "And now shut up, you silly old sod".

The British use the term "yobs" to refer to the readers of such refined press analysis. The word, which became a slang word around the middle of the nineteenth century, is simply the word "boy" spelled backwards and was not particularly pejorative to begin with. Today it refers to a kind of violent and aggressive thug, a type rapidly increasing in number. Drunken yobs are the reason the British team was excluded from the European soccer championship, and were in evidence during the

European championship in Germany. Timid yobs go on Club 18-30 holidays that promise parties "more destructive than the atom bomb". Yobettes wear acrylic, sport bare legs no matter how cold it is, and dream of appearing on the legendary Page Three of *The Sun*, bare-breasted wearing a jockey hat with the caption "Oh, wouldn't we love to be Susie's horse". They are the backbone of another sad statistic: today one third of British girls get pregnant out of wedlock. The undisputed idols of British yobs are English cricket champion Ian Botham and Samantha Fox who began her career as a Page Three girl and now earns £4000 for opening a supermarket.

The problem with yob culture is that it is not always inoffensive. When confronted with the constant brawls of football fans, a few have begun to wonder from what remote depths in the British psyche this desire for fisticuffs comes. Anthony Burgess advanced the theory that these brawny lads are what made the army strong in days gone by. Now that they are no longer letting off steam at the undisciplined subjects of the Empire, these yobs have turned on each other. "From Agincourt to Port Stanley, history books are full of descriptions of our main talent: having a good fight," writes the journalist David Thomas in *The Sunday Telegraph*. One detail worth noting is that once they turn thirty, these brawling youth change into respectable citizens and start to worry that a new generation of yobs might mess with their daughters when they reach adolescence.

Luckily for Britain not every working class family is bringing up hooligans. In the north, despite high unemployment, some of the poorest sectors of the working class maintain a dignity that has sustained them since the Industrial Revolution. The miners, for example, preserve a kind of rock hard purity that made them the object of admiration during twelve months of pointless strikes in 1984-85. Every summer, miners from Yorkshire and Wales take their family to Blackpool for a holiday, and there their children bathe in a tobacco-coloured sea, they spend the evenings under neon lights and sleep in bed & breakfasts. For the British, Blackpool is a kind of working class sanctuary with its own beauty and decency. Yobs, on the other hand, prefer places like Benidorm in Spain where they head every summer to get drunk in the sun and learn the language (*tequila, señorita, pesetas*).

Along with northern beaches, other British working class traditions are in jeopardy. If you want to see where the last of the workforce that built the British Empire goes, you had better hurry. The great granddaughters of the sailors of Liverpool, the weavers of Manchester and the steel workers of Sheffield, for example, go less and less to the bingo halls, so beloved by Andy Capp's long-suffering wife, Alice. Until only a few years ago, the Church and bingo – and bingo more than the church – were places of refuges, where a wife could go while her husband went down to the pub. Today, only a few old-age-pensioners will put up with these melancholy evenings spent with a shandy and five bingo cards for 25 pence. To survive, owners of bingo halls have introduced cabaret-type entertainment, videogames, food services and roller-skating. Alice, who doesn't roller skate, is gradually retiring to the sidelines.

The same fate is befalling another British legend, fish & chips, the only meal you can get for a pound. The crisis of fried fish and chips began when a law was passed prohibiting the use of newspapers to wrap the fish and chips. Deprived of the flavour of ink and tempted by fast food, the working class abandoned the whole enterprise, to the great displeasure of Italians all over England and Scotland who had something of a monopoly on fish and chip sales. In London, though, fish & chips have become fashionable among young trendies, suddenly convinced of the worldly virtues of greasy fingers.

Two great institutions that have resisted the winds of change are pubs and television. The British continue to drink with enthusiasm. Every day they spend £35 million on alcohol, more than they spend on clothing, cars or household goods. Annual per capita consumption, according to the latest figures, is around 270 pints of lager, 20 bottles of wine, 9 litres of cider and 10 litres of spirits. Since even in the United Kingdom there are tee-totalers and newborn babies, it is plain to see that someone is overdoing it.

The same can be said about television. The average male citizen sits in front of the tube 26 hours and 4 minutes a week, females more than 30 hours. Only three families in a hundred have a dishwasher, but 23 have a videocassette recorder. There are no special statistics for the working class, but many surveys would lead you to believe that dependence on the telly is total. The soap operas *East Enders* on BBC and *Coronation Street* on ITV, draw record-breaking audiences. Their main characters, all resolutely working class, have become popular heroes and the escapades of the actors who play them, especially if extra-marital, are enthusiastically reported in the tabloids.

Tabloids and television are responsible for an-other characteristic of the working class, a genuine lack of interest in anything that happens beyond the Channel. You can't even call it xenophobia, because this would assume at least some knowledge of other countries on their part. The working class simply ignores foreigners. Other countries are interesting only in so far as they produce cheaper hi-fi's (the Japanese), drink more beer (Germans), lose wars (the Argentines) or can be insulted. When *The Sun* talks about the French, they don't call them French, but "frogs". At the top of the black list of Britain's working class is the European Union, accused of all sorts of perversity. One of Margaret Thatcher's greatest strengths was to see this clearly. A few insults to the EU and the promise to maintain nuclear weapons, and the British armies of old, now under a different name, were behind her.

HAVE YOU EVER HEARD OF PUNJABI POP?

Miss Sakina Punjani and the Pakistani owner of the Fairaway Foods shop have been more helpful than any television program or lecture in educating me about minorities in Britain. Miss Punjani is an Indian from Kenya who wears a sari and sells newspapers in Ladbroke Grove, Holland Park in London. Like any respectable newsagent, she also sells stationary, ice cream, cigarettes, birthday cards heavy with sexual innuendos, half-price paperbacks, batteries, city maps and disposable nappies. As if that weren't enough, Sakina has also opened a post office substation at the back of the shop and installed a telex on the first floor that you reach by passing through a kitchen full of relatives and cooking smells.

What links Miss Punjani to the owner of Fairaway

Foods in Kensington Church Street is not only their Asian heritage but also the number of hours they work. The news agency in Holland Park is open from six in the morning till nine at night. The mini-market in Kensington effectively never closes although some in the neighbourhood insist that the owner secretly closes for a few hours every night, when he figures that no one will be in for a frozen hamburger, Bulgarian wine, toothpicks, deodorant, light bulbs or shoe polish.

The English are appalled by this kind of behaviour. The convenience of being able to buy eggs at midnight, however, tends to make them hide their horror and forces them to admire such zeal. The pluck of Asian small businessmen, certainly, creates a fascinating mystery. For example, no one knows exactly what the Indians and Pakistanis do with the money they earn. Sending it to relatives in India and Pakistan seems unlikely since most of their families are here. Buying Britain on the instalment plan, however, does seem possible and the day of their final payment must be near.

Race relations, like cricket and the queen, are subjects the British feel strongly about. Like cricket and the queen, the subject goes through moments of highs and lows. Race relations were widely discussed after riots in London, Liverpool, Birmingham and Bristol in 1981 and 1985. It was the topic of conversation again recently after the government decided to introduce entry visas for Indian, Bangladeshi, Ghanaian, Nigerian and Pakistani citizens, all of whom, up till then, as members of the Commonwealth, were able to fly to London and once there, convince immigration officials of their right to stay in England. Fearing they might miss the deadline for the changes in the laws, unwisely announced by the Home Office, thousands of Indians, Bengalis, Ghanaians, Nigerians, and Pakistanis landed at Terminal 3 at Heathrow in London, completely overwhelming it. The British government behaved as if it were sleepwalking. From New Delhi Rajiv Gandhi accused it of racism, in the House of Commons the Labour Party ranted and railed, while television crews wandered through the airport filming newborn babies sleeping in wastebaskets. In the end, the government put all the new arrivals up in hotels, costing the country thousands of pounds. It wasn't the government's finest moment.

The uproar that accompanies such episodes, besides striking a residual imperialist nerve, has led many to believe that the non-white population in Britain is enormous. It is not true. According to a census taken in 1987, it is only two million four hundred thousand people, less than 4% of the population and of this 4%, some 40% was born in the United Kingdom. According to the 1981 census, immigrants are concentrated mostly in the capital where 5% of the population looks to the Caribbean or Africa as their country of origin, 5% come from India and Pakistan and 6% are from other places (Portugal, Italy, Hong Kong, Cyprus – there are more Cypriots in London than in Nicosia).

Non-white Britons can be divided into two basic groups: blacks of Caribbean origin and Asians from the Indian sub-continent. Both came to the centre of the empire at the end of the fifties and the beginning of the sixties, at the same time as Italians were leaving Naples for Turin. In both cases, the reasons were similar. Industries needed manpower and they looked for it where they could. In Italy it was the car industry, in Britain, it was the construction industry in London and the textile industry in the north.

Most immigrants did not expect to settle in Britain, but they ended up staying. If this phenomenon interests you, visit Bradford in Yorkshire. Out of a population of four hundred thousand inhabitants, ninety thousand are from Pakistan, Bangladesh and India. Unlike the Poles, Ukrainians, and German Jews who preceded them, the new arrivals have not assimilated. They continue to eat, dress and behave as they always have and to build mosques (there are already thirty in the city). Since the Asian birth rate is four times higher than that of non-Asians, today one student out of four is non-white. In nineteen of the seventy-three state schools, 70% of the students are non-white.

Ray Honeyford, a Conservative born into a working class family from Manchester, was the headmaster of one of these schools. In an article published in an obscure magazine, Honeyford wrote that ethnic education, adopted in the area, was a disastrous idea. To teach Urdu to students and let Muslim girls swim in pyjamas to protect their modesty was absurd, "since the immigrants' decision to become British citizens implied that they wanted a British education for their children". If the families wanted to pass on Indian and Pakistani culture, Honeyford wrote, "they shouldn't attend state schools in the United Kingdom". The argument was not a popular one: educational authorities were indignant, the city in revolt, and Ray Honeyford was forcibly thrown out. In Yorkshire to the great satisfaction of their parents, Pakistani girls continue to swim in their pyjamas.

When the Muslims of the world rose up in February 1989 against the book *The Satanic Verses* by Salman Rushdie, a British citizen, most Pakistanis, Indians and Iranians in the United Kingdom were in no doubt about where their loyalties lay: with Khomeini and his loyal followers. Interviewed in many cities throughout Britain they repeated over and over that they were willing to personally kill the writer as the Ayatollah had ordered. At the Italia Café in Bradford, groups of coloured youth allowed themselves to be photographed wearing baleful expressions while they cried out for revenge and employees in corner shops in London waved their fists and pronounced invectives. The editors of large daily newspapers came down from their clouds. One after another they declared "we British thought we had at least taught you tolerance".

It is hard to know where to place immigrants within the class system. Even though the Race Relations Acts of 1965 and 1976 give minorities absolute equality, they don't fit into any one category. Someone has written that blacks, some of whom play football for Tottenham and many of whom spend their salaries in pubs, feel solidarity with the working class. Asians do not seem to feel solidarity with anyone although a certain respect for their bank accounts would suggest they belong in the middle class. Deeper observation demonstrates that such an affinity does indeed exist. Until they are rich enough, Asians float above the class system. When they land, they land in the middle class and take up middle class values with enthusiasm. The success of this process is well described by the protagonist of the film *My Beautiful Launderette*, set in the London suburb of Lewisham. When he is accused of being too attached to money, he replies, "I'm a professional businessman, not a professional Pakistani".

The middle class, however, is the highest class a minority can hope to attain. British institutions remain impenetrable. The first non-white member of Parliament wasn't elected until 1987, there are no black judges, only a handful of black or Asian journalists work for national newspapers, the Anglican church has ordained only one black bishop in Britain, the Catholic church has no coloured parishes and of the one hundred and fifteen thousand British police, only about a thousand are not white. The Policy Studies Institute ran an experiment, based on job applications by people of various races. The results showed that it was four times more difficult for a black or Asian to find work as for a white. All the figures – whether on unemployment, housing and violent crimes – paint the same picture: according to a study by the Home Office, for example, blacks will suffer "racial aggression" thirty-six times as often and Asians fifty times as often as whites. In the London boroughs of Southall, Tower Hamlets, Newham and Waltham Forest, many families of Pakistani origin find that excrement through the letterbox and rocks through the windows is even more convincing than statistics.

But these same neighbourhoods in Southall or Newham, where a third of the population is coloured, exhibit something new that is interesting. Here young Asians, a large number of whom were born in Britain, say they prefer simply to live in peace rather than become integrated into British society or work for the future of British Islam. In other words, they are not looking for acceptance. That's something they leave to Italian and French immigrants, whose touching attempts to imitate their hosts they are not even aware of. Young Asians simply want to be left to themselves. Pop music is a good example of this. Not long ago there was a concert given by an Asian group called Alaap at the

Empire Theatre in Leicester Square which drew two thousand teenage girls, covered in jewellery, wearing chunnis and long chiffon scarves, in from the suburbs. Accompanied by brothers, husbands, brothers-in-law and cousins, the young Indian and Pakistani girls paid £10 a piece without batting an eye to cheer their idols, who had conquered the West End. In short, if they were of no interest to the English, neither were the English of interest to them. The concept was simple, so simple it could be expressed without saying a word, bobbing to the rhythms of Punjabi pop.

TRIBES

As we all know, British kids like to hang out in gangs. Gangs form, they develop a sound and a style, the press takes notice and parents worry. The kids figure if the press is taking notice and their parents are worried, then they've got the clothes and music right. For many British over sixty, the post-war period was defined not by the prime minister of the time, but by the groups. In the fifties, there were teddy boys; in the first half of the sixties, there were mods and rockers; at the end of the sixties, there were hippies; in the first half of the seventies, there were glam rock and the sexually ambiguous David Bowie; in the latter half, punks; in the early eighties, new wave; and at the end of the eighties, acid house.

In more recent years, music-inspired groups have faded – only punks have managed to hang on, mostly by turning themselves into tourist attractions. But other types of groups have mushroomed. Particularly healthy and indisputably eccentric are the groups of young rich, who don't like to think of themselves as part of a group. The well-off left survives and suffers in silence, pretending to have no interest in fashion and lamenting the state of the Left. The well-off right – in Britain there is no particular stigma attached to the term – is flourishing.

Under its banner march the eggheads who advised Margaret Thatcher and the City "whiz-kids" who place salary above ideology, and whose greatest worry is another drop in the stock market.

The various groups we'll look at – diverse in terms of wealth, history, social habits and personal cleanliness – have two things in common. Their members take themselves very seriously and they demonstrate that fashion in Britain is anything but a simple pastime. The government is too efficient, the weather too lugubrious and the British too serious for it not to become a full-time occupation. In the sixties British hippies made lack of hygiene and long hair a profession; their Italians counterparts donned tunics and sandals and headed for the beach in daddy's car. Ten years later, British punks appeared, ferociously foolish but authentic: when they cut their noses with razor blades as a sign of protest, the nose and the blade were real. Aspiring Italian punks came to England and were horrified; in the end all they could manage was to dye their hair, a notoriously painless activity.

PUNKS FOR PURISTS, PUNKS FOR TOURISTS

No one talks much about punks these days, but around 1977 they were a powerful phenomenon, raising spitting in someone's face to an art form. If what the English critic Bevis Hillier wrote in the catalog of an exhibition about the cynical seventies is true, that "good art can only be born from an act of bad taste", then punks can claim they did their part, by providing music of questionable taste and behaving abominably. The scruffy prophets of this strange creed were four members of a group called the Sex Pistols. Britain was introduced to them one summer evening in a program on live TV during which they spent a full half-hour insulting a poor presenter named Bill Grundy. They were very young and disgracefully dressed, with wild hair, stained teeth and glazed eyes. During their half hour on TV they sniggered, they yawned and they stuck their fingers up their noses almost to their knuckles. They caused such uproar that the big record companies – whose sales had been stagnant since the Beatles – fell all over themselves to sign them up. EMI got there first but almost immediately was forced to pull out of the contract because the Sex Pistols, blithely continuing to vomit on the front row seats and insult the queen, were ruining the company's image.

The new movement, called "punk", was spurred on by various groups and individuals hoping to capitalise on their success. The Left claimed that punks symbolised the hopelessness of the new generation: unemployed and with no prospects in a country squeezed by the austerity measures imposed on the Labour government by the International Monetary Fund. The extreme right, delighted by the swastikas that turned up on the vests of the new rebels, also embraced them. Punks ignored all the attention, which in any case was probably over their heads, and continued to perfect their "mischievous wind-up", the brand of theatrical violence that made them famous. Their only real political act was boarding the Queen Elizabeth and sailing down the Thames on a "Jubilee cruise". Its sole purpose was to make fun of the real Jubilee organised to celebrate twenty-five years of Queen Elizabeth's reign. The action was meant to be a supreme insult to the queen, whom the punks considered insufferable, rather than a revolutionary act.

The leaders of this movement were the Sex Pistols' singer Johnny Rotten and the bass-player Sid Vicious. Johnny Rotten's chief characteristic was that he couldn't sing: his music teacher, when interviewed, recalled that Rotten – whose real name was Johnny Lyndon – would hide in a corner and keep his mouth shut. If he was forced to sing, he "howled". Sid Vicious turned out to be aptly named: he knifed his girlfriend Nancy Spungen. Arrested and released on bail, he killed himself with an overdose of heroin in New York's Greenwich Village.

Perhaps it was Vicious's unexpected death that transformed the movement from a momentary fad into something deeper. Punks are still around today, carrying on and celebrating their years of glory like war veterans. The life of Sid and Nancy, for example, has been made into a film directed by Alex Cox. It is a kind of punk version of *Gone with the Wind*, even though the two survivors who collaborated on the project, the model Debbie Juvenile and the writer John Savage, insist that nothing in the film is true. Jamie Reid, the boy from Liverpool who designed the album cover of *God Save the Queen*, got caught up in the Millennium frenzy and is working on a project he calls "Leaving the Twentieth Century". His reply when asked if it was going to be a musical, a record or a film was, "Maybe all three".

What's happened to Johnny Rotten is even more interesting. The ex-singer – as it were – of the Sex Pistols is thirty-four years old now, has a German wife who is already a grandmother and lives in Marina del Rey outside Los Angeles, in a castle built for Mae West in the twenties. His conversion has been complete. He sued his ex-manager Malcolm McLaren for a huge amount of money, drives a big cream-coloured Cadillac and openly admits that "to direct two real estate companies might be a bit much for an ex-punk". You only need to mention the punks of today who roam the Kings Road in London to get him started. "Complete idiots! Pathetic jokes!"

Punk holdovers of today, of course, have no idea of the scorn their idol heaps upon them. Convinced of the rightness of their cause, they are still sticking safety pins through their noses. They shamelessly take advantage of the changing times, willingly posing for tourist photos. There are two spots in London where they exhibit themselves like animals at the zoo: Trafalgar Square under the statue of Nelson – who surely would not approve – and in the King's Road. Here on Saturday mornings, punk couples spread themselves out on the pavement and wait for the busloads of Japanese tourists who treat punks with the same enthusiasm they previously reserved for the changing of the guard at Buckingham Palace. Their fees have long been the same, £1 per photo, £2 for camcorders, £5 for a simulated fight. If the tourist refuses to pay – Italians are always trying to get away with it – the ringleader, who keeps a mirror handy, flashes it at the camera lens and snarls. The tourist quickly gets the message: pay up or leave.

Needless to say, all this ferocity is pure theatrics. Punks of the nineties are eccentric, but harmless. Occasionally they even provide edifying material for the press. One decided to start a new life and sold all his old clothes to the Somerset County Museum. A punk couple from Bournemouth wanted to get married with a rat sitting on their heads during the ceremony (the rat's name was Bulldog, in case you are interested). Another couple from Farnborough in Hampshire went to court after their three-year-old son was expelled from nursery school because his blue hair was distracting the other children. A punk sailor from Portsmouth asked his MP to intervene when the Navy refused to allow him to keep his mohican haircut while on submarine duty, claiming it was an obstruction.

Curiously, it is the Italians, when they arrive in London to follow a fashion that has been dead for almost eight years, who take it all the most seriously. The tabloid *The Sun* wrote about Baron Andrea Belluso di Monteamaro, the twenty-three-year-old son of a diplomat who had learned to use lipstick and mascara and wear studded leather in London. I came across Cinzia Borromeo on the King's Road. She was from Pordenone and she revealed her Friulian genes when she strolled through the snow bare-legged, wearing only a micro skirt. When we asked her why she had come to England ten years too late, she seemed unabashed. She explained that coming from Pordenone to London to follow the call of the Sex Pistols seemed like the most natural thing in the world. When you think about it, her answer makes perfect sense. If Italians can go to Kenya to search for a savage Africa that no longer exists and take off for Moscow dreaming of a socialist system that never was, they can also go to London to keep the tourists happy.

YOUNG FOGEYS, OLD BY CHOICE

In Britain, only the Devonshire moors are more silent than the young rich. There is nothing here like the pilgrimages Californians make to places like Melrose Avenue, a Los Angeles street where thirteen-year-olds consider themselves adults because they can buy cocaine all by themselves. In Britain the young rich look down on such things. They may buy books that describe such goings-on but they still consider the cars and the tans vulgar.

Their rules, their manners and their clothes are different. Take yuppies, for instance. The term "young urban professional" was coined by Americans a few years back. On the other side of the Atlantic, American yuppies are young and well-off, without the encumbrance of children, and extremely self-indulgent in matters of cars, exotic holidays and clothing. An attempt was made to import the concept to Britain. After all, there must be single twenty-eight-year-olds there earning £100,000 a year who want to spend it all. Inevitably, of course, someone wrote a book that gave a name of their own to these young Brits: yaps. Young aspiring professionals. The author, Pearson Phillips, wrote that their provenance was obvious. They were "the children of Margaret Thatcher" and they formed a new elite, based strongly on money, merit and appearance and little on social class. Such a thing was previously unheard of in Britain.

For a few months these young people were the centre of enormous interest. It was decided that a yap worthy of the name would have a German car and a girlfriend who wore Italian clothes; he would eat nouvelle cuisine in French restaurants; he would have a credit card and would live in certain neighbourhoods. In London these would be Islington, Fulham and Notting Hill. Into these pretty neighbourhoods from which the original inhabitants, richer and contented, had fled, came the young aspiring professionals and they began to clean up the streets and façades. The camp followers

– fellow yaps who opened cinemas, cafes and gyms to help their neighbours spend their salaries – soon followed.

No one talks much about them anymore. The whole thing was too American and too conventional and yaps didn't really have all that much money. Behind the retreating army there marched a new much more English one: the young fogeys. Their main characteristics are always and in every manner to praise the past, to live in the country, to write only with a fountain pen and to detest Margaret Thatcher for her lack of restraint. Young fogeys adore architecture, particularly neoclassical architecture. He who has not hurled insults at the Bauhaus or fought to keep the old red telephone boxes cannot count himself a proper member of the group.

The appearance of the young fogey is recent. Alan Watkins, a columnist for *The Observer*, coined the term in May 1984. In an article destined to stir up the young champions of a peevish and constantly vaguely disgusted right, he wrote: "The young fogey is a libertarian, but not a liberal. He is a Conservative, but has no time for Mrs. Thatcher. He is a disciple of Evelyn Waugh and tends to be unsentimentally religious. He hates modern architecture, and fusses about old missals, old grammar books, syntax and punctuation. He moans over the difficulty of buying decent bread and cheddar worthy of the name. He loves to go for walks and travel by train". The young fogey's bible is *The Spectator* whose former director Charles Moore is one of the extreme examples of the species. The greatest young fogey of them all is their idol Prince Charles who won the title by popular acclaim after he told the architects of the Royal Institute of British

Architects to their faces that their planned extension to the National Gallery was like a "carbuncle on the face of an old friend".

The term "fogey" struck an immediate chord, not only with the press which launched the new category with enthusiasm, but also with the targets themselves. In magazines like *The Field* and *Country Life*, aimed at the land-owning gentry and full of photographs of wild-eyed horses, the young fogeys were immediately glorified while the more traditional press investigated their political beliefs. They turned out to be "romantic Conservatives", the grandchildren of Disraeli and Salisbury. Their philosophy is fairly simple: it invokes a return to the Merry Olde England of yore before it was systematically destroyed by industry and horrid commerce. Geographically, it goes no further than Dover; nothing of importance happened beyond that point anyway. They were hostile to the construction of the Channel Tunnel, not for being dangerous but for being useless.

Faced with this kind of phenomenon, the British publishing world has not sat idly by. Today you can buy *The Young Fogey Handbook* by Susan Lowry and *The New Georgian* by Alexandra Artley and John Martin. Both have drawn up long lists. For example, things young fogeys don't like are the sixties, television, rock music, computers, electric typewriters, telephones, modern architecture, the European Union and sociology, and not only because it is often confused with social work. Here's what they do like: a reputation for being erudite, witty, aesthetic and vaguely irascible, ancestors, house parties, hunting and beautiful intelligent women. The money naturally comes from the last on the list.

Their outward appearance is no less interesting. Young fogeys adore dressing in outmoded clothes and they secretly devote a good deal of time and energy to this passion. Shirts should have huge floppy collars, suits should not be starched and even when they are almost brand-new, they must look like they've been worn for generations (one of the better known English fogeys, the writer and critic A.N. Wilson maintains that you only change your suit when it stinks); one's tie should be slightly askew, the perfect haircut is the one sported by the protagonists of the film *Chariots of Fire.* Useful accessories are braces, waistcoats and for riding a bicycle, an activity that young fogeys claim to adore, cycle clips. Never a beard, of course. A moustache like Anthony Eden's is acceptable, but risky.

You may be wondering at this point how female young fogeys dress and act. I'm sorry to say they don't exist. Fogeyism is exclusively a men's club. This does not mean that there are no rich, erudite and beautiful women who share a world view with the young fogeys. As sister, wife or colleague they can partake in the liturgy, indulge in their obsessions and sleep in their beds. Some, like the post-feminist Germaine Greer, who converted from rebellion to pro-creationism, enjoy great esteem. If they have old-fashioned Italian names like Arabella, Griselda or Hortensia, even better. The problem lies elsewhere. Young fogeys, who have not yet decided if sex is a sacrament or a nightmare, recall that in the merry England of yore, women stayed quietly in the background. This too, they feel, should remain the same.

The name "New Georgian" is taken from the era between 1714 and 1830, when four kings named George from the house of Hanover sat on the English throne. In those days, furniture was elegant, architecture sombre, hygiene virtually non-existent. Today, there are young English men, not many but certainly eccentric, who consider that era exquisitely English and try to recapture everything that came from the period. This is not done with detachment; indeed it is a virtual obsession. The New Georgians, often from good families, convinced that Victorian architecture is feeble and modern architecture a disaster, buy decrepit old houses in the worst parts of London and move their families in. Called "creative conservationists", they want to save, protect and restore everything and they can date a chimney or a chair leg at a glance. Their motto is "Let the Greens worry about Nature, and leave the rest to us". Their rigorousness has brought them many admirers but few imitators. In Italy where old houses abound, few would be interested in copying their endeavours.

Since the house is the great passion of the New Georgians, we'll start with it. Anyone who knows London (or Dublin or Edinburgh for that matter) will know the kind of building we have in mind: the façade is flat, often with the brickwork revealed. The windows are all the same size and symmetrical, with no shutters. The door, with fanlight and crescent over it, is a few steps above the pavement. Georgian houses are often in terraces. The sight of an early eighteenth-century terrace to a New Georgian is like an aphrodisiac. He is so obsessed with this type of building that he doesn't care what the rest of the neighbourhood is like (here is where he parts company with other well-off young people, happy to live in the dustbin of a basement flat as long as it is in Kensington or Chelsea). Since the most elegant Georgian neighbourhood, Bloomsbury, is beyond the means of most of them, New Georgians end up in some of the less salubrious neighbourhoods of London like Clerkenwell, Hackney, Islington and Spitalfields. The last is the most extraordinary of them all. Behind Liverpool Street Station and tucked around a wholesale fruit and vegetable market and the early factories of the East End, it covers a tiny area. Yet there live some of the most extreme adherents to the faith. And there one must go to believe it.

Spitalfields, dismal as a Hogarth print, is a monument to English eccentricity. New Georgians decided to set up camp there some twelve years ago after ninety of the two hundred and thirty buildings protected by the National Trust had been demolished and another nine were threatened with the bulldozer. A group calling itself the Spitalfields Trust organized a sit-in, raised the money to buy two houses, restored them and sold them. After that, they were able to save 80% of the remaining houses. Not long again a pure example of Georgian architecture on Wilkes Street went on sale. It had no bathroom or plumbing or electricity and it sold for £225,000. When it has been restored it might sell for as much as £425,000. Five years ago, it would have gone for £40,000.

The follies of the New Georgians are particularly interesting because, like all crazed people, inconveniences roll off the backs of these well-heeled bohemians like bullets on an armoured car. If you can't put in heating because you don't want to ruin the original wood paneling, just stick it somewhere else. The president of the Spitalfields Trust decided to transform a hollow bronze statue into a radiator. If respect for authenticity (which obsesses the New Georgians) means no electricity, there are Spitalfields residents who will live by candlelight (most compromise with a 25 watt light bulb).

A cottage industry has grown up around the New Georgians. There are architects who specialise in Georgian bathrooms and an expert on the colour of bricks (deep red until 1730, burnt umber after 1730, yellow – in London – after 1800). One expert studied microscopic flakes of eighteenth-century paint before ordering the plaster for his walls. The prize for authenticity though must surely go to Dennis Severs, a thirty-nine-year-old Californian who lives in a 1724 house on Folgate Street – five stories, nineteen rooms, one hundred and twenty candles –, keeps hay for the horse outside his door and organizes paid tours (which might suggest that rather than obsessed, he's clever).

There is little furniture in the most rigorous of these uncomfortable New Georgians houses and a great deal of disorder (the French call it *desordre britannique*). Exotic odours waft in from outside. The New Georgians share Spitalfields with a lively Indian community for whom art is no deterrent to a curry. Other odours coming from within are less mysterious. As the architect Neil Burton, a specialist on the period points out, authentic Georgian life was rather smelly, and not just because a hot bath was considered a cause of impotence and migraines. The New Georgians – who after all are British – have adapted to it quickly and with little difficulty.

These are the purists. But the phenomenon has

also caught the attention of others. The appeal of Georgian buildings has touched the hearts of estate agents all over London, who have thrown themselves like hungry wolves at these houses. If you should want to own one, besides the money, you will need to practice self-denial: a little row of Georgian houses will often be surrounded by run-down tower blocks and council housing. This was the case in Cassland Road in Hackney in London's East End, where £60,000 got you a basement flat consisting of two rooms plus kitchen and bath. For those who can't afford the original, there are copies. A good example is Grafton Square in Clapham, south of the river. And if a copy just won't do, you can always rent. A house in Dorset Square (NW1) goes for £3250 a week.

If you can't afford the original, a copy or to rent, there is always theft, thanks to which you can turn a house that isn't Georgian into one that is. According to the police, the disappearance of objects from that era is reaching epidemic proportions. Doors disappear (market value £500), along with chimney pots (£50), cast-iron bathtubs (£200), and especially fireplace surrounds (up to £25,000 for a Robert Adam original). One night not long ago all the inside doors and the staircase banisters disappeared from 42 Upper Grosvenor Street. Nearby, three individuals were apprehended who, pretending to work for the city, were removing the old paving stones from the sidewalk (market value £20 per square metre). In their defence they quoted the New Georgians' motto as written by Henry James: "Of the present we can only see the profile, it is the past we can look face on".

Of the many whingers whom the British Left
indulges to show that though it may not get many
votes, it does have a heart, there is one particularly
entertaining group. It is the "drabbies", young socialists who have chosen shabbiness and the mystique
of noble poverty as a way of life. In a country that,
right or wrong, considers itself a breeding ground
for new trends, they are taken very seriously.

Ideologically, drabbies are children of the
sixties. They are ecologists, pacifists, and feminists.
They are rarely extremists but they are almost always outraged. They will take any job as long as it
doesn't pay well. They drive third-hand cars and
dress as if they chose their clothes with their eyes
shut and then stomped on them a bit to rumple
them. They are anti-yuppies *par excellence*. They like
Indian music, politics and macrobiotic food and
are proud of it.

Supporting them and their brand of grass roots
socialism is a chunk of the Labour Party. Against
them are all the trendies who fill up London night-
clubs, write articles in magazines and invent all
kinds of harmless new styles that we copy a year later
in Italy. Their main criticism of the drabbies, whom
they reluctantly concede are lefties, is this: drabbies
are the last gasp of the sixties and the sixties killed
off any style socialists might have had. Take Wood-
stock, they say. It was a bacchanal and those sweaty
bodies were definitely in bad taste.

Michael Foot is a supreme drabby and an ex-
leader of the Labour Party who took on Margaret
Thatcher in the general election of 1983. During
the campaign he would appear on television wearing a corduroy jacket, chequered shirt and wool tie

and sporting an Albert Einstein hairstyle. His trouncing at the polls is partly attributed today to his dishevelled appearance. Peter York, the author of a book called *Modern Times*, holds that "the Warrior Queen (Mrs Thatcher) projected on to the nation her style, one which exuded strength and purpose, while Michael Foot dragged on in his worn-out jackets, pretending to be an ordinary person. But ordinary people didn't want an ordinary prime minister". York, better known as the author of the *Sloane Ranger's Handbook*, asserts that only executives in airlines ads wearing silly grins rate lower than drabbies.

People who detest drabbies call for a new kind of socialism and they are constantly finding new prophets. One of the noisiest is Robert Elms, the editor of *The Face*, a magazine of "fashion and trends" snatched up by Italian kids the minute they set foot in England (it's true that they hardly ever understand the English, but there are always the pictures). Elms, who modestly considers himself "the most elegant man in London," seems to be convinced of the need for a holy war against the shabbiness of the left. In an article that came out in *New Socialism*, entitled "Style Wars: Let's Ditch the Drabbies"., he argues, for example, "Style and the Left used to be synonymous; style came from our very roots. It is time we go back to them". He noted how "in international history, socialism has always been aware of the power of style. From the stark simplicity of the red flag to the Sunday best miners used to wear to go out dancing; from the revolutionary propaganda of the Russian activists to the designer chic of the Italian Euro-communists. But in England the pacifist look has taken over and the comrades with their turtleneck jumpers want to convince us that style is a dirty word".

Socialist style is also examined regularly by two London weeklies, *City Limits* and *Time Out*. *City Limits* is the bible for drabbies, who like the fact that it is in black and white, that the paper is not slick and that graphics are used sparingly; *Time Out* is beloved of yuppies, young, newly rich and with no children to support. The editor of *City Limits* has accused *Time Out* of not being the true voice of the radical left in London and for siding against progressive movements. *Time Out* editor, Tony Elliot, maintains that these insinuations are the ravings of a madman and his magazine has always been on the left. It was just that *Time Out* was not dreary and didn't play up to all the misery guts in the capital.

A similar but perhaps even noisier battle has been fought in the world of rock music. Two groups, one called "Style Council" and the other called "Red Wedge", were both trying win over British youth for Labour through their music. Red Wedge adored Neil Kinnock, the leader of the Labour Party; Style Council supported the "trendy left". The singer Paul Weller, apart from a few questionable ideas like wanting to turn the flip side of a record into a political proclamation, is educated, intelligent, and wears his hair short, as *The Face* dictates. Thanks to him, it looked like the Left had managed to find a comfortable place next to Boy George and Wham!, when along came a new rock group which claimed to represent the *true* left, more interested in class war than in the class of shoe. The new voices of outrage were called "Redskins" and they recently put out a CD with songs like *Kick over the Statues*, *The Power is Yours*, and *Keep on Keeping On*. Only drabbies – and not even all of them – buy their records, but that doesn't seem to bother them much.

The problems of "the left in search of a style" don't end here. Being in opposition left the Labour Party with time on its hands and so they refashioned their image, like other socialist parties in Europe. But they are miles behind in spite of their determination. It adopted a new slogan ("People First"), new colours (no longer red but grey) and a new manifesto ("Freedom and Fairness"), sure to depress many Bolsheviks. There is also a proposal to ban the singing of the *Red Flag* from the party congresses and replace it with something more modern. If the proposal to replace it with *Sailing* by Rod Stewart is voted in, drabbies will go into mourning.

TURN RIGHT FOR REVOLUTION

Start with privatisation of the nuclear industry, legalisation of incest and prostitution, castration for rapists. Continue with the abolition of income tax, social security, the National Health and privatisation of all public services, including the police and prisons. Finally if a revolution has not yet broken out, legalise euthanasia and abolish civil marriages, "a pagan and disrespectful institution". These and other ideas were part of a manifesto put out by the British Federation of Conservative Students, one of the noisiest refuges of the New Right that grew vigorously during the eighties. These Conservative students, who still hang about at Tory party conferences handing out leaflets, were a thorn in Mrs Thatcher's side. They were proof of the advice: keep your extremists under control, or they'll end up embarrassing you.

The war of attrition between the Conservative Party and its youth organisation started up again during the electoral victory of 1979. Extremely enthusiastic about the new prime minister, whom they dubbed the "Warrior Queen", the members of the Federation of Conservative Students reduced the young Conservatives, traditionally more moderate, to silence and began their march to the extreme right. The old guard of today loathes them and the feeling is mutual. In one of their programs they planned the immediate expulsion of the ex-prime minister Edward Heath, considered shamefully wet, while of John Biffen, the ex-head of the parliamentary group and for a brief moment aspiring opponent of the Warrior Queen they said, "he should be locked in a cage and hung from the ceiling in the Commons".

The manner in which these Conservative students managed to get themselves constantly talked about cannot have pleased the Conservative Party. For example, Federation vice president David Hoile chose to spend his holiday with the Contras in Nicaragua armed with a Kalishnikov. The Federation recently did some other unscripted things like distributing bumper stickers and pins that read "I love South Africa". At the 1985 congress the Conservative students chanted "Thatcher, Reagan, Botha, Pinochet!", when it was clear at the time that the lady would have preferred, both for herself and her friend Ron, other companions. After the Congress they damaged some of the buildings at the University of Loughborough, ended up paying fines and were made to promise never to return.

If they represent the more colourful side of British Conservative youth, there are more presentable groups on the New Right who still can provoke attacks of bile among traditional Tories, who prefer a dialogue with organisations like the Institute for Policy Research, a left-leaning think tank founded in 1988 and directed by Baroness Tessa Blackstone. The most fascinating of these organisations is perhaps the Policy Unit. There is probably no other group in the world of twenty-somethings who work hand in glove with the head of a government and give advice on how to put the country back on track.

If you do not think that Britain is unique, read on. Members of the Policy Unit really did work hand in glove with the prime minister – indeed, they worked directly overhead, as they had offices on the second floor of 10 Downing Street. There were eight members in all. One pair came from Trinity College, Cambridge, while others were prodigies lent by the administration or transferred from the private sector (such as Shell, the Rothschild Bank, British Leyland). Their brief was to advise the prime minister on economic and social matters, in the hopes that on any given day, she would allow herself to be advised. They were led by Brian Griffith, a professor at City University of London, an economist and the inventor, author, and framer of the theory of "Christian and moral justification of the production of wealth" which Margaret Thatcher treasured. Griffith was the third director of the Policy Unit, an organisation born in 1983 with the transformation of the think tank, the Central Policy Review Staff, that Lord Rothschild had set up at the beginning of the seventies. The young eggheads who cycled to 10 Downing Street were very young indeed and also very brainy. One of them, Christopher Monckton was described as a walking anachronism because he always appeared in public wearing a waistcoat, bowler hat and carrying a rolled-up umbrella. It was his idea to abolish all rent control in the private sector. Monckton,

Viscount Monckton of Brenchley's heir, when asked by the British *Who's Who* to list his hobbies, wrote "nihil humanum a me alienum puto". *The Face*'s suggestion that he "join his contemporaries and go out and eat a pizza" seems not to have been taken.

These young braves of the New Right are still carrying on Mrs Thatcher's crusade: privatisation, pension reforms, and efforts to reduce unemployment. They all know and help each other. Of five friends from Trinity College, Cambridge, two went to the Policy Unit, two were personal advisers to junior ministers and the fifth, Charles Moore, was the editor of the conservative weekly *The Spectator*, a kind of bible for the intellectual right, before taking over *The Daily Telegraph*, the main conservative broadsheet.

It is not hard to find other watering holes for the New Right. In Lord North Street, Westminster, there is the *Salisbury Review*, one of those magazines that everyone refers to but no one actually buys. The soul of the publication is Professor Roger Scruton, just forty and considered the newest and most philosophical of the new British philosophers. Scruton has many original ideas. He maintains, for example, "the country must first get rid of coarse intellectuals, wets, and the loony left". That done, "the government of the nation can be handed back to the messy, incompetent and shamefully inactive politicians". Then he and his colleagues can "return to their desks to read, write and listen to good music". You might think he would want to get his ideas across to as many people as possible. You would be wrong. Scruton happily concedes that the *Salisbury Review* is the least read journal in the country, selling only one thousand copies every three months, but "this does not matter, at least as long as everybody believes we are important". To keep his adversaries stirred up, Scruton also writes a column for *The Times*. Among other things, he wrote "Nelson Mandela is a man stained with shameful pride". He prefers to save his deepest thoughts for the *Salisbury Review*. For example, "Thatcherism will sweep clean the New Corruption, the rot of self-perpetuating privileges in the maze of the Welfare State". Or "Socialism is a temptation of the human mind: it is wrong, but it must be dealt with".

Space allows us to name only a few of the holy shrines of the New Right. One would have to be the famous Centre for Policy Studies, cradle of Thatcherism, set up by Sir Keith Joseph in 1974. Its current director, David Willets, a thirty-something Oxonian, uses football metaphors to illustrate the aims of his organisation. "Our scope is to push on to the right, to create enough space in the centre, to allow Ministers to score." Another is David Frost's Institute for European Defence and Strategic Studies, affiliated with the Heritage Foundation in Washington DC. Its aim is "to promote western values in international affairs". And let's not forget the Adam Smith Institute, which would privatise the monarchy if it could and at the moment is studying the success of small enterprises and the misdoings of "the small clubs that control British public life". Lastly, there is the Coalition for Peace through Security whose objective is to "unmask the fronts for Communist propaganda". Its director, Julian Lewis, not yet forty, was famous at one time for having infiltrated one of the extreme left factions of the Labour Party, moving it to a more moderate position and then escaping before his colleagues discovered they were consorting with an egghead of the New Right and skinned him alive.

LONDON. CAPITAL ADVENTURES

To illustrate the transformation of this city, it might be useful to look at the way Notting Hill has changed. This neighbourhood is familiar to Italians, who go there on Saturday mornings, especially when it rains, eager to buy the second-hand junk worth its weight in gold to the Portobello merchants who sell it. It is also well-known to Londoners who see it as a reflexion of the ups and downs of the capital. In the middle of the nineteenth century, Notting Hill was the preserve of a wealthy middle class. Close to the centre of town, near Hyde Park, it was full of whitewashed houses facing communal gardens. More elegant than Chelsea and more accessible than Belgravia, it seemed like the ideal city neighbourhood. During the second world war, the houses, by now too expensive to keep up, were requisitioned as housing for refugees. After the war the rich didn't return and immigrants from the Caribbean took note of its central location and reasonable prices and decided to settle there. When they rioted in the hot summer of 1958, they did it in the streets of Notting Hill.

The only whites who had the nerve to stay on were the ones who couldn't afford to move: the poor, artists, and starving intellectuals. They in turn attracted more of the poor, more artists, and more starving intellectuals. They then attracted young well-heeled liberals. The young well-heeled liberals drew the simply young and well-heeled – City traders and lawyers with their families – who felt very adventurous living somewhere that wasn't South Kensington. In 1975, a first floor flat, three rooms, kitchen and bath, went for £15,000. In 1985 it would go for £200,000. The Caribbean immigrants have fled, often with pockets full of cash.

What took place in Notting Hill is called "gentrification" and it has also happened in parts of Islington and Clapham. At cocktail parties in London it is considered quite a *coup* to have bought a house somewhere in London before gentrification and the subsequent explosion of prices. This sort of risk is mostly confined to the British; foreigners hardly ever take it. French diplomats and Italian bankers, knowing they will be staying in London only a few years, are not in a position to experiment and prefer to live in a neighbourhood that is already established. The mews houses of Belgravia and the basement flats of Kensington are consequently full of young foreigners who claim to be happy, while British families willing to spend an hour on public transport in the hopes of someday making a killing in the property market, move into Victorian houses around Clapham Common, south of the river and far from everything.

The rise in property prices has been vertiginous and is only just slowing down. For several years the increase was at about 20% a year and rents followed suit. Five hundred pounds a week for a flat in a fashionable neighbourhood (Belgravia, Knightsbridge, Chelsea, Kensington and Holland Park) is nothing unusual. A recent news item that shocked the nation found that a two room flat in the centre of London cost as much as a castle in Scotland, grounds and all.

The one hundred and twenty-three-year lease of what the British describe as a one bedroom flat (sitting room, bedroom, tiny kitchen and bath) in Chelsea was on the market for £155,000. Meanwhile selling for the same price was the sixteenth-century Monboddo Castle in Scotland which not only inspired the poet Robert Burns but was big enough for him to have got lost in, with its eight bedrooms, four halls, various bathrooms and two acres of land.

The house price increase has created some bizarre situations. A good example is the search for cemeteries in London, of which there are many (one hundred and three). When it comes to these plots of land – where, as the Italian poet Ugo Foscolo noted, the British come to bury their dead and then hang around for a chat – the greed of the speculators is blinding. Not long ago, even the City of Westminster got involved. It sold three cemeteries (Mill Hill and East Finchley in north London and Hanwell in the west suburb of Ealing) for the token sum of 15 pence to an estate agent to avoid paying £300,000 in yearly maintenance costs. The land was passed on to another company aptly named "Cemetery Assets Ltd" and finally ended up sold to a Swiss company. When the three cemeteries were put on the market, the asking price was £2 million as a long-term investment (you never know, reasoned the owners, the local authorities might someday give them a building permit). Protests were immediate from the families of those interred there who had paid for the upkeep of the graves in the price of the plot and from Westminster City Council rate payers who thought the price of 15 pence ludicrous and wanted to know when the other £1,999,999.85 was going to be collected.

It must be said that the skyrocketing cost of life in London has also had less funereal consequences. One is that the population is growing smaller. In 1970 it was around 11 million – we are talking here of greater London – and now it is closer to 9.5 million. Company directors refused to move to the capital even if it meant a promotion. Companies responded with generous "London weightings" even for those who work in Dover, Oxford or Southampton. Rising house prices have encouraged tenants to follow the government's advice and buy up the council houses they live in. The phenomenon has inevitably divided the lowest classes. Those with jobs have been able to get a mortgage and become property owners. Others, equally poor but unemployed, often find themselves out on the street because the Conservative government doesn't want to spend public money for council housing. Many families have ended up in bed & breakfasts in Bayswater and Camden at the local government's expense with whole families living in a single room and sharing a communal bathroom. The situation was highly popular with the owners of the bed & breakfasts who were making a fortune out of the misery of others but it was less so with the local governments. The borough of Camden was on the verge of bankruptcy after running up hotel bills of £23.5 million.

Very different and much quieter are the suburbs. In Richmond, actors, bankers and retired professors are willing to ignore the airplanes flying overhead that mess up their television reception for the pleasure of living near Richmond Park, where Henry VIII used to hunt deer. The ones who can't afford to live in Richmond, live in Putney. The ones who can't afford Putney, live in Wimbledon. When the BBC needs to film the British lower-middle class in action, it goes to Ealing. There the houses are all the same, with their bay windows, rose gardens and flowery-patterned sofas and carpets that camouflage countless suppers in front of the TV. This part of the city, which tourists pigheadedly ignore, has not changed in sixty years. The critic Cyril Connolly a few years ago wrote "if slums make good breeding grounds for crime, middle class suburbs are hothouses of apathy and insanity". Of course he wasn't familiar with the suburbs of Naples and Palermo.

Londoners have strong feelings about their neighbourhoods and are loyal to them. It is unusual for someone to say "I am a Londoner" but you do hear "I live in London", followed by the name of a neighbourhood. Saying "I live in Hampstead" says you are upper-middle class. To admit to living in Battersea, south of the river, means you would like to live in Chelsea but can't afford it. Even the residents of Streatham, a borough in the southeast, are proud of their neighbourhood, while in Hammersmith, in the west of London on the way to Heathrow, you can spend an evening with locals who will wax eloquent about the joys of Sunday lunch along the river, report that they just discovered that the poet Coleridge lived in the neighbourhood and try to convince you that the West End isn't far by tube.

To be honest, public transport is an obsession for everyone and a legitimate source of pride. Londoners love their underground system, in spite of tragedies like Kings Cross in 1987, in which thirty people died in a fire because the Underground had not replaced wooden stairs in one of the exit routes. They know it is the oldest system in the world (1863), the most extensive (more than four hundred kilometres of track) and it has wonderfully named stations like Seven Sisters, The Angel, Elephant and Castle. There are two hundred and fifty stops from Acton Town to Woodford on nine different lines. The famous Underground map, a contorted drawing that looks like the work of a high-strung child, was designed in 1933. It ignored actual distances and topography for clarity's sake and it hasn't changed since. The London Underground, which the British call the Tube and Americans call the subway, transports seven hundred million passengers a year (not many compared to New York, Moscow or Paris). Some of the stations have been voluntarily tarted up under the guise of modernisation so you get Bond Street decorated with little tables and umbrellas, Baker Street with souvenirs of Sherlock Holmes, and Tottenham Court Road with colourful mosaics, perhaps to cheer up the victims of pickpockets. The cleanest lines are the newest, the Victoria line completed in 1971 and the Jubilee line which is still being constructed. The Piccadilly line that goes to Heathrow is the most efficient. Cynics say it's to impress tourists while the opposition Labour Party claim it is because the government has plans to privatise the Underground and so maintains the Piccadilly line as a kind of showpiece to attract future buyers. The smelliest, worst maintained and least frequented is the Northern line, which cuts a vertical path north through the city and seems to be a favourite for suicides. Commuters call it the misery line and amuse themselves with running commentaries on its defects. "Good heavens, the stench at Elephant and Castle this morning is rather strong, the platform at Euston is more crowded than usual, the wait at Kennington longer and more inexplicable…"

Everything about the Underground fascinates Londoners. A recent event that provoked indignant letters to the editor had two buskers as protagonists. Bongo Mike and Extremely Frank Jerry, alias Mike Kay and Jeremy Helm, not content with playing their music in the corridors of the tube, had taken to boarding the cars and entertaining the passengers inside. When they were arrested, they raised a stink, and denounced the police who arrested them. Playing music on the Underground was no offense, they argued. They weren't forcing the passengers to pay anything and no one had ever complained during their performances. Kay and Helm claimed they were professional musicians of "situation music, i.e. music which matches various circumstances". Their greatest success, *This train is bound for Heathrow* changes to *This train is bound for Cockfosters*, once the train reaches the airport.

Even with the extensions under construction, the Underground will not be able to resolve London's transport problems. Some zones of the city, such as certain parts of the East End near the Thames, are just not well enough served by public transport. Efforts have been made to improve matters, like building the Docklands Light Railway connecting the newest part of London, born out of the ashes of the port destroyed during the war, to the rest of the city. City Airport, built closer to the City, has regular flights to Brussels and Paris, although only a small plane, the Dash 7, can use the runway built along the old wharves without bursting the eardrums of residents. A while ago, some particularly perspicacious investors noticed there was a river in London and it occurred to them to develop an express riverboat service. Soon a hydrofoil will link Chelsea with Greenwich. The journey will take thirty minutes and make seven stops along the way.

The idea of using the Thames, which winds through the city from west to east, occurred to planners in the nineteenth century as well, but it was abandoned when steam boats killed more people than were killed in a colonial war. Between May 1835 and November 1838 there were twelve collisions and seventy-two people drowned. In 1847 the *Cricket* blew up (thirty dead). In 1878 the *Princess Alice* sunk (seven hundred dead). One hundred eleven years later the tragedy was repeated. In August 1989 the *Marchioness* sank, with fifty-seven victims among those on board for a dancing party on the river. Today, while London waits for a public boat service, there are private riverboat services available. The owner of the *Daily Telegraph*, in an effort to lure journalists away from Fleet Street to his new headquarters in Docklands, has provided a ferry that runs daily between Westminster and Canary Wharf. On winter mornings one can see the journalists, like poor souls on the Styx, boarding Charon's boat and disappearing into the fog.

It has taken the ever-worsening traffic problems to convince Londoners that the time has come to use their river. In the last few years, innumerable reports and studies have documented that the number of cars driving into the capital is ever increasing, traffic jams are ever more frequent – mind you, this is by British standards. In Italy they would just laugh – and the lack of legal parking spaces is ever more problematic. The key to the whole traffic problem in London, according to the

Metropolitan police, is Hyde Park Corner. If it is blocked, Park Lane and Marble Arch become jammed in a matter of minutes. Shortly after, Bayswater and Edgware Road become blocked, while in the south the paralysis quickly spreads to Victoria, then Westminster and the Thames. Not long ago it was calculated that this mega-jam spread from the centre to the periphery at a rate of seven kilometres an hour, faster than a car during rush hour.

Some optimists thought that all the problems would be solved by building a ring road around London, the M25 (one hundred and ninety-two kilometres, £125 million and fourteen years to complete). They were wrong. Shortly after it was opened, the M25 turned out to be clogged with traffic during the day and at night filled with mad drivers in Porsches who were hoping to set speed records for the full circuit (sixty-eight minutes at the moment, if you're interested). Even this is a sign of the times. Fifty years ago, cars driving down a new road would have stopped to admire the flowers in the dividing strip.

For the most passionate point of view on London traffic, talk to a cab driver. You hardly need to bring the subject up and they are off and running. Cabbies loathe cyclists because they are small and stealthy, buses because they are big and awkward. They consider "so-called messengers" on motorbikes criminals, minicabs illegal, and the administrators of Heathrow who levy a 50 pence tax on black cabs, dishonest. But most of all, London taxi drivers hate pedestrians. A cynical old cabbie, interviewed on television, explained his theory. "When pedestrians do not cross on zebra crossings, they are calling your bluff. If you let them pass, two hundred of them will cross in front of you, the foreigners all looking the wrong way."

There are fourteen thousand black cabs in London, most the old model FX4. The new Metrocab is not popular and has been compared to a hearse. The eighteen thousand cab drivers – some share a cab – are as tightly-knit as masons. And like masons, they have strange rituals. The apprenticeship is called *the knowledge* and consists of memorising the name and location of every street in London. A *butter boy* is someone who has just passed his exam on the knowledge. "I have been legalised" means "they didn't leave me my 10% tip." Thirty years ago, one cab driver out of seven was Jewish. Now you see women and black cab drivers. The fares are not unreasonable. It costs less than £4 to cross the West End. Using taxis and public transport, Londoners can comfortably get around the city. No one has suggested closing the centre off to traffic, especially since the lack of parking spaces and the droves of traffic wardens make it virtually impossible to drive in the West End during the day anyway.

Only in the evening do Londoners get in their cars and head for the centre of town. In theory, it is to partake of the capital's nightlife – if such a thing exists. Over the course of the years, sleepless German executives, penniless French artists and wifeless Italian businessmen have all remarked on the same phenomenon. London shuts down just as Paris wakes up and Berlin starts to function. The hours for pubs and cinemas and the last Underground trains, along with sadistic restauranteurs, conspire to send Londoners home and foreigners to their hotels just after eleven at night. Of course, there are exceptions: night clubs where members of the royal family behave like peasants and peasants behave like royalty; saunas; badly lit Chinese take-aways; and clubs for sadomasochists where you're only admitted if you're wearing leather and covered in spikes.

If late night entertainment is insipid or sordid, evening entertainment in compensation sparkles – at least, given its calm and civilised character, as much as it can. Theatres are in good health, annual attendance figures have grown by a million since 1982, and a series of extravaganzas constantly beat all records (*Me and My Girl, Liaisons Dangereuses, Starlight Express, Cats, Les Miserables, The Phantom of the Opera* and *Miss Saigon*). But if you look below the surface you will discover that all that glitters is not gold. For a start, almost all of the successful productions are musicals and a third of these musicals are the work of one man, Andrew Lloyd Webber. The audience is composed mostly of new theatre-goers – people who think that "foyer" is the name of the orchestra's conductor – and tourists. American attendance alone has increased by 70% in just four years. Recently a ticket to see the original cast of *The Phantom of the Opera* just before it changed was going for up to £1000.

There is less cause for celebration in the traditional theatre. Often a production in the West End is forced to close after only a few performances and some companies struggle to survive. The Royal Shakespeare Company has had some disastrous seasons at the Barbican and is thousands of pounds in debt. The director of The Old Vic, worried about having included such obscure names as Ostrovsky, Lenz and N.F. Simpson on the playbills, said that London was becoming a cultural desert because of the philistine tastes of tourists and their insane passion for musicals. This seems a bit excessive ("never believe anyone in the theatre," said George Bernard Shaw). Anyway, the best works are at fringe theatres. A good example is *Serious Money*, a very popular play that happily lambasted the City and the people who worked there.

Film is in good shape and what is surprising in a city where 50% of Londoners have VCR's and are confirmed couch potatoes, the number of film-goers has doubled since 1984. In those days people complained that the national film industry was near bankruptcy. Today when the film industry is making a comeback, they are still complaining, saying the films are too depressing. The debate began after an attack on the last wave of British films by an Oxford historian named Norman Stone who accused the filmmakers of portraying a Britain that didn't actually exist. The films in question were *The Last of England, Sammy and Rosie Get Laid, My Beautiful Launderette, The Empire State* and *Business as Usual*. Most are set in decaying metropolitan outskirts, they ooze sex (homosexual if possible), abuse, violence and misery. *The Last of England*, directed by Derek Jarmon, doesn't even have a plot. It consists of a series of apocalyptic images of London, inhabited by bands of wretched people who meet along the banks of the Thames. Public opinion is divided. Liberal youth maintain that post-Thatcher Britain is very diverse and it was about time that British cinema produced something other than films like *Gandhi* and *Passage to India*. Conservatives declare themselves disgusted and have demanded that their subsidies be cut.

Except for films, evening activities are age-oriented. If you are over twenty-five with adult tastes but little money, classical music is very popular. There is a lot on offer in venues like the Barbican, Queen Elizabeth Hall and the Royal Albert Hall and it is hardly ever difficult to find seats, even for big events. Not long ago, when Arturo Benedetti Michelangeli was in town, an Italian woman bought two tickets by phone on the morning of the concert and the thrill of being able to tell her friends in Milan was almost too much to bear.

Even more popular than theatre, films and concerts, is going out for a meal. Londoners have always loved eating out and continue to enjoy it in spite of the huge financial sacrifice it entails. Dinner for two in an ethnic restaurant can cost £15 (the favourite is Indian, it is usually in the suburbs and has a name like "Standard" or "Star of India"), £20 for a Greek restaurant around Tottenham Court Road that includes retsina and waiters who threaten to play the guitar; £25 for a Chinese restaurant in Soho or Bayswater, £35 for an Italian meal with spaghetti drowning in sauce. (If you complain, they tell you the British like it that way.) For £100 you can eat at the Japanese restaurant Suntory on St James's Street, which was recently taken to task by the *Good Food Guide* for raising its prices by 21% after it won a Michelin star. Even more devious are the restaurants that call themselves Anglo-French (the quality is Anglo, the French is just an excuse to raise prices), especially in big hotels.

Needless to say, the younger generation doesn't usually go to over-priced restaurants. They prefer to spend their money on drink, rather than bad food. Young trendies like to go clubbing and to make it difficult for the uninitiated, they have invented one-nighters, spots that are open just one night a week. The foreigner then must know not only *where* to go but *when* to go. At the Hippodrome on Charing Cross Road, where you'll find the winners of free trips to London sponsored by Italian furniture makers and au pairs on their evening off any day of the year, the best night of the week is Thursday (Mondays for gays and friends). The Mud Club, begun in 1981 and the spot most resistant to fashion, is open on Fridays. If you're hoping to see something to top the Australian transvestite got up as a soft-boiled egg (yes, that's right, a soft-boiled egg), go to Taboo on a Thursday night. On Friday evenings the most popular place with actors and rock stars is The Wag Club on Wardour Street. It recently changed its password to "The seventies are back" and an obedient public suddenly appeared in bell-bottomed trousers on the streets of London, much to the delight of magazines like *The Face, Time Out* and *i-D*, always on the look-out for new absurdities. Nineteen-eighty-eight saw the start of Acid House and it works something like this: hordes of invaders dance for hours to the obsessive rhythms of music produced by a rotation of in-house disc jockeys (hence the term "house music"). Proper attire is a T-shirt with a happy face on the front and some sixties-type psychedelic allusion on the back. The fact that the followers of Acid House take a hallucinogenic acid called "Ecstasy" has brought Scotland Yard into the picture and caused the BBC to prohibit the word *acid* in any transmission, including the *Top of the Pops* hit parade.

When you talk about nightlife in London, you can't avoid the subject of prostitution. Fans of this sort of entertainment insist that the British capital is a disappointment and not only because fear of Aids has created a "look, don't touch" reaction in potential patrons. Take Soho, once considered the red light district by tourists. After a frenzy of laws and clean-up acts, it is now acceptable to families with children just about any time day or night. There are, however, still clubs that cater to foreign businessmen and their credit cards (a famous one is the Gaslight of St James's), you can find a few young ladies from Liverpool who hang out at Paddington and there are always escort services, about which there is a body of literature. Highly esteemed is Paul Theroux's novel *Dr Slaughter* and the film starring Michael Caine that followed it, *Half Moon Street*. If nothing else, you can always find flyers stuck in the telephone boxes promising a "whipping without mercy" and "spankings by the headmistress" – this reveals a lot about English sexual tastes – if you care to phone them. Appointments by phone are necessary since it is against the law in Britain to solicit on the street. Foreigners, who are ignorant of this but insist on their right to sin, end up wandering aimlessly through the night.

The more than three hundred thousand Italians who visit London every year usually spend their time on other pursuits. It is easy to figure out where we go and what we do. According to the British, we are instantly recognisable. The uniform of choice for the tourist from Milan or Rome consists of a leather overcoat in the winter, a pullover in the summer, a pair of Timberland look-alikes, a pocket-sized map of the Underground, a collapsible umbrella, and a comfortable number of famous sayings in his head, usually beginning with Samuel Johnson's comment "When a man is tired of London, he is tired of life". (More apt and less drastic these days would be Thomas De Quincey's "A duller spectacle this earth of ours has not to show than a rainy Sunday in London".)

Our tourist, who if allowed would explain London to the British and if not, will explain it to his wife for the fourth time, has lately found himself in a bit of a jam. Certain customs which he found puzzling in the past and therefore came to love seem to have changed. Pubs, for example, can now remain open all day. The Home Office justified this by explaining that the traditional hours, from 11 to 3 pm and from 5:30 to 11 pm were introduced during the first world war to insure that workers at munitions factories would not fall over drunk at work. Since that war ended a few years ago, he concluded, we decided to change the law. The official forgot one small detail, however. Tourists come to Britain, in spite of the constant rain, because they enjoy these strange British customs. If the British start to introduce sensible laws that eliminate the strange customs, there will be nothing left for the tourist but the rain.

There are other surprises. The hurricane of October 1987, for example, changed the look of the parks in London. Some good soul took the time to count the victims of that night of 160k/h winds: 300 trees in Hyde Park, 285 in Kensington Gardens, 31 in St. James's Park, 17 in Green Park, 350 in Regent's Park and 700 in Richmond Park. The total number of trees blown down in London was 3,000 while another 2,000 were uprooted and had to be cut down as potential dangers. Kew Gardens looked like it had been attacked by a giant with an axe. In Syon Park, 80% of the trees were uprooted. The Italian tourist may not have gone into mourning as deeply as the average Londoner for his *davida involucrata* or his *ailanthus altissima*, but he could certainly recognise a disaster when he saw one.

Other tourist fixations disappeared years ago but there are still tourists who refuse to believe it. One example is Carnaby Street, a symbol of swinging London during the sixties. It is useless to explain to your Italian friends that Carnaby Street is just a little back alley where no Brit would dream of setting foot. Friends set off full of memories and video cameras and soon find themselves surrounded by tourists underneath an archway which says something like "Welcome to Carnaby Street, famous throughout the world". Sharp-eyed Pakistani shop owners, lying in wait behind piles of T-shirts that say "University of London", spy the new arrivals with glee. We have tried in vain to explain to our more sophisticated friends that the only good feature of the street is that, involuntarily, it has become a kind of museum of British fashion trends over the last thirty years. The shop owners have warehoused the leftover raincoats and jackets from the mod years (1962) to which they've added Indian shirts from the era of flower power (1968), skinhead vests decorated with the Union Jack (1973), punk-style spike-studded collars (1977) and the little black jackets of New Wave followers (1980). The only novelty on Carnaby Street may be this: Mary Quant, mother of the miniskirt, has opened a store here, convinced the street will make a come back. If this happens, the Italian tourists patiently waiting these twenty years, will in the end be proven right.

Other stops on the tourist trail are undergoing radical transformations probably with the aim of confusing them. The controversial Albert Memorial, built at the behest of Queen Victoria as a memorial to her husband, is on the verge of collapse. A series of leaks corroded the iron structure and engineers who examined it predicted disaster within the next few years (that such a collapse would be a disaster must still of course be proven). Piccadilly Circus has a shiny new face. Construction, carried out at a snail's pace, is finally finished after eight years of work, as is the constant displacement of little Eros, a national mascot and the gift of the seventh Lord Shaftesbury (though why a Victorian philanthropist would choose a naked cherub to represent him is anyone's guess). Other revolutionary changes have taken place at Harrods, a name Italians usually can't pronounce but still love to show off on their green plastic bags when they arrive at Linate and Fiumicino. The owner, an Egyptian named Mohamed al Fayed, decided to spend £25 million to return the store to its original Edwardian fittings. The project was carried out by a platoon of interior decorators using old photographs and archives. The work, begun in 1987, went on for five years and covered ten hectares of departments and corridors.

When they are not getting lost in the food halls of Harrods, Italians enjoy open air activities. At Portobello market on Saturday mornings, there are so many Italians these days that you can no longer talk to your companion in a loud voice, which is always one of the pleasures of a foreign holiday. A better place to go now would be the Caledonian Road market on Friday mornings and Camden Lock on Sundays. Another hit with Italians is the modern musical, a superb British creation which you can understand even if you don't speak a word of English. One of the most popular, for reasons unknown, is *Starlight Express* where a dozen madmen on roller-skates skate around in circles. Unfortunately they never fall down. Other favourite places to visit are the various nineteenth-century buildings like the House of Commons, which tourists insist on believing is medieval (one has to admit the Gothic revival was a great marketing idea). We have willingly participated in some of the most embarrassing pastimes of Italians in London, such as Talk of London, a dinner theatre in Covent Garden. Here innocent groups, dragged along by ruthless tour guides, end up at the mercy of fat dancers and magicians with rabbit tricks. This bit of London will not change, not in the nineties, not in the year two thousand. Indeed, for the Italians who still fall for it, a Millennium party will probably be organised, with thinner dancers and more rabbits.

GOING NORTH

FROM THE CHANNEL TO THE HEBRIDES IN A SILVER MONTEGO

Brighton is a good place to start an end-of-summer trip through Britain. The city is English enough, southern enough and gloomy enough to make you want to get away from it as soon as you can. Not even Graham Greene wanted to stay. When he wrote *Brighton Rock* in 1938, he did it from a safe distance, although in his descriptions of Mexico and Indochina he was more scrupulous. Brighton's curse is its day-trippers who arrive in the morning from London, a fifty-five minute, seven-pounds-forty-pence-return train trip, and return in the late afternoon. They visit the Brighton Pavilion, an enormous pile of kitsch architecture commissioned by George IV when he was the Prince of Wales. They eat a hamburger cooked in a microwave. They wander around a little and they leave. The real tourists are retirees in tweed jackets. They arrive in their Austin Cambridges, watch the day-trippers with disapproval through the windows of their sea-side hotels and venture out only in the evening when they feel it is safe.

We leave Brighton and the south coast and head north on the A26, blending in like natives, we hope, in our silver Montego, steering wheel on the right. For maps we have the completely incomprehensible Ordnance Survey, a Baedeker and the Automobile Association's *Illustrated Guide to Britain*, this last a bit like the pillow Italians always keep in their cars – not much use, but everyone has one.

The road runs along the downs of East Sussex and passes near Glyndebourne, where every summer the rich from all over Europe plus a few opera lovers arrive in evening dress for a picnic among the sheep. Our aim is to avoid driving through London by going east on the M25, crossing the Thames through the Dartford Tunnel. The river Thames divides England into two worlds. To the south, lie the counties of Sussex and Kent, rich and green; in Tunbridge Wells it would be easier to come across a camel than a Labour Party supporter. Thanks to its thermal baths, the city enjoyed moments of glory during the eighteenth century, which lasted until someone discovered that breathing sea air was socially and physically superior and the smart set moved on. As a consolation, Tunbridge Wells was granted the right to add "Royal" to its name and became Royal Tunbridge Wells. North of the river are the outer fringes of London's East End, where local taste leans towards tattoos, lager and buxom girls. On summer weekends East Enders travel en masse to the Essex and Suffolk coast, to the kinds of seaside towns that the fashionable set who picnic at Glyndebourne and go to Ascot would never dream of setting foot in. The very thought of blaring tape decks and the smell of chips makes them shudder, they tremble at the possibility of bumping into their plumber in a state of undress, and they have absolutely no interest in spending 95 pence on a ballpoint pen that reveals a topless model when you turn it upside down. All of which, of course, seemed to us good reasons to go there.

Clacton-on-Sea on the Essex coast is one of those kinds of places. In the sixties, mods on motor scooters, wearing suits with drainpipe trousers and winkle pickers, and rockers on motorcycles dressed in leather jackets with studs would meet up for rumbles over Easter and other holidays. Today's visitors are calmer. The working class of London brings its children here to spend their days valiantly digging for worms in the sand on the beach. For dad, there are the pubs; for mum, there is bingo on the boardwalk. In the bingo parlours, the caller doesn't just read out the numbers, he chants them: "two and two, twenty-two-o-o, four and three, forty-thre-e-e". Looking bored, the women sit at their tables checking their cards. They have broad hips, stiletto heels and vividly painted toenails. Around them, prizes look on menacingly: giant stuffed animals, the likes of which disappeared from Italian country fairs ages ago.

Clacton-on-Sea also offers other amusements. The most obvious is the pier, complete with amusement park. At the far end, a restaurant serves eggs and bacon and cheese and pickles all year round. The cheese is invariably cheddar and the pickles are a mahogany colour that immediately makes you want a beer. But of course you can't drink beer here. For that you have to go to a pub. And the pubs are back on the boardwalk. At the entrance to the pier, a band of musicians in their forties plays rock music at full blast, their loudspeakers resting on the pavement. The bass player sports a Tom Jones-style hairstyle and the drummer is a bit winded but no one seems to mind. This is British popular music. Their audience of old-age-pensioners tap their feet in time to the music and they seem to enjoy it.

From Clacton, thanks to our Silver Montego and in spite of the Ordnance Survey Map, we reach Walton-on-the-Naze, a gloomy little village where the BBC recently came to do a documentary about the British seaside of the fifties where the English go to carry out their annual summer rituals: the dozing adults, frolicking children and bored teenagers. Today is the day of the village fete and the surrounding villages have decorated floats. Each village has three queens, a little girl of five, a young girl of around twelve and a twenty-year-old. Seated on their flowery thrones, they wave their hands at the crowds. The twenty-year-olds look like they are on death row, but the crowd isn't taking much notice. It's two in the afternoon and the pubs are full, the parents inside drinking and the children outside waiting.

Just to the north of Walton, beyond the river Stour, lies the county of Suffolk, famous for having the laziest people in the country. You can still spot "Please, don't rush me, I'm from Suffolk" bumper stickers on some of the older cars. Like the rest of East Anglia (Norfolk and Cambridgeshire) Suffolk is wealthy. Small industries have sprouted up all over. Felixstowe is the fifth largest container port in the world and Lowestoft, the easternmost town in Britain, has an impressive fishing fleet. Great Yarmouth, another big tourist destination, is also an important port city. The bed and breakfast where we stay is called Marine View, although you can't actually see the sea from our room. In compensation we have flocked wallpaper. When we look at the guest book we notice we are the first foreigners for a long time. The owner however swears he remembers a South African guest at the beginning of the summer.

Great Yarmouth has a splendid beach, dotted

with windbreakers to break the force of the gales blowing in from Scandinavia, well-tended little gardens, and a boardwalk full of lights, noise and couples walking arm in arm. There is also plenty of so-called wet weather entertainment for when it rains, which it does often here and all along the coast. We meet Eileen George of Brixton, a seventy-two-year-old tourist, who tells us that this year she has gone on day trips to Margate, Brighton, Eastbourne and Southend organised by her nursing home and it has rained on every one of them. There is a wax museum in which, if one tries really hard, it is possible to distinguish the members of the royal family from the cast of *Dallas*; there are ghost trains and several amusement parks with strange names. A ride on a flying saucer costs 10 pence. One problem with the place, though, is the sea itself and the problem is not a minor one, considering that Great Yarmouth is a seaside town. The water quality here does not meet the minimum standards of cleanliness set by the European Union. However, no one seems concerned about this and the minute the sun comes out, the children dash out into the grey-coloured waves.

We leave Great Yarmouth on a Sunday morning and head inland towards the Norfolk Broads, thirty shallow little lakes connected by canals and rivers. The Broads were created by the earliest settlers in the area who dug up the countryside for its peat, which they used as fuel. Today the Broads are frequented mainly by tourists out to enjoy fairly risk-free boating. As was explained to us by a couple from Norwich, sitting on the stern of their sailboat, enjoying the sun and a bottle of white wine, the boats all have sails but they also have engines to avoid collisions.

In the westernmost part of Norfolk, in a flat

landscape full of canals that looks more like Lombardy than England, lies King's Lynn, which the locals call simply "Lynn". It is a pretty little town on the banks of the Wash, with buildings whose names recall its mercantile past: the Hanseatic Warehouse and the Greenland Fishery House. The atmosphere here is calm, almost Dutch in tone, like much of East Anglia. A bit to the north of King's Lynn one can draw an imaginary line that would connect the Wash in the east with the Bristol Channel in the west, and, in an often repeated over-simplification, divide the rich South from the poor North. Yet the first county we come to north of the line is Lincolnshire and it doesn't seem at all poor. A mostly agricultural economy probably saved the region from the problems caused by the industrial crisis in Yorkshire and Lancashire.

Along the A1, the first city one comes to is Grantham. For many people, this name evokes just one thing: Margaret Thatcher. Mrs Thatcher was born here on October 13th, 1925 and she lived above her father's pharmacy in the town. Her father, Alfred Roberts, besides being the local chemist, was also a city councillor, judge and founder of the local Rotary Club. A few years ago the family home and shop was sold to an entrepreneur who turned it into a restaurant, The Premier, that specialised in Victorian food. Whether it was the name or the Victorian specialities, it didn't work in the East Midlands countryside. The place was put back on the market again, this time for £180,000. The Pakistani newsagent who related all this to us said he would never buy a place like that. On a moonlit night, walking through the rooms, you might come across her spirit.

His lordship, the tenth Duke of Rutland, like the owner of any self-service snack bar, sells light refreshments to his guests. The only difference is that his food is served in Belvoir castle amidst the forests of Leicestershire. (For reasons known only to the English, Belvoir is pronounced "Beevor".) Here are the prices of a noble lunch. Two pounds ten buys you brown bread and butter, jam, a teacake and a pot of tea. For an extra 85 pence you get that plus an egg salad sandwich. For £3.60, you can have a complete orgy of food with a ham sandwich, brown bread, butter, jam, a piece of cake, fruit and ice cream. The duke, who lives in one wing of the house and has no direct contact with the public, is not for sale. But nearly everything else is. The entry fee is £2, a guided tour £1, and two plastic swords £4. At the exit, by the souvenir shop, a sign invites you to have your ancestors traced for £3 "because 96% of surnames are related to a titled family". We duly paid our £3 but we are still waiting to find out what happened to the Severgninis of Leicestershire.

The visit to this stately home, not counting lunch, cost £7. In one year they have over a hundred thousand visitors. This means they must take in something like £700,000 yearly, more than enough to maintain the house and grounds. If you throw in a few medieval tournaments and other money-making events, the income should be even greater. Our entrepreneurial duke must make Margaret Thatcher proud. We check our calculations with an ancient employee, wearing a tweed jacket, in the hall of the house. He replies in monosyllables, obviously suspicious of foreigners who want to talk about money instead of about the fifth Duke of Rutland, who rebelled against Elizabeth I and ended up in the Tower of London.

North of Belvoir lies Sherwood Forest, where a certain Robin Hood led a happy existence making life a misery for the church, the rich and the Sheriff of Nottingham. People are still talking about the man who could split the branch of a willow tree with an arrow at four hundred paces. His name is everywhere. Two forests compete for the honour of being his birthplace, Barndale in Yorkshire and Sherwood Forest. The former claims to have proof that a certain "Robyn Hode", son of a gamekeeper, was born in Wakefield in 1285 and with the Duke of Lancaster took part in the uprising against Edward II in 1322. In Sherwood they consider this a vulgar lie and to prove that Robin Hood belongs to them, have erected statues of their beloved robber all over Nottingham. Tourists come, even though there isn't much left of the forest to see, they spend money, and the local government is happy.

Tourism is a source of income for York as well, though not its only source. York is separated from Nottingham by coal mines in the south and two of the most impressive graveyards of the industrial revolution: Sheffield, where the steelworks died and Bradford, which saw the death of the textile industry. Leeds was only saved, in spite of the decline of the manufacturing and clothing industries, because the local economy was not tied to a single industry. York's fortune lies in its cathedral, something the Japanese and Koreans, even with the best of intentions, cannot imitate. Every year two and a half million people come to see it. The most successful northern city, York was able to withstand the crisis that hit the manufacturing industries that resulted in two million workers being laid off between 1978 and 1981. The reason was fairly simple. York has Rowntree, the manufacturer of "After Eight" and other confections; Birmingham has British Leyland, the car manufacturer. During a recession, people around the world still eat British sweets, but they buy their cars from Germany.

Above northern Yorkshire, full of cyclists who speak an incomprehensible dialect, you reach the Northeast, consisting of Durham, Tyne and Wear and Northumberland counties. The region has the dubious distinction of having the highest crime rate, the most deaths caused by cancer, and the highest unemployment – if you exclude Northern Ireland – in the country. Its citizens are called Geordies, they speak with a strange accent, and use words that are Scandinavian in origin. According to a local Labour MP, Austin Mitchell, there is more vomit per square yard here from drunks than anywhere else in Britain and wife-beating is still one of the local sports. Aids, on the other hand, is almost non-existent. An acquaintance from the region told us that in the northeast gays are for beating up, not for taking to bed. In spite of that, he says, people here are generous, they will throw themselves into lost causes and they are the last real repository of working class culture.

The capital of this strange paradise is Newcastle, population 285,000. We arrive in the rain, and even through the foggy windows of our Montego (we've begun to believe they are manufactured this way, to make the British feel at home), there is something appealing about this town, though we can't quite put our finger on what. You reach the city by crossing the river Tyne over an iron bridge that looks like it is made from a giant Meccano set. In the centre of town, perverse urban planners allowed an enormous windowless shopping mall to be built. In nearby Gateshead, across from the council houses in Scotswood, there is another one – they love shopping malls in the north – called Metrocentre. It is supposed to be the largest in the European Union, as everyone constantly reminds us. What the largest shopping mall in Europe is doing in one of the most depressed regions is anyone's guess. For Margaret Thatcher, it was enough that it existed. For years when accused of neglecting the North instead of paying off the debts of the industrial revolution, she would reply by exalting Metrocentre. The city fathers say the shopping mall thrives because people in the region have so little faith in the future that no one saves and no one invests. They prefer to spend their money. Local Labour Party members say that Metrocentre's success is an illusion. The crowds of people aren't buying. They're just looking.

We ask Peter Carr whether this is true. Carr is the head of the City Action Team, one of those official bodies set up to promote the local economy. An amiable fifty-something chap with the air of a retired army officer just back from the colonies, he coordinates a team made up of people from the Departments of Trade and Industry, Employment and the Environment who help out the local authorities. He firmly believes Metrocentre is a success. Built in record time on some of the worst land in Newcastle – an old steel dump –, it used only local labour and materials. Carr has faith in the region's future. "We must convince people here that the days when the yards employed fifty thousand people are over; jobs must now be found elsewhere. Obviously it would be great if factories were to move up here from the south; costs are 30% lower than in the London area." Luckily, he says, the Japanese have arrived, and have chosen the English northeast as their foothold in Europe. The car manufacturer

Nissan employs two thousand people near Sunderland; Komatsu, the second largest producer of excavating equipment in the world, is in Birtley. The Geordies have found the work habits and rituals of the Land of the Rising Sun a bit odd, but a pay cheque is a pay cheque, so they have adapted and now are disciplined about doing their Japanese exercises during their tea breaks.

Next we talk about the future of Newcastle with Martin Eastel, the head of the Northern Development Board, a body made up of trade unions, industrialists and the local authority. In his forties, with a lively sense of humour, Eastel is a Londoner and still dresses like one, but he claims he is happy with his transfer to the north. "Here," he says, "I live better, I can afford a bigger house and more leisure activities." The existence of one hundred and fifty different organisations all trying to stimulate employment leaves him baffled. As long as businessmen in the south look at the north with dread and the government raises interest rates at the slightest whiff of inflation, he claims the northeast will not rise out of its morass. "We mustn't rely on the landed gentry: they prefer to look through their castle windows at a quiet undeveloped landscape, not at a factory. A lot of the civil servants whom the Government sends up here to get the economy going are administrators who've returned from the colonies: they mean well but they don't have enough funds," complains Eastel while we have lunch in a deserted pink brasserie with a French name, the most delightfully out of place restaurant one can imagine in Newcastle-upon-Tyne.

If the Scots knew that an Italian driving a Montego would be coming to write about Britain, in particular a Britain shaped by Margaret Thatcher, they would not be very pleased. First of all, they would point out, this is Great Britain only in a manner of speaking. The collective name was tolerable when Scotland and England took on the world together in the glorious days of the Empire. But today, with no treasures to divide, the two countries politely ignore each other. Margaret Thatcher was ignored straight away – she was about as popular as the measles and the Scots wasted no opportunities to remind the world of this. In the General Elections of June 1987, the Conservatives lost eleven of the twenty-one Scottish seats they were defending, out of seventy-two seats over all, and among the seats they lost were two held by Scottish office ministers. Once Thatcher was out, some of the rancour disappeared. With John Major, the fortunes of the Scottish Conservative Party picked up again, although only somewhat.

We drive to Scotland via Newcastle, taking the longer route, going first west to Carlisle, then along Hadrian's Wall, which to the joy of the local tourism office is still standing. Then we head south, to a region known in the Middle Ages as Galwyddel, meaning "the land of the Gaelic Celtic foreigners" in Welsh. Today it has been divided into two administrative counties, Dumfries and Galloway. The countryside looks like a romantic watercolour, but it is home to the most stubborn of all the Scots. In the middle ages, its inhabitants fought English feudalism; in the seventeenth century they signed the Solemn League and Covenant in which they swore to "allow wind to whistle through their bones" rather than accept the bishops appointed by the king of England; in the eighteenth century, after the Union of the Crowns, the so-called

Levellers went out by night to tear down the walled enclosures to protest against agrarian reform.

We reach Lothian following the Tweed river valley. Its capital, Edinburgh, is holding its annual summer arts festival, a chaotic event. Good reason to continue on towards Stirling, centre of "Silicon Glen", so-called after three hundred electronics industries set up plants here. Some seventy of them are American and apparently they are very satisfied with the arrangement. The *Washington Post* reported that the employees who come from the United States "love to write home that they were late to work because they got stuck behind a flock of sheep". A little farther north, the Scotland of picture postcards begins. The A84 takes you towards Fort William, at the foot of Ben Nevis, the highest mountain in the United Kingdom, full of people with backpacks and an air of exhaustion. Another forty-six miles on tiny roads and we are in Mallaig. Here we can smell the sea air and it's time to stop.

Mallaig is first and foremost a port and it lives on fishing and tourism. Understandably, the local population counts on the former more than the latter, if only because it provides an income year round. Tourists show up only in summer and even then stay just a few hours before catching the ferry to the Isle of Skye. The Anglican vicar, who runs a somewhat untidy bed & breakfast and forgets his slippers on top of the guests' bedside table, tells us that the fishermen follow the herring and hake six hundred miles out into the Atlantic beyond the tiny British island of Rockall and stay out for days. At the docks, the owner of one of the refrigeration plants, amused by these foreigners who want to know the difference between whiting and haddock, confides that winters are cold, but at least it doesn't snow. There is, however, a lot of wind, so in the evenings folks gather at the Royal National Mission to Deep Sea Fisherman, sit around the formica tables and watch television. In the O'Clamhan pub on the main street, local kids drink their pints, oblivious of the tourists in their embarrassing tartan neckties; meanwhile a group of folksingers sings, *Let's take the boat over to Skye*. Since the island is visible beyond the Sound of Sleat, we take their advice and cross the sea.

The first thing we notice when we arrive in Skye is that everyone seems to be named MacLeod or MacDonald. These two clans dominate the island and occasionally indulge in bloody fights with each other. The place abounds with strange legends of fairies and elves and magic cloths that will produce babies when spread over the marriage bed. The local hero is Bonnie Prince Charlie, young heir to the Stuart clan who in 1745 set off to win back the crown in Scotland with seven men and eventually assembled an army of Highlanders to fight George II. Defeated at Culloden, he fled to Skye disguised as a woman. Bars, restaurants, sandwiches and newborn babies on Skye are all named after Bonnie Prince Charlie.

Apart from the Bonnie Prince Charlie fixation, the local population is friendly and innocuous. Tourists are drawn here in summer by the landscape: heather-covered hills, dark steep mountains running down to the sea and castles. In Dunvegan, the decision to open the MacLeod castle to the public was considered to be an excellent one, especially by its owner, who pockets £2 from every visitor and lives in Aberdeen. In Skye overall unemployment is 23%, but in Portree, the main village, we are assured that this is a joke. The local folk cash their unemployment cheques and then go look for some work. In good weather, it might be tending sheep or fishing. In winter they work as plumbers, painters, and handy men in the hotels and bed & breakfasts. The owner of one of these B&B's, a woman named MacLeod (naturally), tries to persuade us that there is a night life on the island apart from the fairies and elves. In the sitting room next to the fake wood fire, she displays a collection of books about the royal family. Mrs MacLeod assures us that Prince Charles looks very elegant in his kilt and firmly denies that his ears stick out.

From Uig, the northernmost seaport, a ferry service called the Caledonian MacBrayne links Skye to the Outer Hebrides. The crossing takes three hours and the locals spend that time in the ship's bar. The boat docks in Tarbert, the one and only inhabited village on Harris. Its name means "the narrow strip of land between two bays in which boats can be towed" and that's probably what the villagers have done over the centuries to pass the time. On Harris, there are only sheep, white sandy beaches, freezing deep blue water, midges that seem to thrive on insect repellent and more sheep. The locals speak Gaelic, observe Saturday closings and try not to meet up on the single road that runs through the island. It is one lane only with the occasional passing place. The passing places are mostly filled with sheep.

Andrew and Alison Johnson moved into this unique paradise in the seventies. Oxford graduates, they decided to trade in their friends, family and career for a hotel on Harris. They found an old parish house, Scarista, facing the bay. Alison, small, with dark curly hair and wearing a thick grey wool pullover, looks more like someone from the south of

Italy than an Oxford intellectual. She has written a book about their adventures, *A House on the Shore*, which has enjoyed a certain success in England: it has become a kind of gospel for people who fantasize about making drastic life changes after an argument at work. The book has brought disciples to Alison Johnson and guests to Scarista House. "They come here and just stare at me, awe-struck," says the authoress. "Luckily when autumn arrives, the weather drives them away – the wind blows from the north, it blows from the south, it blows from the west, it blows the cars off the road and it rains all day long."

North of Harris is the isle of Lewis. Flat and barren, its main town is Stornoway, home of the well-known Harris Tweed. The town has two famous public conveniences that are very popular on Friday nights after the pubs close. One is called the Old Opera House and the other, the New Opera House. They were given these names because people go in bringing their bottles with them. Then they stay on and sing. Stornoway, in spite of its size, has a newspaper, *The Stornoway Gazette*, which comes out every Thursday. A recent edition was dominated by the story of Dave Roberts's discovery of a new kind of bat (seven columns, including photos) and the fear that the Outer Hebrides might be used as a nuclear waste site (three columns). From Stornoway, under the watchful gaze of a family of seals, the ferries of Caledonian MacBrayne sail on to Ullapool, a Scottish port founded by the British Fishing Federation in 1788. It recently celebrated its bicentennial and sells T-shirts that say, "We've been fishing for two hundred years". From Ullapool the A835 crosses the Highlands towards Inverness. Here is where Loch Ness ends and the fun begins.

For three days in the autumn of 1987, a group of American and British scientists combed these waters using motorboats equipped with sonar apparatus. While the operation, called Deep Scan, did not manage to scare up the Loch Ness monster as hoped, it did send a lot of local Scots off the deep end. A certain amount of hostility towards the project was understandable. If the American sonar didn't turn anything up, it would have meant a third of the population around Loch Ness, four thousand people who swear they have seen the monster, was crazy. If the instruments had unequivocally established that the legendary monster was merely an oversized seal or a giant carp, it would have been a disaster for the tourist trade: who would want to go on holiday to see a large fish?

Aware of this, the locals worked discreetly to sabotage the experiment. First they made only twenty-four motor boats available to the scientists, instead of the forty they had promised. This meant the boats were never able to cover the whole lake at once, so the fact that they didn't find anything might have meant only that Nessie was never in the same spot at the same time as they were. Scotsmen, wearing kilts and tartan berets, attended all the press conferences, noisily protesting if anyone so much as hinted that the monster might be just an invention of the tourist office. Press conferences were scheduled for six o'clock every evening at the Clansmen Hotel's pub, which proved to be a mistake. The Scots took up their stations there an hour beforehand and by the time the press conference began, they were completely drunk and constantly shouted out their disapproval.

Fortunately, it all ended well. The Lowrance Electronics sonar equipment registered three strong "mid-water contacts", one at 80 metres, one at 170 metres, and a third, the clearest, at 180 metres. Each time they were only able to establish contact for a few minutes before it was lost, implying that the object, whatever it was, had moved. Similar conclusions had been reached in an earlier study carried out in 1982 with less sophisticated sonar equipment. Naturally there were all sorts of opinions as to the identity of the Loch Ness resident. According to an organiser of the 1987 expedition, a shaggy-haired naturalist named Adrian Shine, it was probably a huge predator fish at the top of the food chain in the lake, a fish so large that it could eat all the other fish without being eaten itself. The Lowrance Electronics experts respectfully noted that a fish would have to be enormous to produce a signal of that magnitude at 180 metres, and they could not imagine what it would be doing at those depths since there wouldn't be any food that far down. Darren Lowrance, the company director, said the readings reminded him of "a gigantic shark". These opinions scandalised the purists. Sween MacDonald, "clairvoyant of the Highlands" declared that the next expedition would prove that a family of plesiosauruses lived at the bottom of the lake – it wouldn't be the first time an animal previously believed extinct was rediscovered. Ronald Bremner and Anthony Harmsworth, founders of the Official Loch Ness Monster Show, were particularly disturbed by the "big fish" theory. "It's just one man's opinion," they were heard to say.

There has certainly been no shortage of theories. The modern age of the Loch Ness monster began in 1933, the year the A82 motorway from Fort William to Inverness was opened along the western shore. Before that there were legends. Gaelic folklore has it that a monster named Eioch Uisge lived in the lake, formed four hundred million years ago when northern Scotland slid a hundred kilometres to the southeast. Saint Columba came up against the monster in 565 A.D. and prevented it from devouring a Pict, one of the early inhabitants of the area. Cromwell's soldiers, especially after an evening at the taverns, often spotted "floating islands" in the waters. In 1933, the new road took travellers along the shores of the river and they began to see things too – heads, tails, fins, scales. Interest mounted to such a pitch that in 1934 the *Daily Mail* sent a Mr. Weatherall, a famous big game hunter, to Loch Ness to solve the mystery once and for all. He arrived with great pomp and ceremony and after only a few days discovered an enormous footprint. When asked how he happened to have such good luck, he replied that nothing was ever too difficult for an ace hunter. Another newspaper, *The Times*, wrote that the whole affair smelled fishy. The British Museum jumped into the fray and declared that the footprint was a hippopotamus's. Local inhabitants discovered that the footprint was made with the base of an umbrella stand in the shape of a hippopotamus foot. The great white hunter feigned innocence, let a few days pass, and then declared he had found another monster, one that looked like a seal. He was recalled to London.

Over the years there have been plenty of photos to thrill the public and make the sceptics more sceptical. In one photo dubbed "the Surgeon's" because it was taken by a doctor on holiday, you can see a head and neck emerging from the waters. In "MacNab's photograph" an enormous half-submerged shape appears in the waters below the ruins of Castle Urquhart. In 1960 Tim Dinsdale, an aeronautical engineer, filmed a large animal swimming in the lake. The film was authenticated by NASA and the RAF and roundly applauded by the "pro-monster" faction. Through the Loch Ness Phenomenon Investigation Office, believers from all over the world have met to conduct a series of so-called "scientific" experiments around the lake. Here is a sampling. An airship was sent to the lake in the belief that aerial exploration would resolve the mystery. It had already started its journey over the lake when someone pointed out that the waters were so dark it would be impossible to see anything even a yard below the surface. In another experiment, Dan Taylor holed up in a yellow submarine christened the *Viperfish* and descended into the lake in front of video cameras. After a few minutes he resurfaced, saying that by eight yards he couldn't see anything, that the submarine made an unbearable racket, that it barely crawled along and that he couldn't control it. The *Viperfish* was equipped with two harpoons that in theory at least should have made it possible to get a sample from the flesh of the monster for research purposes. The results of the entire operation were so disastrous that someone suggested that they harpoon the director of the Investigation Office, but this idea also came to nothing.

Other interesting episodes followed. In the seventies a school of dolphins was released in Loch Ness bearing video cameras and sonar equipment. The RSPCA intervened claiming the dolphins would suffer in the muddy waters of the lake. The dispute became irrelevant when the head dolphin died of a heart attack during an experiment. A few years earlier even the mechanical model of Nessie, used in the film *The Private Life of Sherlock Holmes*

(1969), sunk ignominiously. This wasn't necessarily a disaster. At least we know there is now one monster for certain in the lake.

Today research continues around Loch Ness. Going down the longest and least travelled road on the eastern side, we meet entire families attempting to catch a glimpse of the monster. This is how they spend their holidays: Dad sits immobile with a pair of binoculars, Mum is nearby, camera at the ready, the children take turns sitting on a collapsible chair, eyes peeled on the dark waves. When we stop and ask them how things are going, they seem delighted to explain to a couple of novices the simple pleasures of a stake-out on the lake. An insurance broker from Glasgow, never lifting his eyes from the lake, declares that the hunt for Nessie is an ideal weekend pastime. It is inexpensive, it is time spent out in the open air and it is a relaxing way to spend the day since nothing ever happens. The only problem, he says, is with the children, who are totally bored: they don't believe in the monster.

UP NORTH

DEATH BY STEEL: HEROIC SHEFFIELD

What is striking is the simple yet spectacular collapse of these northern cities. An industry reaches a point of crisis. Its decline affects the fortunes of other local businesses. Unemployment spreads. Soon there are signs of economic collapse everywhere: deserted docks in Liverpool, ghettoes in Birmingham, and here in Sheffield, the red brick steel works with broken windows, filthy yards and "For Sale" signs, heartbreaking to see because it is clear, especially here, that disasters are not something you can buy or sell.

You don't have to understand economics or the current problems of the steel industry to see that something enormous happened here. To imagine Sheffield as it once must have been, you need only drive through the lower valley of the Don, the river that runs through the city. There the streets, with names like Vulcan Road, are reduced to canyons dividing the shut-down steelworks. Hadfields Steel, closed. Firth Brown, closed. Jessop, closed. Darwin Balfour, closed. Once each mill had a pub where the workers would go before and after their shifts. When the workers left, the pubs closed. Near the Carlisle Works there was the Alexandra Palace with its green walls and decorative glass. We meet Lawrence Grimsdale, a retired school inspector, born and raised in Sheffield, who tells us that twenty years ago it took half an hour to get through the neighbourhood. "Now there's so little traffic, it only takes ten minutes. It makes me sad."

Looking down from Tinsley Viaduct, where the road to Barnsley and Leeds begins, the only things moving are the bulldozers looking for a way through the piles of detritus and gypsy camps. A few kilometres on down the road, in two areas called Attercliffe and Brightside, there are two British Steel plants still in production, but one wonders for how much longer. The Sheffield Forgemaster, the largest private company, has managed to lose £16 million a year. Between Sheffield and Rother-ham, a nearby city that has had both steel and coal industries, there has been a reduction in the labour force from sixty thousand to twenty-five thousand jobs. Nationalised by the Labour government in 1967, the steel mills of Sheffield have since been privatised by successive Conservative governments, but today ideological arguments seem irrelevant compared to the present disaster. This is summed up with great simplicity by Irvine Patnick, a leader of the much diminished local Conservative Party. "There is no need for all that much steel in Great Britain and it is now cheaper to import it from Japan than to produce it on the spot."

The "For Sale" signs remain and optimism is confined to promotional colour brochures about the city which they insist we pay for at the town centre. Its glorious history also remains. Sheffield became the "steel city", after Benjamin Huntsman in 1740 invented a technique that made it possible to produce steel of such uniform quality that it revolutionised manufacturing industry. Sheffield's success might be blamed on Huntsman and also perhaps on the abundance of coal and the proximity of the North Sea. As the Reverend Alan Billings, the city's eccentric Marxist deputy mayor, said, "If we hadn't produced guns for the German navy in 1914 and steel for the English navy thirty years later, we might not be in this mess".

Sheffield's decline has more everyday dimensions as well. Besides warships, it also produced cutlery. This was manufactured in another part of the city, towards the centre and it was a natural spin-off of the production of special alloys. Only a few years ago, Sheffield blades were found in every kitchen in the world. Then the city committed hara-kiri. Confident that the label "made in Sheffield" gave them the edge over competitors, local manufacturers began to import unfinished blades from the Far East, where they were cheaper, and finished them in Sheffield by attaching the handles and stamp. It didn't take the Japanese and Koreans long to realise that they could do the same thing themselves and they had no qualms about doing it. Today 98% of the world market of so-called "volume cutlery" is in their hands. As one of the people we spoke to said, "First the Japanese sent their cutlery to Sheffield to have it finished off, then they thought they could use it to finish Sheffield off".

For the cutlery industry as well as for steel, the dimensions of the disaster are immediately obvious. You don't need to go to the "industrial museum" that the city recently opened. History is down every street. What happened to the workers who made the blades for scissors and then delivered them to the workers who put them together? What happened to the workers who produced only blades for carving knives? The answer lies in the yard that used to house five laboratories and now has only one. Or in the ruins of Viners, the most famous steel work of them all. It was torn down a few years ago, to the cheers of neighbourhood children.

Now Sheffield is clinging grimly to the last industry left, quality cutlery. In the town centre, between tourist agencies promoting cheap holidays to Tenerife and shop windows full of shiny polyester jackets, the establishments specialising in knives are hanging on. For example there is Sheffield Scene, which claims it has only one policy: no Japanese imports. When people stop buying Sheffield's famous Kitchen Devil knives, Mrs Robinson, the owner, says she will close down.

Sheffield's politicians toss the blame back and forth. In the city council, the Labour Party has been in power for fifty years and accuses the Conservatives of "short-sighted and deflationary politics". The Conservatives answer them by saying that given that the Labour Party has always been in power, it's their responsibility. Irvine Patnick, the local Tory Party leader, says, "Instead of flying the red flag on the Town Hall on Labour Day and twinning with Bulgarian cities, the Council should have declared Sheffield a 'free enterprise zone'. Then we would not be in such a state".

Patnick is short, chatty, outgoing, and Jewish. He interrupts his Yom Kippur observances to meet with us. He has very precise ideas about the Labour Party in power in his city. Sheffield, in his view, is "the capital of the People's Republic of Yorkshire". He refers to the town hall as "our little Kremlin". We follow him down corridors and up staircases to the top floor of the town hall and there with the city below and no one to overhear us, he confides, "Do you know that Labour councillors turn up at council meetings with Jesus sandals and bring their dogs and children with them? And that two months ago, during my speech, the councillor opposite me was breastfeeding her baby?". As we go back down the steps, he indicates with disapproval a secretary with bare feet and stops to sigh in front of a marble statue of the catholic Duke of Norfolk, mayor in 1857.

According to Patnick, Sheffield is falling apart. Reverend Alan Billings, the deputy mayor (the sensible face of madness, in the minds of the Conservatives), disagrees. He believes the city is on the road to recovery. In anticipation, the council provides many free services and spends a lot more money than it takes in. This has provoked furious confrontations with the government and to some, if Sheffield has been abandoned, this is the reason. One thing is certain though: the poor living in ugly tower blocks behind the railway station are genuinely poor. We drive up. From here, you can see where the houses in Sheffield end and the green countryside of Derbyshire begins. From up here the city also looks less ugly. Its calm is unnatural, almost clean, without the smoke from the mills. This complex of tower blocks, dubbed "Hyde Park" by one witty architect, was built when the city was lively, dirty, and rich. Everything is different now. The only thing that hasn't changed are the young girls in white nylon anklets, walking silently down to town, their arms folded across their chests.

MANCHESTER. NICE MEMORIES, BIG LOOS

Of the many records it has held, Manchester is left with only one: that of having the longest public lavatory in Europe. It is not literally true – it is what locals disparagingly call the Arndale Shopping Centre, built in the seventies. The structure would be ugly enough if it were set down on the outskirts of any American town, but here in the midst of what was once the most exciting Victorian city, it is dreadful. Journalists from the local *Manchester Evening News* have an interesting theory. They say that it is a monolithic piece of cheese – same shape, same colour, same veining – dropped down from heaven to punish the city for some horrible misdeed.

The misdeed must have been truly bad for Manchester, along with the rest of the north, to have the kind of luck it has had. Like its sister cities, Newcastle, Sheffield, and Liverpool, Manchester is another victim of the Industrial Revolution. Today the North – a vague term that the British use for everything north of Birmingham – suffers from higher unemployment, higher rates of mortality, fewer home owners, and worse nutrition than its neighbours in the South. Of the fifty most prosperous cities in the country, forty are below that imaginary line that runs from the Wash to the Channel in Bristol, north of London. The first city in the north to earn the classification of "prosperous" is Aberdeen in Scotland, in nineteenth place, and only because of North Sea oil.

It may be hard to believe it today but Manchester was once a great city. At the beginning of the nine-teenth century it led the vanguard of the Industrial Revolution and mounted a challenge to London. At the time, 10% of the British population lived in London and agricultural and commercial produc-tion was concentrated in rural England and Wales. Manchester built up a textile industry while Sheffield chose metals and Liverpool developed its sea port. In 1830 there were one hundred and eighty-five textile mills, twenty-eight silk factories, and dozens of small industries where a bit of everything was manufactured, from Charles MacIntosh's waterproof cloth to Joseph Whitworth's special screws. In that year the first steam-powered railroad was inaugurated and it gradually began to replace the old system of canals built in the previous century. There was steam and work for everyone. Professor Brian Robson who teaches geography at Manchester University says that the line that Yeats wrote about the Irish rebellion of 1916 was equally true for those early years in Manchester: "All changed, changed utterly: A terrible beauty is born".

We meet Robson one Friday afternoon on the deserted campus. The professor, who has written a pamphlet entitled *Where is the North?*, explains that the decline in this part of England was due to the short-sightedness of the local industrialists at the beginning of the twentieth century. It was their lack of imagination along with the first world war that dealt the blow from which the region has never recovered. Since then Manchester has inexorably declined along with Britain's manufacturing industry. In the past fifteen years, the decline has been steep. Figures are boring but they help paint a picture. In the decade 1974-84, when industrial production grew 22% in Italy, 42% in America and 61% in Japan, in Britain it fell by 4.3%. In Manchester the big collapse began in 1979 when new investments stopped. Today the population has fallen by a third compared to 1951, unemployment in the city is around 30% and among those under twenty-five, it is as high as 50%.

The city centre carries the most visible signs of

this violent transformation. It looks as if the Victorian city suddenly died and the new town was never born. One quarter of all its housing, according to the housing officers themselves, is sub-standard and a good part of the housing built in the sixties to replace the slums (sixty-four thousand houses were demolished in ten years) is now in need of serious repairs. Lately there have been problems with the sewers as well. Built for many people but few cars, they are collapsing under the weight of traffic. The city council, in an effort to avoid a repeat of 1979 when there were fifty accidents, replaced the sewers with new ones able to withstand the weight of double decker buses. Perhaps this time they'll have it right.

In Manchester the most miserable neighbourhood is Hume, just to the south of the centre, beyond the railway. It is a jungle of high rise tower blocks, which are not very common in Britain, built where textile workers once lived. One huge block, looking like some strange animal balancing on dainty feet, is known as the "bull ring" and no taxi driver will go there at night. It is not only Hume that is surprising. Downtown, the streets open up from time to time into wide car parks, like freight docks. There, they tell me, everything was torn down, but nothing was built to replace it. No one wants to live there now to become a pioneer in the nocturnal wasteland of the inner city. For their part, the Labour government is ideologically opposed to giving up any of the land. If it is forced to, it will declare the land " of historical significance", thereby tying developers' hands. Those who are stuck living in the centre, live in rented accommodation, and don't bother to pay their rent. Manchester City Council confessed sometime ago that it was owed some £8.4 million in back rent. There are a few new industries (the first computer was built here back in 1949; electronics are thought to be the only hope for Manchester), and they need space, which they find outside the city. The middle class has also moved outwards in search of bigger houses, followed by the shopping malls, in search of the middle class.

The urban centre, therefore, has become the place where the poor live. It is full of pleasant memories and ugly monuments, like the huge red brick warehouses on Whitworth Street, and the Arndale Shopping Centre that looks like a public convenience. There are dismal conversions, like the Corn and Produce Exchange in Fennel Street which has become the Vesuvio Restaurant and Pizzeria, the old train station which has been converted into an exhibition hall and the Royal Exchange which is now an avant-garde theatre. Bombay Street and Bengali Street look like they've been recently bombed and perhaps they have been, if historical events can be considered explosive.

LIVERPOOL AND THE GIRLS AT THE ADELPHI

If there were disaster tours, like there are lakes and mountain tours, I would recommend Liverpool. The city is England the way the Labour Party would like it to be so that they would have a focus for their indignation. And it is what Conservatives hope never to see, a moribund port, a decaying city and the promise of a revolution never fulfilled.

The last Conservative MP for Liverpool was Anthony Steen. After he was elected in 1979, he and forty willing housewives founded Thatcher's, a tea shop where even today you can have a cup of tea and cake under a portrait of the ex-prime minister. Steen stood again at the next general election, but he left Liverpool for a seat in Devon. He knew that he would never be re-elected in Merseyside. The city has six MPs at Westminster, five Labour and one Liberal Democrat. The pride of Liverpool used to be its two football teams, Liverpool and Everton. The tragedies of the Heysel stadium disaster in 1985 and Hillsborough in 1989 diminished even this pleasure.

But disasters do not make Liverpool less fascinating. In fact, just the opposite. One watches the city dying a languid death, British-style. And it is dying. Forty years ago, it was one of the most important commercial ports in the world and eighty years ago, it was the second most important city in the Empire. Today it is only considered a great city in the out-dated guidebook by Touring Club Italiano. If you read their descriptions of it standing in front of the deserted river Mersey, you have to laugh. "This is one of the most prestigious trading centres for the import of cotton, timber, grain, fruit, and tobacco and the export of cloth and machinery." The truth is that when trade with America ended, the city didn't adapt to the changes as Rotterdam did. When Britain joined the European Community, ports on the English Channel were favoured. Unemployment, which in the Southeast is less than 9%, here reaches 30%. And while in the Southeast, those 9% get £30 a week on the dole as well as finding odd jobs to support themselves, in Liverpool the favourite sport of the unemployed seems to be just hanging out.

Liverpool's problem, to put it simply, is that it is closing up shop. If you arrive by train at Lime Street station, it doesn't take long to notice that while the nearby buildings may testify to an important past, they are "so jumbled up today that they look like the crooked front teeth of many of the local citizens," as Mario Praz observed. Like certain Eastern European cities, traffic in the middle of the morning is light, shop windows are dreary and the clothes of the people are shabby. Down at the docks, there is nothing left to see but the chains that bound the African slaves as they waited to sail for America. The Cunard shipping line has left its grand offices and moved to London. The Irish Steamship Company closed down the ferry to Belfast when it realised no one was taking it anymore. The next to go will probably be the ferry that connects the two shores of the Mersey, the river that cuts the city in two. On the north side is the centre of town, on the south side is Birkenhead where youngsters used to go during the last world war to bathe and to watch the ships full of American soldiers arrive. A committee to save the ferry has been set up and is presided over by Maurice Packman who believes that Liverpudlians have seen their city wither in the last ten years and don't deserve this final humiliation.

A ferry implies water and water, no matter what colour it is in the last bit of the river, fascinates Liverpudlians. The Merseyside Development Corporation was set up to convert the old wharfs on the Albert Docks into small flats and was inundated with requests for information. These renovated buildings on the old docks are now finished and are a source of great pride for the city. On Sundays entire families sit at tables outside in the wind and the fathers tell their children that if Liverpool succeeds in this enterprise, there is hope for Merseyside. Members of the government and the royal family repeat this litany – with perhaps less conviction – when they visit Liverpool for a morning and then depart.

135

Along the rest of the river, the landscape is diverse. Wharfs stand like great empty cathedrals, tall and full of broken windows. Today only ten million tons of goods pass through the port a year, just 4% of what Rotterdam sees, and most of it goes to nearby Seaforth on the other side of the Irish Sea. Only the dockside pubs seem to want to remember that things were once different. They bear names like the Dominion, the Victoria, and the Rule Britannia. The Baltic Fleet is one of the most famous. It was built in the shape of a ship, and aligned to look out on the other ships on the river. Nearby the melancholy inner city holds out its arms. Half demolished mansions, dilapidated little houses and vast wastelands wait for the money and the interest to build something here. Inside the Soviet-style building of the *Liverpool Echo*, the afternoon paper, they talk about the time when the Minister of the Environment came from London. After a bit of pressure, they got him to admit that the city centre was in a disgraceful state. To the government's lack of interest you can add the arrogance of the Labour administration, led for years by Derek Hatton, a spitfire dressed in polyester, who was expelled from the party as an extremist after a series of fiscal irregularities. Hatton and his followers refused both cooperative and private aid. Only public money is welcome here, they declared – but, of course, there was none.

Toxteth, a dilapidated neighbourhood sitting high on the river, run down, yet almost beautiful, is a good example of what has happened to Liverpool. Here in 1981 violent race riots broke out and they have been repeated on a lesser scale every year since. During one of these confrontations, the crowd burned down a little art nouveau theatre, the

Rialto, that has now been added to the list of pleasant memories of the city. Nearby is the beginning of Catherine Street with its brothels. Here is where Rod Stewart's "Maggie Mae" lived. Times are hard for the girls too. Sunday morning, their day of rest, they meet at the corner pub, Peter Kavanagh's, and reminisce about the good old days when Polish sailors would come up to Toxteth. Today they have to go down to the docks themselves when the ships come in. In another pub, the Philharmonic, opera lovers meet. The men's room, its walls covered with coloured ceramic tiles, is considered so fine that on Tuesdays it is also open to the ladies. Here too, between a lager and an insult to the government, is the confirmation that Liverpool has become the capital of the "other England", as David Sheppard, the Anglican bishop, calls it when he gets excited during a sermon.

An example of the fact that Liverpool is not going through its best period, if statistics and empty docks don't convince you, is Beatles City. Hardly anyone visits this attempt at a museum on Seel Street, built by the city to honour its four famous sons. At the entrance a young woman sells scarves and T-shirts, or at least she would if anyone would buy one. Inside you pass through a kind of chamber of horrors that consists of tapes of *Love Me Do* and film clips from the sixties. The museum now closes five months of the year during the winter. If it continues to be deserted, they may end up selling the whole thing, from John Lennon's first guitar to Ringo Starr's Morris mini with the enlarged boot to hold his drums. The Japanese have already said they are interested.

Another fascinating bit of decadence is the Adelphi Hotel, near the train station. It was sold in

1983 by British Rail to a private consortium which attempted to return it to its former Edwardian splendour, full of stucco and mirrors. When it first opened in 1914, it was declared to be one of the five most beautiful hotels in the world. The rooms on the lower floors had enormous bathrooms and were inspired by the staterooms of first class passengers travelling to America on the great transatlantic liners. The Adelphi was where people met to say good-bye before the long voyage and later it was where Harold Wilson waited for election results on polling day. Today an advertisement inside the lift promises discounts for a "dirty week-end", a sexy Saturday night to remember in a luxury hotel. It is aimed at kids from the north, who have no memory of what the Adelphi once was and have no interest in knowing their parents' Liverpool, only twenty years ago.

IT'S RAINING IN GLASGOW ON THE CASA D'ITALIA

One rainy day in Glasgow (and most of them are rainy), we decide to visit the Casa d'Italia. Besides providing shelter from the rain, it is a good place from which to observe an unusual side of Scotland and a melancholic bit of Italy. The Casa d'Italia is a time machine. In this Victorian mansion at 22 Park Circus in Kelvingrove Park, you see ties and jackets that went out of fashion in Italy twenty years ago and Naples football fans who may admire Maradona but say that the Brazilian Faustinho Cane could kick a goal more accurately and tell you they remember when they brought their children to the stadium with their faces blackened with shoe polish in his honour.

138

The director of the Casa d'Italia is from Barga, in the province of Lucca. He shows us around, turning on lights in cold rooms that are no longer used. Of the three hundred and fifty members, few come here and even fewer pay their dues. The discotheque in the basement has turned into a blue catacomb full of dust. The restaurant is papered in red velvet plush and two Salvation Army officers are there eating, while the "function rooms for entertainment, wedding receptions, dinner dances and all sorts of parties" as described in the souvenir brochure, are closed off so as not to waste heat. At the bar they explain that the club was founded by the Italian fascists in 1935, requisitioned by the British authorities in 1939 and returned to the Italians in 1946. The director says the Casa did well in the fifties when Glasgow was "black with soot and birds didn't sing, they coughed". Then the birds stopped coughing, and things went from bad to worse. "The Italians are all in the fish and chips trade, which is the poor man's food. When the poor ran out of money, we Italians ran into trouble."

Certainly, things have been hard for ordinary people in Glasgow. It is enough to know that every industrial sector has had to lay off people and that traditional employers like the shipyards, steel and textiles industries employ half the number of people they did in 1971. At the beginning of the nineteenth century, one ship in four – in the world – was launched from one of the twenty-three shipyards along the river Clyde, including all the great transatlantic liners that sailed from Liverpool (Cunarders). Today it is one ship out of one hundred and thirty.

In the past Glasgow's advantage was that it lay right on the open sea. The clipper ships of its tobacco merchants could reach America long before their London competitors: the London ships had first to slip past pirates lying in wait for them in the English Channel. Today Glasgow is still in the same place, but the markets have moved on. The city, with half of Scotland's population, has become a depressed area, the only one in Scotland besides Dundee. The Conservative government, in essence, props up the city and the good citizens of Glasgow repay it with a lot of contempt and not many votes. The Scottish Labour Party holds a huge majority of the Scottish seats in Westminster; the local government has been Labour since forever. In 1922, when the fascists were marching in Italy, there were ten powerful orators here called the Red Clydesiders who subsequently became Scottish MPs. They were so incendiary that their followers rose up against the then prime minister Lloyd George during a visit, forcing him to send in the army. Little remains from those days, apart from Harry McShane who is now ninety-four and was once secretary to John MacLean, the first local consul appointed by the Bolsheviks in Britain. McShane says that for a Marxist like himself Glasgow is a textbook case. "That woman [Margaret Thatcher] thinks she is Adam Smith. Every man a capitalist: daft stuff, son, daft stuff."

It must be said, Glasgow has done everything possible to encourage the Marxist hopes of McShane. The Gorbals, a district synonymous with misery, bad language and prostitution, has been cleaned up but the squalid working class neighbourhoods built in the fifties and dotted around the centre, have survived, thanks to which Glasgow continues to head the list of most violent cities in Europe. We go to visit these neighbourhoods one Sunday afternoon with a hulking great taxi driver who immediately tells us the names of all the streets where he won't go because people will stone and break his windows. "They hide behind those concrete walls, the bastards, and hurl stones at anything that moves."

We drive around the centre clockwise. Possil-park is in the north and from a distance looks like a single enormous concrete building. As you get closer however, you can see it is made up of many buildings, all horribly the same, with staircases smelling of piss, walls covered with graffiti and spooky pedestrian passages connecting the build-ings. They say anything can happen in these parts. Not long ago, four young boys went into the house of a mentally handicapped young girl, raped her and then went on to paint the walls blue with their bare hands. British Steel Engineering used to be in Springburn; now the police station is like a bunker and a billboard on the street urges you to "invest in gold". At Roystonhill there is a fish market and the only pub in Britain that opens at seven in the morn-ing. Young people drive around in red and black second-hand Morris Marinas waiting for something to happen, just as they do in southern Italy. The same look, the same elbows hanging out the car windows, the same music playing on the radios. This is the most Irish neighbourhood of Glasgow, where IRA terrorists hide out before crossing the channel. If this is the best housing the Bauhaus archi-tects of the Weimar republic could have dreamed up for the working class, give me the small single family homes of the nineteenth-century bourgeoisie.

Luckily, there are also a few pleasant surprises to be found in Glasgow. The city government has launched a campaign to promote the city, much like New York's with its "I love New York" slogan. Its distinctive posters, plastered on buses, proclaim "Glasgow's miles better". Whether it is miles better than Ankara or Belgrade or just better than Edinburgh, is not clear, but the campaign seems successful at least as far as stirring up controversy among the public which still hasn't decided whether to admire the city government or just think them mad. The university is old, quiet and clean. The city centre, sloping down from West George Street, is full of drunks being sick on Saturday nights, according to the good citizens of northern Britain, but it could be worse. Catholics and protestants who shoot each other in Northern Ireland simply get into fights here after a football match between Celtic and Rangers at Park Head and Ibrox Park, in memory of the days when the protestants were rich tobacco merchants and the catholics, coming down from the Highlands or from Ireland, carried the tobacco on their backs down to the ships.

Other good news is that jobs lost in industry – some two thousand a month starting in the seventies – are being replaced with jobs in service industries, banks, insurance and newer fields like electronics. In Scotland some two hundred companies have followed the lead of IBM, Honeywell, and Hewlett-Packard. The people with jobs aren't interested in the squalid outskirts and they've created a kind of fashionable and modern inner city. ("The Berlin effect", Jim Murdoch, a young law school lecturer, assures us.) Around the local BBC offices and the university, there are some twenty sophisticated French restaurants, the kind where you spend a lot and eat very little. They bear names like Lautrec's, Geltrude's Wine Bar and La Bonne Auberge. At the

Ubiquitous Chip in Ashton Lane, you can eat Scottish grouse in what seems to be a conservatory, surrounded by beautiful well-dressed blondes of the kind you'd find in London, discreetly gossiping and laughing. From this vantage point Glasgow seems to be optimistic and full of confidence and the suburbs of the East End and the closed shipyards seem light years away. No surprise then that the Italians of Casa d'Italia, proud of the photographs taken with Italy's former president Giuseppe Saragat and worried about the future of fish and chips, never set foot in this part of town.

BLACKPOOL: KISS ME QUICK, NEVER MIND THE SEA

Not long ago, people in the north of England had two pastimes. One was maligning the south of England, the other was holidaying in Blackpool. Today, unluckily for Blackpool, only the first pastime, which doesn't cost anything, is still enjoyed. In Blackpool's chilly resort on the Irish Sea, the number of guests is sadly declining. Miners from nearby Yorkshire and their families still arrive every summer and find enough bright lights and lager to get them through their holidays. And every autumn the political party congresses and the trade unions still fill the place for a week. But that's not enough for Blackpool's tourism industry just as it's not enough to call the city the "Las Vegas of Lancashire", with its 10 pence slot machines and three thousand five hundred bed & breakfasts, £7 for a sea view.

There are obvious reasons for Blackpool's decline, the tourist industry will reluctantly tell you. The North has always been poor. And there is high unemployment. The poor and the unemployed don't have money for holidays. Those who can, save up for a holiday in Spain – every year eight million British holiday-makers board charter flights and return a fortnight later with a sunburn and a silly hat. A week in Benidorm costs only £99, including airfare. Blackpool simply can't compete with these prices.

Before those in the tourism business realised this, they tried everything they could think of to lure people to Blackpool. The city fathers promoted Blackpool as the only truly English seaside resort, full of fish & chips shops, and the smell of fried food and suntan oil. Why go to Spain where they treat you like animals, they said. Come back to Blackpool, as you've been doing since 1770. Here you can drink beer and chase girls on the Golden Mile, the boardwalk down by the sea (just five hundred metres long despite its name). A few years ago the tourist office published a brochure with the title "Come to Costa Notta Lotta", hoping to lure holiday-makers away from the Spanish resorts. They increased the number of amusements inside the four hundred and fifty foot Tower and allowed strip shows in the clubs on the boardwalk (in the ordinance they are defined as healthy family entertainment). They also did everything they could to keep customers away from the sea itself, which was a good idea. According to the 1988 Water Report from the Ministry of the Environment, the sea around Blackpool didn't meet minimum standards of cleanliness as established by the European Union. The tourism office even dreamed up a "Sauerkraut Festival" in the hopes of attracting German tourists. Not surprisingly, they were doubtful about travelling a thousand kilometres north in search of sun.

Thanks to these efforts and to drastic price cuts,

Blackpool will probably survive. Each August five hundred thousand eggs are fried in the bed & breakfasts, according to the local tourist office, which suggests there is someone there eating them. But Blackpool's future depends on the prosperity of the areas surrounding it. If new industries in technology or service move into Manchester and Merseyside to replace the defunct industries, it may stem the flood of people going south in search of jobs. It might even change the mentality that the CBI (the Confederation of British Industry) described as "discouragement coupled with a certainty that it is always somebody else's responsibility: it is up to the South, to Europe, to the Japanese, but it is never up to the northerners themselves".

In Lancashire, they are not convinced. The North is doing badly, people say, because the southeast, London and its surrounding areas, would be delighted to cut off the North from the rest of Britain and cast it adrift in the Atlantic. Blackpool asks only for a little help. For example, why not pass a law allowing children to enter pubs with their parents? It's not allowed now. The head of the family has to go in alone and drink his beer while his wife waits outside with the children, noses pressed against the window like something out of a Dickens novel.

Every spring in Blackpool, they say that this summer will be the decisive one. Every summer, the poor man's Las Vegas has the same smutty postcards, the same "Kiss me quick" caps and the same discount shops where girls in high heels drag their boyfriends drunk on beer to look at appliances for their future homes. London, four hundred kilometres away, seems like the capital of another country. To give you an idea of what people here think of the government down there, the wax museum on the boardwalk melted down Mrs Thatcher not long ago and replaced her with Boy George.

QUIRKS

PLUMBING THE DEPTHS OF THE BRITISH SOUL

A few simple souls believe that the most fascinating topic of conversation for a foreigner in Britain is the royal family or Margaret Thatcher, or, maybe, castles in Scotland. Nothing could be farther from the truth. The most interesting topics for us are some of the extraordinary customs of the British that have baffled the finest minds in Europe. No one for example has yet to explain convincingly why the British persist in installing sinks with two widely spaced taps, one for hot water, one for cold water, placed at the very edge of the sink, so that when you want to wash your hands, you either scald them or you freeze them, but you never manage to wash them. This is such an ingrained tradition that even a recent publicity campaign in the papers, meant to encourage people to save energy, featured a sink that you would find only in some backwater in the Italian mountains.

The mystery of two taps is closely connected to that of the bidet. The reason the British continue to ignore its existence has been widely debated. One explanation links it to Protestant Puritanism, which detests the bidet as a symbol of unmentionable intimacies. We're not convinced. We would argue that a more likely explanation for why the bidet has been ignored is that the British are convinced that if they were to install it, they would have to use it. A certain aversion to this type of activity is suggested by a series of statistics (British, of course) meant to prove the opposite: it seems that no other country in Europe consumes as much water between 7 am and 9 am as Britain. Now, apart from the fact that its people might simply enjoy the sound of running water, remember that half of all British families have pets. My theory? In the morning, they run water and bathe them.

The disconcerting relationship between the British and their bathrooms goes back over the centuries. We can't delve deeply into a history of plumbing here, so we'll limit ourselves to noting that in the Middle Ages, the British employed various euphemisms to avoid using the word "toilet". Among the nobility and the clergy there were prudish phrases in vogue like *necessarium* or even stranger, *the garderobe* or "cloakroom". The cloakroom, in finer homes and castles, was carved directly out of the thick outer walls or was situated in a small extension that protruded from the exterior wall, allowing the waste to discharge directly into the space below. In this way, moats, built as defensive measures, ended up offensive, at least to the nose. In 1313, Sir William de Norwico ordered the construction of a stone wall to conceal the discharge of the so-called cloakrooms. Many of the "secret rooms" and "private chapels" that tour guides show visitors to castles and stately homes were actually latrines. At Abingdon Pigotts, near Royston, for example, it is easy to spot the "altar stone" with its decidedly suspicious hole in the middle.

In Victorian England, the deteriorating state of

baths almost changed the course of British history. It seems that after a stay at Londesborough Lodge, near Scarborough, the Prince of Wales and several of his entourage were struck down by an attack of typhoid fever. The Prince survived but the Earl of Chesterfield and his valet died. The country was genuinely shocked. The heir to the throne had nearly succumbed to the inadequate sanitation of the Earl of Londesborough's house. Legend has it that Edward, once recovered, publicly announced a crusade for better sanitary facilities and declared to his future subjects that if he had not been prince, he would have liked to have been a plumber.

If he had become a plumber, he would have had his work cut out. When the British threw themselves into the acquisition of new enamelled bathroom fixtures after the first world war, they didn't install them in proper bathrooms. Middle-class terraced houses built in the nineteenth century had only two large rooms on each of three or four floors and it didn't occur to the British at the beginning of the century to provide for anything as optional as a bathroom. After the war when households no longer had servants – during the war, servants found more lucrative work in the factories and were reluctant to go back into service – the situation grew worse. Terraced houses were divided up into maisonettes, small apartments and studios, and tenants were forced to grope their way down the stairs in the middle of the night and knock on the door of the communal toilet, which was often carved out of a space on the landing. This placement had its advantages. The stairwell served as a perfect resonating chamber for the sound of flushing so that everyone was able to keep up to date on the state of their housemates' bowels.

Things are not much different today. If you take a stroll through Bayswater in London, and look carefully at the backs of houses, you will find that bathrooms are still put in strange places. A visit inside one of the beautiful white houses in a crescent in Notting Hill will demonstrate that bathrooms were the last things on the minds of the proprietors for generations. When they weren't built on the landing, they were stuck in the attic or in a corner of the bedroom. These architectural acrobatics mean that a window in a British bathroom is considered optional, like a Jacuzzi. Almost everywhere, you will run into the "plumber's delight", the name for the glass shelf just below the mirror, which is precariously balanced on two brackets so widely spaced that you need only touch it for it to fall merrily to pieces in the sink.

Along with the practicality of taps, which we have already mentioned, the lack of decent showers and the irascibility of the water closet must be mentioned. "How many water closets flush the first time you pull the chain?" asks Lawrence Wright in his work *Clean and Decent*, published in 1961. Even the Duchess of York brought up the subject during a visit to Los Angeles in 1988, much to the delight of the Americans present, who expected almost anything from a member of the British royal family except a dissertation on the workings of the WC's at Windsor Castle.

If hygienic standards were maintained, one might say that British houses have a certain charm, as long as you consider it charming being the last person in the evening to use a windowless bathroom in a bed & breakfast. Unfortunately, the scant amount of interest in bathrooms would seem to be reflected in their maintenance and cleanliness.

This reminds me of something that happened to me the first few months I spent in London, which I look back on with a mixture of nostalgia and horror. I was staying with friends in Clapham and I noticed that the inside of the communal bathtub was a kind of mossy green. Thinking that the most common colour for pre-war plumbing was white, I asked if by chance the tub wasn't home to some sort of plant life, interesting from a botanical perspective but worrying from a hygienic point of view. The reply after some pressure was that the tub was green not white and there was no need to worry. Unconvinced, I took advantage of my hosts' absence one Sunday afternoon and experimented with a sponge and cleanser. After a few hours of work, it was clear that the tub was white. My hosts, however, remain convinced that I replaced it with a white one and that continental Europeans are psychopathically obsessed with cleanliness.

We Italians have always been thrown by things like this. No sooner does it become clear that getting into a bathtub in Britain is the beginning of our adventures – with the exception of grand hotels where guests are offered "extras", like a bidet (though not necessarily a window) – than we realise that our exploration of bizarre Anglo Saxon customs has begun.

A headmaster from northern Italy recently wrote wanting more information about "the English girls who go tightless in the winter and so walk around with deep blue legs" whom I had mentioned in an article. I must say the question is one of the most perplexing I have ever been asked. For my readers' sake, I decided to delve deeper into the subject. My tightless friends – I did have friends who wore tights – insisted they did this because they weren't cold. I then asked, if they weren't cold, how come their legs turned blue. They pointed out that a leg could turn blue even if it wasn't cold. I then thought perhaps it was a matter of economy, but I discarded that hypothesis when I saw that an English girl who went tightless would go dancing and spend the equivalent of five pairs of tights in an evening. Still not satisfied, I continued my research and here's what I discovered. Middle-class girls wear tights more often than their working class counterparts; girls from southern England wear tights more often than girls from the north; London transvestites wear tights more often than anyone.

I also knew – and here perhaps was a clue – that many English girls think they are attractive without tights, and that they are even more attractive in repulsive pointy-toed fake leather stilettos, which squash their feet and turn them bright red, which go perfectly with their navy-blue calves. Here are a few more noteworthy theories: generations of English schoolgirls, forced to choose at boarding school between bare legs and woollen stockings – nylon was banned – opted for the former, and the habit stuck. Another explanation: the English, punished by their climate, yearn for contact with nature. Girls run around with bare legs; on the first warm sunny day, men strip down to their underpants in the parks. One last theory is that English girls are way behind their European counterparts and are still dressing like Italians and French girls after the war. If this is correct, they will adopt tights somewhere around 2020, and who knows, by then there might be bidets and single taps too. But this, I must admit, is wishful thinking.

For a certain breed of Englishman, the gentlemen's club is like a lover. A Frenchman or an Italian might throw himself into the arms of another woman; an Englishman prefers his leather armchair. The analogies don't end here. Like a lover, a club doesn't come cheap and like a lover, it can fall out of favour. At the moment, clubs are going through good times and it's not just because sex, since the advent of Aids, has become as dangerous as parachuting, which makes the choice between an armchair and an adventure that much easier for an English gentleman. These days the older clubs have waiting lists that are a source of pride to their members, they keep their books balanced and have replaced roast beef and Yorkshire pudding with ersatz French cuisine. Along with the menu, the regulars have also changed. Retired colonels are still part of the furnishings but there are younger men now with good manners and very good salaries, often from the City, who have been persuaded that £400 a year is a reasonable price for a bit of polish.

Before we look at how gentlemen's clubs have come back into fashion, it's worth examining how they became successful in the first place. Anthony Lejeune and Malcolm Lewis, authors of *The Gentlemen's Clubs of London*, write of the "need for the well-to-do Englishman to get away from women and domestic worries". This explanation seems convincing, especially if you consider the great lengths men went to, to keep their life's companions out of their clubs. In his club a gentleman intended to read without interruption, smoke without being scolded, drink without being looked at askance and discuss politics with someone who showed some interest. In other words, he didn't want his wife around. The fear that one day wives might break down the fortress doors lasted a century. The story is told of how General Sir Bindon Blood, dozing in the smoking room at Brooks, was jolted out of his sleep upon hearing the swish of a skirt not six inches from his nose. He opened his eyes and saw Queen Mary whom the secretary of the club was showing around. Unperturbed, he closed his eyes again and said in a loud voice to his neighbour, "My friend, it's the snowball that will start the avalanche".

The habit of living in close quarters with members of the same sex, which began in British public schools, made life in these refuges even more agreeable. Bruce Scambeler, the secretary and historian of the Travellers' Club, 106 Pall Mall, has no illusions about the lifestyles of the founding members around 1820. "They would have late lunches, visit their tailors, sneak out the back door and spend the rest of the afternoon in Savile Row's brothels. They would come back in the evening to eat, drink and play cards." A popular explanation for the success of the various Whites and Reforms is this: the club was not a place where an English gentleman would go to meet his peers, it was a place where he could go and be reasonably certain his peers would leave him in peace. It is why the Royal Automobile Club of Pall Mall, wittily nicknamed The Chauffeurs' Arms and always as crowded as the village square on market day, is now looked on with disdain, while Hurlingham isn't even considered a true club, just a place where foreigners hang out when Harrods is closed. There is a famous anecdote about a retired colonel back when the Royal Automobile Club was still in its glory years. He arrived one day saying, "I had a full life and I intend to end it in peace. I have come here to die and my only wish is to pass away peacefully and quietly in the comfort of this old armchair". According to legend, his wish was granted.

There may be many elderly gentlemen snoozing in libraries who secretly share those feelings, but the clubs, as we said, have changed profoundly. There are many reasons for this. First of all, they have undergone a process of natural selection: the various crises in the seventies when London was poorer and more socialist weeded out many of the less viable clubs. Members left orphaned moved to other clubs whose survival was thus insured. The Naval and Military, affectionately known as the In and Out, absorbed the Cowdray, the Canning and the United Services (nicknamed The Senior). Brook's took in members of the St. James's, while Cavalry joined the Guards becoming the Cavalry and Guards. Among its three thousand two hundred members are many from the army. Even today the annual dues are equivalent to a day's pay for a member with a rank lower than captain, and two days' pay for ranks of captain and higher.

Another explanation for the better health of the clubs is the acceptance of women. Until recently they were allowed in only through the kitchen windows; from there they were taken directly to bedrooms on the upper floors. Of the larger clubs, only the traditionally liberal Reform Club at 104 Pall Mall has accepted women as members and even then, only since 1981. Others – though not all – limit themselves to accepting women as guests only. Brook's opens its doors after 6 pm and says that this concession has kept its dining room in the black. Wives, fiancées and secretaries, properly attired, are admitted at the Naval and Military, where they have a separate entrance, and at the Army and Navy and the Reform, where they have a separate cloakroom. At the Garrick at 15 Garrick Street, the club that boasts of the best dining room and is a meeting place for lawyers, journalists and others of their kind, women are welcome. But not at the Athaeneum, home of the church establishment, whose hardly scintillating atmosphere drew this comment from Rudyard Kipling: "It is like a cathedral in between services". There are other similar anecdotes about the place. For example, this announcement was said to have appeared in one of the daily newspapers: "The Athaeneum has been reopened today after its annual cleaning; members are back in their original places". Sir James Barrie, the creator of *Peter Pan*, on his first visit to the club asked an octogenarian biologist seated in an armchair where the dining room was. The old man burst into tears. He had been a member for fifty years and it was the first time anyone had spoken to him.

Along with women and restructuring, the reasons that London clubs are coming back in full force are essentially economic. First of all, the clubs' administrators have changed. Instead of retired colonels, masters at waging war in Malaysia but less successful at finance, there are new young managers with experience at big hotels. Thanks to them, the large clubs are almost all in the black today. The Reform, where such illustrious visitors as Gladstone, Palmerston, Asquith, Churchill and Lloyd George used to come for drinks, showed a profit in 1986 of £190,000. The dining rooms and lodgings have helped keep these London clubs in the black. Faced with the high prices of restaurants and hotels, members saw that the clubs were a bargain and have begun to use them as their *pieds-à-terre* in the capital. Here are sample prices. An annual membership costs around £400, lunch £10, dinner £20 and a single room for one night £25. The credit for having finally taught economics to the upper classes must of course go to Margaret Thatcher, whose government also made something else clear. No matter how splendid their buildings, the clubs were going to have to become self-sufficient. Club managers faced reality and got organised. Some said that as a tribute to the Thatcher government, their members should be urged to vote Conservative. Since they already did, this hardly seemed necessary.

All the changes we've described shouldn't lead you to believe that clubs like the Pall Mall and the St. James's have turned into Holiday Inns. With the books balanced, they have jealously preserved their idiosyncrasies. For example, the oldest, White's, which originally began life as a pastry shop in 1693 owned by an Italian named Bianco who anglicised his name, has never seriously considered accepting women as members. At the Garrick, they were not happy that some members read newspapers over lunch, so someone set fire to *The Times* an unlucky member was reading. When one joins the Reform Club, along with his dues the prospective member must swear allegiance to the Reform's liberal ideals. A few years ago Arkady Maslennikov, the *Pravda* correspondent in London, applied for membership and declared his acceptance of the clause; no one would believe him. Members of the Traveller's had to prove that they had travelled at least five hundred miles away from London as the crow flies. Today members, many of whom come from the nearby Foreign Office, are discomfited when American guests are hesitant to leave their bags and hats in the cloakroom for fear they will be stolen. In a gentlemen's club, such a thing could never happen. But if it did, there would always be a face-saving way to show that it hadn't. At the entrance to one of the clubs on Pall Mall not long ago, there was a notice that read "Would whoever might inadvertently have taken a blue cashmere coat and left a lightweight jacket in its place, please report in confidence to the secretary".

MAKING WODEHOUSE HAPPY

The servant problem in Britain has been tackled with much the same aplomb as the problem of the Empire was in its day. Back then when their subjects protested, the government simply made them citizens of the Commonwealth and that was that. When the idea of domestic service became controversial in the sixties, the establishment simply changed the way they referred to such workers and called them domestic help instead. However, by then there were far fewer of them. A sense of collective guilt, the advent of time-saving appliances and basements, euphemistically described as lower ground floors or garden flats, rented out to foreigners signalled the end of that delightful British game called "upstairs, downstairs". In that old world, servants lived downstairs and could gossip and smoke as they wished, while their employers lived upstairs and could throw vases and produce an heir without being interrupted.

In the eighties, the newly rich British gradually overcame their shock at this state of events and began to employ butlers, waiters, cooks and gardeners again. Naturally the numbers, the style, the relationships and the salaries have all changed. A twenty-three-year-old financier, after making a fortune in the City, can now hire a butler to explain such vexing questions as the correct number of buttons on the sleeves of a jacket. Jeeves looked after Bertie Wooster in much the same way – P.G. Wodehouse would no doubt be fascinated by this turn of events.

Let's begin with some statistics. In 1851, servants were the biggest single category of workers in Britain after farm workers and they formed the largest trade union in London. Only six British cities had total populations larger than the 121,000 servants – half under the age of twenty-five – working in London alone. Eighty years later, in 1931, there were still 1,382,000 in service in the country. The latest figures furnished by the Department of Employment came out in 1986, and show that today there are 181,000 domestic workers, breaking down into 159,000 women and 22,000 men. This figure, which includes nannies, au-pairs and cleaners paid by the hour, is of course bogus. For tax purposes, nannies are called personal assistants and to avoid problems with National Health administrators French au-pairs are officially "guests", a category that doesn't prevent some of them from being treated like slaves.

"Butler" must surely be the category of service worker that has profited most from the revival of Victorian values. For the newly rich young City workers who enthusiastically employ them, the British butler has become administrator, sommelier, driver, and spiritual counsellor. And, what's more, he earns at least £1500 a month in addition to room and board. Ivor Spencer founded Ivor Spencer's School for Butlers in 1981 in south London.

He claims that the students who graduate from his four-term course have their choice of jobs and countries, so highly in demand are they. At school they learn to serve champagne, keep their breath fresh and their eyes lowered when they serve the mistress of the house her morning cup of tea. An interesting note is that the school offers not only classes for aspiring butlers but also courses for aspiring bosses to learn how to treat their new butlers. Every four months, the whole group, students, teachers, and future bosses, move to the Dorchester Hotel in London to put into practice what they have learned.

These are also good times for nannies. Their services are needed by young professional women who have no intention of giving up their careers or free time. The young women who come to their homes look nothing like Mary Poppins and they can be divided into two categories, professionals and amateurs. The former come from specialised schools like Norland Nursery Training College in Hungerford. They earn £125 a week and are in great demand. Their only fault is that they are too perfect and occasionally show a vague contempt for their young employers.

The amateurs bring a different set of problems to middle class families. If they are girls from upper class families looking for something to do, they may sniff at their employers' table manners. If they are girls from the north who come to London looking for work, they may suffer from homesickness and spend their free time crying over a photo of their boyfriend. Some give up and return to Liverpool, while others carry on, ask for raises and end up as professionals. This progression is well-known to young Italian employers who come to London, put an ad in *The Lady* and then set about interviewing prospective candidates. Some are lucky and find a British girl with a good disposition who likes children; others, less familiar with English accents and manners, turn their children over to hellions who plot to steal the family silver and run off with the bouncer at the local discotheque.

In London a full-time nanny earns about £75 a week plus room and board. Families looking to do it on the cheap hire foreign nannies. The Home Office has been tight-fisted about giving work permits to Asians, which is a blessing to Spanish and Portuguese girls, members of the European Union. Au pairs also enjoy a certain popularity, especially those from Australia and New Zealand, who are reputed to work harder and complain less than their French and Italian counterparts. Swedish teenagers have always been popular with husbands and for that reason have been almost completely banished by wives.

By law an au pair should only have to look after the children and do a small amount of light housework. For this they are given room, board, and about £30 a week. In practice, two British personality traits see to it that this rarely happens. Liberal families suffer from guilt complexes and often treat their au pairs with excessive delicacy. Auberon Waugh, the English writer, tells of a French au pair who, fed up with being treated with kid gloves, began to shout, "*Monsieur, vous avez peur de me commander*". Others seem to forget that their au pair is a young student there to study English and they keep them busy from seven in the morning till nine at night. Rarely are they subjected to the legendary Mrs Beaton's advice in *Cookery and Household Management*: "A lady must not forget the importance of the well-being, both physical and moral, of the people who live under her roof. As for girls it is her duty to keep herself discretely informed about the people they consort with. She must set a curfew, normally at 9 pm and it is her duty to put the young people in touch with a representative of their religion or with a recognised organisation such as the Association of Young Christian Women".

Mrs Beaton would certainly be surprised today by another phenomenon that is changing the face of domestic help in Britain, the agencies set up to meet the needs of the rich, well-dressed single urban professional. Such agencies have mushroomed. One of the best-known is Mops and Brooms, which the *Financial Times* recently singled out for praise. The relationship between the domestic help sent by this organisation and their young employers is a curious one, as they never meet. She arrives after he has left for the office and picks up the dirty clothes of someone she has never seen. Her employer doesn't bother to put her in touch with a representative of her religion; his concern is limited to leaving her a cheque.

THE SEASON

Few things in the world are more fascinating than the spectacle of the English at play. It is a field of endeavour at which they excel. Not only did they invent a fair number of modern day games, but they developed variations on the theme. The best example in winter is the gentleman's club – men of a certain age drinking, smoking and gambling at a safe distance from their wives. In the summer, it is the Season.

162

As consolation for miserable winters and unreliable springs, the British turn all their attention to a series of open air activities during the hot (so to speak) season. The main ones are Wimbledon which runs from June to the beginning of July, Glyndebourne from May through August, Ascot in June, the Henley regatta and the garden parties at Buckingham Palace in July. There are hundreds of unwritten rules for each occasion, which thrill the British who know them, and terrify foreigners who don't. The foreigners invariably betray their ignorance by clapping too much or asking a particularly stupid question, thereby exposing themselves to the person next to them as being from Modena or Aix-en-Provence and not Richmond. The hordes of foreigners who manage to insinuate themselves into every event and the noisy troops of *nouveaux riches*, enjoying the spoils of ten years of Thatcherism, are extremely interesting material for a visiting journalist and for the gentry, they are an equally good reason to stay at home.

Let's start with Wimbledon. No matter how much they love it, tennis is not the main reason fans go through the gates at the All England Lawn Tennis & Croquet Club, in SW19. The four hundred thousand spectators go to tuck in to 8 tons of salmon, 4 tons of steaks, 12,000 bottles of champagne, 75,200 pints of beer, 300,000 cups of coffee and tea, 5 tons of cake, 190,000 sandwiches, 23 tons of strawberries and 1,400 gallons of cream. Strawberries and cream, the symbol of Wimbledon, are consumed out of a sense of duty, even by those who don't want them; they represent a social pleasure available to all.

Then there are the enclosures of the privileged. The most exclusive is the royal box, facing centre court. From the reserved seats in the Members' Enclosure, guarded by elderly men in blue blazers, you can see as many as twelve courts. At the far southern end of the grounds are the marquees belonging to companies, each of which can host up to thirty people. The names that count (ICI, Barclays, IBM, Heinz) are in numbers 1 to 24 and they spend up to £100,000 to entertain their friends and clients. The upper-middle class of business and industry is concentrated in Orangei Park at the north end. Outside the grounds are the tents of the rest of the world and they are so numerous that Wimbledon authorities have had to intervene to keep the site from turning into a campground.

At Glyndebourne, on Sussex Downs, high society has not yet set up private tents but they would if they could. For fifty years, the British have been dressing up in black tie to listen to opera and dine on the lawn in the garden. The organisers pretend it is an opera with a picnic during the interval but in fact it is more like a picnic with a bit of opera around the edges. As always, it is the ritual that counts. One catches the train from London to Lewes and the champagne toasts begin before the train has left Victoria Station. From Lewes, a bus takes the guests to Glyndebourne where, in the middle of the countryside, there is an opera house built in the thirties by an opera buff named John Christie. Tickets are hard to come by since the five thousand members of the Glyndebourne Festival Society have first choice (membership has been closed for years) and the two hundred and twenty-five corporate members get the pick of what is left.

Once you get to Glyndebourne the ritual becomes esoteric. In the middle of the afternoon, groups and couples in evening dress, under the indifferent eyes of flocks of sheep, look for a private spot to leave their hampers and rugs. The day we went, the opera began at 5:15 pm, a lively production of *Così fan tutte* with Claudio Desderi as Don Alfonso. It included the traditional seventy-five-minute interval when everyone wandered out to the spots where they had left their picnic baskets. The old guard, enjoying the Arcadian atmosphere and the chance to drink with friends, sat on blankets or around a small portable table. The *nouveaux riches*, flown in by helicopter or driven in their Rolls Royces, showed off with silver candelabra and tucked into lobster served by their chauffeurs, now playing the part of butler. After an hour and a quarter, the rich and the noble, like souls in purgatory, meekly filed back to the theatre for the second act.

If Glyndebourne is the most genteel and cultured of the British summer pastimes, Ascot is the most worldly, crowded and spectacular. The two share a desperate hunt for tickets and a picnic. At Glyndebourne, you wear evening dress and have a picnic on the lawn; at the horse race you wear a morning coat and you eat your picnic from the back of a car. The fact that the British have succeeded in convincing the rest of the world that it is extremely chic to have lunch on the grass in a parking lot shows one more time that if Britain were to put its genius to work in industry as it has put it to work on social matters, Britain would now be the Japan of Europe.

At Ascot more than anywhere else the real British upper class struggles to keep a certain distance from the *nouveau riche* or, as *Tatler* sees it, the "real smart set" does not want to mix with "brash new commerce". Once they would have been safe in the Royal Enclosure where only the personal guests of the queen were invited. The criteria for admission then were very rigorous and delighted the more worldly British. For example, if you were divorced, you were not allowed in and you had to watch the races from the Iron Stand above the bookies. This ended up being a kind of enclosure reserved for abandoned marquises and duchesses. Today things are different. Thousands of people are invited into the Royal Enclosure; all you have to do is pay the £25 entry fee. Even so, tickets are not easy to come by so the thousands of ladies in hats can still feel they are part of the privileged few. Nigel Dempster, the best known society journalist in Britain argues that Ascot has become overrun with social climbers. He complained that he recently had the misfortune to run into Linda Lovelace (*Deep Throat*) in the Royal Enclosure, a woman who "cannot tell one end of a horse from the other".

When all is said and done, however, most people who attend Ascot are actually interested in the races. At Henley on Thames, where the Royal Regatta takes place at the beginning of July, most people cast only a distracted glance at the boats and turn their attention instead to the champagne. Here the place to be is the Stewards' Enclosure with its very rigid dress code – men were only allowed to remove their jackets once, in the torrid heat of the summer of 1976. It is for members only, that is, those who have raced at Henley before, and their guests. The enclosure looks over the finishing line and from there you can see – if you're interested – the winners of the various races. Most people don't find this very important. After a day in the sun, drinking champagne and Pimms (forty-one thousand bottles over a weekend), they can hardly tell a boat from their own car.

This is another ritual that clearly separates the old from the new. On one side of the river, members in their enclosure look at the attire of the people around them and remember the days before they had middle-age spread when they could still fit into a canoe. On the other side of the river dozens of businesses have set up tents to entertain friends and clients. Until a few years ago, that spot was reserved for the band and no one on the other side would have dreamed of setting foot over there.

Finally there are garden parties at Buckingham Palace. The Queen doesn't make an appearance here as she does at Ascot nor does she lend the word "Royal" as she does at Henley. She is the hostess. The guests, permitted to bring their unmarried daughters, are diplomats, clergy and police lieutenants who are honoured in this way for a life of service. Waiting for an invitation to one of the garden parties – there are three each year in July – is agony for some. For a foreigner to be invited is not easy, but the fact that yours truly has been invited twice means that these days even the Palace isn't that choosy.

THE MATTER WITH TIES

"Pardon me, Sir, your tie."
"What's wrong with it?"
"Everything, Sir, if you allow me."
"All right, go ahead. But I can't help asking myself if ties really matter at a time like this."
"There is no time when ties do not matter, Sir."

P.G. Wodehouse, *Much Obliged, Jeeves*

One's wardrobe doesn't hold the same importance for everyone in Britain. Until recently, it didn't matter at all to the lower classes. Men in the north wore drip-dry shirts and polyester suits that glowed in the dark and the women wore blue plastic shoes more suitable for a doll than for someone with real feet and the need to walk in Newcastle. For the gentleman or those with aspirations in that direction, clothes were an obsession, studied with great care, helped along at times by literature – Oscar Wilde seemed to have an aphorism for every article of clothing – and maintained at great financial sacrifice. Today the situation is somewhat changed. At Marks & Spencer, the chain founded in 1894 by a Polish Jew (Marks) and an Englishman (Spencer), you can buy pure cotton underwear, pure woollen jumpers and honest copies of Barbour raincoats without spending your life's savings.

Marks & Spencer's success – two hundred and eighty-two outlets in Britain and a few foreign acquisitions like the American company Brooks Brothers – shows how the country has changed. Not only are the British richer but they are willing to spend a part of that wealth to dress like other Europeans. Riding the waves of this new interest in clothing is a fashion industry that counts the Princess of Wales as one of its foremost ambassadors. In 1987 the fashion industry – ten years earlier people would have laughed as such a phrase; steel was what the British made – exported goods worth £2 million. When Margaret Thatcher inaugurated London Fashion Week in 1988 she praised its contribution to the national economy.

The former prime minister, whose entire wardrobe used to be chosen by Aquascutum at the beginning of each year, is much better dressed these days than when she was first elected in 1979. In those days she would carry tiny handbags and

wear tweed suits that looked like they'd been chosen
wearing a blind-fold. Today she is more sophisticated (or gets better advice) – an American magazine
generously named her one of the most elegant
women in the world. At public occasions she wears
big hats Gloria Swanson-style and at work she wears
blouses buttoned up to her chin with soft bows at
the neck. In Moscow she delighted her Russian
hosts and photographers by appearing in a fur hat.
She took to speaking about colours and styles ("A
dark shade is a woman's best friend." "The shoulder line is what dates a dress.") with the same passion she devoted to nuclear weapons. One possible
positive influence on her has been Carla Powell,
the lively Italian wife of Thatcher's former diplomatic counsel Charles Powell. Carla has a way with
skirts, blouses and belts and was probably able to
find a discreet way to dissuade the former prime
minister from some of her more unfortunate choices.
Certainly the two women get on well. If it's true –
and even if it is not, it's amusing – this anecdote
demonstrates their closeness. Carla Powell, so they
say, was deeply engaged in a gossipy giggly telephone conversation when her husband asked her
to be quick as he urgently needed to ring the then
prime minister. "Don't worry, darling," said she.
"I'm talking to her now."

There are still signs from time to time that
feminine elegance does not come naturally in
Britain. Even famous figures slip up occasionally.
Diana appeared in a day dress that made her look
like a boiled sweet and Margaret Thatcher wore a
suit that would have been more appropriate on one
of her childhood friends in Grantham. This
happened at an Anglo-Italian summit meeting on
Lake Maggiore. Mrs. Thatcher's dress of big brown

and white checks looked more like a rustic table-cloth than an outfit suitable for a prime minister. Sarah Ferguson, shortly before becoming the Duchess of York, had her share of legendary disasters. She appeared at the Chelsea Flower Show in what looked like a kimono; at Ascot she wore a dress with broad horizontal stripes; she attended a polo match dressed up like Pippi Longstockings; and on other occasions she looked like she had just come down from the farm.

Even more interesting than the royal family's fashion sense is that of the fashion sense of Britain's younger generation. Londoners especially argue that Europeans in general and Italians in particular are pathetic because they all dress alike and mindlessly follow fashion like sheep. There is probably some truth in this observation because passengers who land at Gatwick from Rome and Milan are all wearing the same jackets and shoes and passengers from Italy who land at Heathrow are all business-men wearing the same silk ties. Another Italian custom the British find amusing is that of ostentatiously showing off labels – showing up at a friend's house in a sweater that has Burberry plastered all over it may be chic in Italy but in London it will only produce snickers. Having your monogram on your shirts is also considered rather vulgar, something you might do if you were an estate agent with a flashy convertible and a platinum blonde girlfriend.

Critics don't limit themselves to attacking us Italians, and the attacks can come equally from the left or right. A traditional Conservative may freeze in horror when he sees what he considers bad taste, but the situation on the left is even more complicated. "Fashion," writes Sarah Mower, fashion editor at

The Guardian, "is a moral minefield fraught with nameless dangers, vices and temptations. The seductive power of clothing affects British feelings on matters of class, snobbery, Puritanism, thrift, sex and justice." In other words, don't tell a friend at a party that she looks nice tonight. She'll respond by asking you if you think that normally she doesn't. And don't compliment a young writer on his shirt. Either he will think you are mocking him or he will worry that you don't take him seriously.

If clothing is a minefield, there is at least a way out in men's clothing. Artists, journalists and academics are considered beyond the pale and can dress as they please. A visit to the London School of Economics is enough to see that there is little hope for the last group. The more famous a professor is, the more shabbily he will dress and it will be of absolutely no concern to him whatsoever. Everyone else wears a uniform and this makes them feel secure. The uniform of the City is a pair of black shoes and a suit; it doesn't matter if both are a bit scruffy. In fact, it is better to wear a shabby mixed wool suit than a fine cashmere jacket. On weekends you can dress as you please. A politician will let himself be interviewed walking his dog in the countryside wearing an ancient jumper and everyone seems to find this perfectly normal. The dinner jacket is another basic item in a man's wardrobe, along with a pair of brown shoes for the weekend and half a dozen striped shirts. The choice each morning of which shirt and tie to wear with the grey suit is all the mental effort one needs to make to get dressed for work. You must agree that this is a great boon to the mental health of the country. You will never meet anyone at a meeting who is better dressed than you – at most he will just be wearing a different shirt. Even André Gide, who wasn't English, thought this a good idea. "If men are more serious than women", he wrote, "it is because their suits are darker."

British men are proud of the way they dress and brook no dissent. If tradition demands that the last button on a waistcoat – or as they call it on Savile Row, a vest – should be left unbuttoned, then it is left unbuttoned. If the last button on a double-breasted suit is never buttoned, then pity the man who buttons it. If a French businessman appears in the City in a brown suit, his English counterpart will shudder in horror, even if it has been tailored by Yves St Laurent himself. Brown, in particular, evokes strong feelings. This is a colour considered suitable only for the countryside. A banker of Scottish origin once was paid a visit by his brother who had moved to America and he showed up wearing a rust-coloured suit. The banker took one look and turned his face away, crying with distaste, "Ginger!". Paul Keers, the author of *Classic Suits and Modern Man*, tells of an elderly business magnate who in similar circumstances declared, "Brown looks like shit".

Some might say that the complacency with which the English treat the question of men's clothing shows they are incorrigible and that they still think they are the masters of the world. Such a statement, if permitted, would be ungenerous. In this particular field, Britain holds the title and it can set the rules. The traditional style of men's clothing, virtually unchanged over the years, at least among the best labels, came into being during the Industrial Revolution when men gave up their dandified outfits and adopted the sober look immortalised by the Victorian gentleman. The Duke of Windsor – as duke and for a brief time as Edward VIII – perfected the style and became the standard for the rest of the world. Between 1930 and 1936, his attire during foreign visits started fashions that are still in vogue today: witness the Windsor knot and the pinstripe suit.

We can't go into all the little rules and regulations of British dress that a gentleman so faithfully adheres to, so we will limit ourselves to suits, shirts and ties. Suits should be dark and should never look brand new – Beau Brummel used to have his servants wear them first to break them in. They must have two side pockets, (a smaller third pocket, for tickets, is sometimes found on more sporty jackets) and they must have two buttons in front. There were three at the beginning of the century and during the sixties it went down to one but Savile Row tailors now favour two. Some traditionalists, though, still hold out for three. On the sleeves, there should be four buttons – an invention of Napoleon's to keep his soldiers from wiping their noses on them – and they must be real buttons and real workable buttonholes. At one time this allowed you to turn back the sleeves if you needed to. Now it is the sign of a bespoke suit. Of course, the buttons are never ever unbuttoned. On this subject Richard Sennet in *The Fall of the Public Man* wrote, "It is always possible to recognise the jacket of a gentleman because the buttons on the sleeves can be buttoned and unbottoned. And you can recognise a gentleman because his buttons are always buttoned, so that your attention is not drawn to that detail".

Equally quirky is the question of the shirt. Handsome English shirts with vertical strips are sold on Jermyn Street in London for anywhere from £30 to £50 or more. They came into fashion around 1870 when the first shirts that unbuttoned all the way down were made; before that they had to be pulled over one's head. At first, they were not considered suitable for the office. They were seen as "regatta" shirts, in part because it was thought the stripes would hide grime on the collars and cuffs which the British were fond of. They became respectable only after a compromise was reached: the collar and cuffs had to be white, no matter what colour the rest of the shirt was and this style has been in fashion ever since. The former Liberal Democrat leader David Steel is devoted to them, although they make him look like a schoolboy. Not all the eighty-five million shirts sold in Britain each year – 3.6 shirts per man – are pure cotton. Only about 30% are, while the rest are labelled "cotton rich", meaning they have a higher percentage of cotton than any other fibre. A survey conducted by Harvie & Hudson found that the most popular shirt since the end of the war is the blue and white Bengal-striped shirt, which for purists is a shirt with vertical stripes, both the white and the blue exactly 1/8 of an inch wide. For everyone else, it is just a blue and white striped shirt.

There are precise rules about shirts too, to the delight of those in the know, and it lets the elderly salesmen on Jermyn Street know exactly what sort of customer they are dealing with. These salesmen are an extraordinary lot. The details of all the customers who order made-to-measure shirts are entered into a thick battered notebook and consulted by an assistant in black tails waiting in the shadows of the establishment. This ritual delights Americans who cross the Atlantic just to partake of it – if they were to discover a computer hidden in the depths of this sanctuary they would be horrified. A proper shirt – and they will explain this to you, if they think your vocabulary is up to it – has a collar made of two layers of material, with the underlayer cut into two pieces (originally one piece for each shoulder), no breast pocket, and ample material for the tail of the shirt to reach the front when tucked through the legs. The collar can be a cutaway (wide enough to accommodate a Windsor knot) or, more trad- itionally it can be a turndown, with the collar tips pointing down. The button-down was invented for polo players so that the collar wouldn't flap during a match. The button-down is a particular favourite of Americans. Cuffs can have one button (trad- itional), two buttons (more sporty) or be fastened with cufflinks (decidedly more formal), and if there is a gauntlet, possibly closed by a single but- ton. The combination of buttons and cufflinks is considered an abomination.

We'll close with the tie, as this is where foreigners usually get into trouble. British ties must be chosen with great care because unlike French or Italian ties, they almost always have a meaning. Let me ex- plain. If you go into a Tie Rack in Kensington High Street and buy a polka-dot tie for £3.99, there is no risk involved other than that of wearing a mediocre tie (if it twists up when you hold it from the narrow end, it's been badly cut). In Milan if you wear a tie with little hippopotamuses on a dark background, it's just a tie with little hippopotamuses. In London it means you are a member of the Leander Rowing Club, founded in 1820, and you run the risk of deep embarrassment if you come face to face with a member of the genuine Leander Rowing Club in a restaurant.

Even more dangerous are the ties that identify

you as a member of one of the traditional British networks: an Army regiment, a club, a public school or even worse, a group or team within a public school. The story is legendary of Lord Tonypandy in the fifties when he was simply George Thomas, a young Welsh Labour MP, representing Cardiff Central. Determined to make a good impression on his first appearance in Parliament, he bought a nice black tie with discreet diagonal blue stripes and with this, he made his entrance at the House of Commons. From the Conservative backbenches, there was immediate laughter and such an uproar that the Tory whip, Captain Chichester-Clark, was forced to go over to him quickly and hurry him out of the hall. "My dear boy," he said, "don't you realise you are wearing an Old Etonian necktie?" When Thomas finally calmed down, he revealed that he had innocently bought the tie second-hand at a jumble sale in Cardiff.

If it is any consolation to the foreigners who attempt to cross this minefield, even the British themselves are not always clear on the subject. There are over ten thousand designs with some meaning in circulation (that's how many there are in the archives of P.L. Sells & Co., the largest British manufacturer). Some groups' ties are identical to other groups'. A member of the second Indian Grenadiers might be taken for an "old boy" of Westminster Hospital. Others consider it all a bit vulgar and a sign of insecurity to wear a tie to show the world that you are part of a certain group. Not even the question of where one wears an old school tie has been resolved. The story is told of a young Etonian, who while walking through his club wearing the old school tie, was stopped by an elderly member sitting in an armchair. "I have always been under the impression that one did not wear one's tie in town," he said. The younger man replied, "True, sir, but I am on my way to the country". The old man, unperturbed, responded, "I have always believed that one changed one's tie at the Chiswick roundabout".

VICES

British vices are many and varied and the British know them all. Over a meal among friends, especially when a glass of wine has loosened their tongues and helped them overcome their national affliction, embarrassment, they will list them one by one for the benefit of any foreigner present. Which brings us straight to the first, though not the worst, of them. The British drink too much. About £35 million a day is spent on drink, one fifth of the total spent per day on all consumer goods. At any party, event, ceremony or christening, a guest will find himself with a drink in his hand before he has even taken off his coat. The curse of drinking, the subject of sermons from Protestant pulpits for centuries, is directly proportional to the passion for it. When describing the convivial warmth of a pub before closing time, the British wax lyrical and after their fourth gin and tonic, they radiate sincerity.

The problem is that too often they drink not to quench their thirst, as is the custom in France and Italy, but to get drunk. In many places in England and most places in Scotland and Wales, a Saturday night is not over until you get drunk with your mates and a dinner party with six friends is considered a disaster if there are only two empty bottles on the table at the end of it. The international expression "Let's meet up sometime", in Britain is "Let's have a drink sometime", a sure sign that drink is considered an indispensable part of social life. Certain groups and professions seem particularly exposed to the risk of liver damage; journalists in London, for example, step out for a pint as often as their Milanese or Roman counterparts step out for a coffee (which may be why Italians have a reputation for being high-strung while the British have a reputation for being alcoholics).

The British drink a bit of everything but in recent years, they have shoved off tradition. Beer sales, which forty years ago made up 82% of the alcohol sold, have dropped to 55%. Lager is more popular these days than real ale and is responsible for much of the excess flesh peeking out between belt and T-shirt on a warm sunny day. Wine is also more popular. In 1950 it was only 4.7% of the total amount of alcohol consumed. Today it has climbed to 20% and is the subject of great discussion, especially among people who don't know anything about it. People still drink port, sherry, whisky – a drink they do know about – , and champagne, a drink they pretend to know about. Taste in alcohol, like so many other things, is divided by class. The working class loves beer and the upper class adores French wine whereas the middle class drinks both and denies it.

To their credit the British openly acknowledge their own vices. They admit, for example, they are fascinated by the mix of politics and sex (especially if it's paid sex and even better if it's gay sex) and by spies and crime, even when it is shocking. They are attracted to gambling. They succumb to gluttony after generations of indifference to food. And they are still baffled by Europe which for many remains a mystery and for others is downright scary. But you would be wrong to condemn their vices out of hand as so many foreign visitors do after spending twenty-four hours in Britain. The writer Samuel Butler was right when he wrote in *The Way of All Flesh*, "Half the vices the world most vehemently condemns have the seed of goodness in them and must be practised in moderation rather than aiming at total abstinence". Butler himself was a curious person. The son of a clergyman, he studied at Cambridge and then went to New Zealand to raise sheep. His book came out posthumously in 1903 because the author never had the courage to publish it while he was alive. Hypocrisy is another very English vice.

GET READY, IT'S TIME TO EAT

The British eat worse than they would like to but much better than we think they do. Students coming from Milan and Turin to study English across the Channel turn up their noses the minute they hit the tarmac and never change their minds. Boiled vegetables, mystery meat pies and roast lamb are sources of particular suffering. It's not clear though whether this suffering is genuine or simply a diversionary tactic to avoid explaining to their parents what they were getting up to with their Scandinavian classmates.

The British themselves have been suffering in silence for years. In 1967 David Frost and Anthony Jay wrote what still remains a veritable truth: Britain believes there is a connection between virtue and food. The frightful diet schoolboys were forced to eat produced strong bright-eyed young men, ready to go into battle and heap glory on the nation.

Haute cuisine – like those two other superfluous items, sex and the bidet – had made sissies out of foreigners and therefore was to be avoided. Better to eat tough meat, pies with mysterious ingredients and tasteless vegetables because that's the stuff that made Britain great. Only kings had the moral prerogative to indulge themselves and Edward VII, not by chance a Francophile, had a stomach that was proof he took advantage of his position. For generations overindulged children were looked on with disapproval, fancy foods were viewed with suspicion and the three Quaker families who developed the British sweets industry – Rowntree, Cadbury and Fry – had such strong feelings of guilt that they gave away large parts of their fortunes.

Change came in the early fifties when rationing ended. Italian coffee bars opened and Chinese and Greek restaurants mushroomed. Over the following decades, with the invasion of American fast food, what culinary pride there was in Britain gradually disappeared. They say once you order a family-sized super burger and a king-sized milkshake in a fast food outlet in London, you have lost your dignity forever.

American fast food chains may seem to draw all the customers – Wimpy's, MacDonald's, and Kentucky Fried Chicken earn more than £3.5 billion a year – but they have not yet managed to replace traditional British fare completely. You'll not find a Brit willing to settle for a cheeseburger instead of his traditional Sunday lunch, not even in the outskirts of Newcastle. On the other hand, French food has managed to quietly insinuate itself into British cooking. Every week there are recipes in the food sections of the newspapers teaching British housewives how to make a soufflé. There are Anglo-

French restaurants in which young chefs cross *nouvelle cuisine* with traditional British recipes. The results are sometimes mixed but the public loves it. Italian, Greek and Spanish dishes, with slight interpretations, now form part of the daily diet of millions of families. Indeed, the British often ask why we Italians insist on having pasta as a first course when clearly by the time you have eaten a whole plate of *Pasta Amatriciana* no one could possibly have the energy or room for more. In 1984, the humorist George Mikes imagined a conversation between a Yorkshire miner and his wife. "What's that, Doris, paella? Paella again? Fine, I like paella, but paella every day, bloody paella and nothing else! Why can't we have a good old decent ratatouille for a change?"

The passion for cooking – a desire to finally eat decently, some might say – has had its consequences. Today there are fewer customers in restaurants sending back the steak tartare because it's too rare. Newspapers like *The Times* dedicate half a page of fulsome praise to restaurants (an example is their review of one on the Fulham Road, named Best Italian Restaurant of 1987. They wrote "The risotto is pure ambrosia, it is unbelievable, such delicious risotto should be known by another name".). Harrods's food halls have become shrines, where after they have bought their four ounces of prosciutto, people wander the aisles in ecstasy for hours and it's not just because they can't find their way out. The quality of food in large supermarkets like Waitrose and department stores like Marks & Spencer has improved enormously in recent years, and the British get misty-eyed these days when they speak about Sainsbury's. Television programs in which a plump little man with a French accent spends half an hour describing the sauce he is making are increasingly popular. For many, eating out is their main social activity and apart from Greek restaurants that hold fast to their kebabs and Indian restaurants that stick to chicken curries, menus are as trendy these days as fashion. At the moment, fish is in fashion and one finds it everywhere. Monkfish and mackerel, once reserved for cat food, today inspire learned discussions by gourmets. Melanie Davis, the producer of a cooking program on Yorkshire television in 1989 summed it up nicely when she said, "We used to eat, full stop. Now we actually look at what's on our plates".

But don't let this mislead you. The traditional British diet that convinces many Italians to take their holidays elsewhere has not disappeared. It couldn't, in part because many traditional dishes have deep roots in the collective psyche. Suet pudding takes the British back to their school days; HP sauce and roast lamb with mint sauce reminds them of Sunday lunch, the only moment in the otherwise long solitary day when the family gathers together; crumpets with butter and jam bring back tea breaks at university (though eventually the hot dripping butter runs down their sleeves once too often and they turn to something else). Strawberries and cream mean tennis at Wimbledon, even for the ones who have never managed to get there, cold roast beef and Stilton – a blue cheese that Daniel Defoe, the author of *Robinson Crusoe*, ate with a spoon, maggots and all – is lunch in a pub. The one institution that has changed is breakfast. Working mothers no longer have the time to prepare eggs, bacon, sausage, porridge, toast, mushrooms, tomatoes and so on. Families have decided that it's one thing to have a big breakfast on the table when it's been prepared by servants. It's another thing when you have to get up on a dark morning in a cold flat in the middle of winter and make it yourself.

Only the working class, unfortunately for them, still eat a diet based largely on potatoes, sausages and baked beans. For many British, this threesome could replace the Union Jack as a symbol of the country, along with the coronary and liver diseases that go with them. Not long ago two dieticians from the British Society for Nutritional Medicine claimed to have just discovered that adolescents brought up on junk food like chocolate, ice cream, and other snacks were potential delinquents because their brains didn't function properly. It is not just the odours one can smell wafting out of a football stadium that lends credence to this theory, but also the observations of an excellent journalist, Ian Jack, writing for *The Observer* and *The Sunday Times*. Shortly after the Heysel stadium tragedy in Brussels and at the time of the European Cup final between Liverpool and Juventus, he went to Turin. He planned to compare life in Liverpool and Turin. He came back convinced that the Italian working class could teach its British counterpart a few things, not least about food. "I went to the home of Mr Domenico Lopreiato who works at Fiat and lives in the outskirts of Turin," he wrote. "Mrs Lopreiato told me that apart from tinned tuna she only bought fresh food. She makes her own pasta sauce – tomatoes, olive oil, salt and basil – and has her wine sent up from Calabria, which we tasted over a lunch of pasta, veal cutlets, salad, four kinds of cheese and fresh fruit." In Liverpool a working class family buys all their food at a Kwik-Save supermarket – bread, potatoes, eggs and tins of baked beans. In places like Croxteth, young mothers bring back packets of chips, oil oozing through the paper, for their three-year olds, who eat them cold with ketchup.

SEX IN A TUBE OF TOOTHPASTE

When Henry Kissinger said, "Power is the ultimate aphrodisiac," he might have had the British in mind. Every few years for the last twenty, ministers, MP's and party leaders take turns as protagonist in a sex scandal. One must admit they do it with flair – they get involved with their secretaries, of course, but also with dancers, policemen, and masseuses. Scandals have become as traditional as Wimbledon.

If you exclude Ronald Ferguson, the father of the Duchess of York, who was caught visiting a *very* private club and Mike Gatting, the ex-captain of the national cricket team, guilty of holding open house to all the barmaids in town, the last of the great reprobates must be Jeffrey Archer. An extraordinary character with the face of a boxer, he is a writer by profession and deputy chairman of the Conservative Party by avocation. Margaret Thatcher gave him this job in 1985 in the hopes that he would raise the morale of the troops which was low at the time. Archer made his debut with two or three terrible gaffes ("The unemployed? Lazy people, basically."), but he got better. He organised three hundred fund-raisers throughout England and gave three hundred speeches. The scandal that erupted around him at the end of 1986 seemed almost banal. A thirty-five-year-old prostitute named Monica Coghlan claimed that Archer had taken her to a hotel in central London for sex and then paid her two thousand pounds to leave the country. Archer admitted only that he had offered her the two thousand pounds. The popular press was out to get him, he said, and the only way he could extricate himself was by sending "that girl that had phoned me asking for help" far away. Then a meeting at Victoria station was caught on film. A Sunday paper came out with a front page scoop and Archer offered his resignation as deputy chairman which was immediately accepted. The usual worried musings appeared in the newspapers. In Parliament, the euphoric Labour Party took advantage of the situation to have a bit of fun. Each member in turn asked the same question: Why had scandals like this become more traditional than Wimbledon in Britain?

To answer the question, it might be useful to recall some of the episodes that have helped Britain stay ahead of the game in the last twenty years. Besides a few minor events like young MPs caught in Turkish baths, there have been four juicy scandals: the Profumo affair in 1963, the Lord Jellicoe and Lord Lambton affair ten years later, Jeremy Thorpe's adventures in 1979 and the Parkinson case in 1983. The only scandal that didn't have a Conservative as protagonist, say the Tories with pride, was a homosexual affair (Thorpe).

Naturally the experts are ready to explain this Tory monopoly with endless theories. Gordon Newman, the author of a play on the subject, *The Honourable Trade*, claims that Conservatives are the undoubted champions of sex scandals for two reasons. One is that they were all sent away to boarding schools at a very early age and consequently suffered from a lack of affection as children, so now as adults they are looking for love. Another has more ideological roots. "Conservatives," says Mr Newman, "are in favour of free enterprise. Sex is not much different. When you see your chance, you grab it."

Hugh Montgomery Hyde, author of *An Intricate Web: Sex Scandals in Politics and in British Society*, maintains that instead of more explanations, one should look at precedents: it is simply part of British history. Lord Melbourne, a prime minister in the nineteenth century, was into flagellation. Lord Castlereagh when he was foreign minister would regularly visit the prostitutes in Green Park on his way back from Parliament. Unfortunately the last girl he picked up turned out to be a boy and Castlereagh committed suicide from the embarassment. Lord Palmerston tried to rape one of Queen Victoria's ladies-in-waiting during a stay at Windsor Castle. He was forgiven when he explained that he had gone into the wrong room; another lady was waiting for him somewhere else.

The modern scandals which the British remember with affection began in 1960. The first involved Christine Keeler, a young woman to whom Jack Profumo, a Conservative Party minister, lost his heart, his reputation and his position. The story exploded in 1963, when the nineteen-year-old Miss Keeler was caught jumping between the beds of Profumo, then British War Secretary, and Captain Yevgeny Ivanov, the Soviet military attaché. People still talk about the affair. A film, *Scandal,* based on the memoirs of Christine Keeler, came out in 1989 and even lords and Anglican bishops got their tuppence worth in.

Many believe that the Profumo affair contributed to the fall of Harold Macmillan's Conservative government and signalled the beginning of the sexual revolution in Britain. It also turned the two young women at the centre of the scandal into legends. Christine Keeler today is in her forties and a bit down at the heel but Mandy Rice-Davies, who was also involved in the affair, is still a saucy bubbly blonde. She recently published a thriller, *Today and Tomorrow*, based – no surprise here – on a politician and a hooker. Completely unashamed of having introduced an entire generation of British adolescents to the world of sex, Mandy Rice-Davies continues to enjoy her role. In a recent Tom Stoppard comedy, *Dirty Linen*, she played "Miss Gotobed".

The next scandal came in 1973 and though very colourful, paled beside the Profumo affair. This time it was two lords who were in trouble: Lord Lambton, Minister of Defence in charge of the Royal Air Force and Lord Jellicoe, the leader of the House of Lords. Lord Lambton was photographed in bed with two prostitutes, one white and one black, in a flat in Maida Vale. Lord Jellicoe was called in by Edward Heath, prime minister at the time, and told that proof existed of his involvement in a ring of call girls. The resignations of the two men were very different. Lord Jellicoe said that he deeply regretted having had his adventures. Lord Lambton claimed he was most sorry for his friend Jellicoe. "Poor George, bad luck. Normally he was only with one girl at a time."

After the sad affair of Jeremy Thorpe in 1979 – the leader of the Liberal Party was forced to resign after he was accused of having had an affair with a male model – the country breathed a sigh of relief with the more traditional Parkinson affair in 1983. Cecil Parkinson, Industry Secretary, former Conservative Party head, former member of the inner cabinet during the Falklands War, found a very simple way to commit political suicide. He got his secretary,

Sara Keays, pregnant and when she told him, he promised to dump his wife and marry her. Then he changed his mind. Ms Keays, mortified by his duplicity, met with two journalists of *The Times* and dictated an article headlined "I begged him to tell Mrs Thatcher". Cecil Parkinson resigned. He then made an historical comment that almost escaped notice: "What can you do? You can't put the toothpaste back into the tube".

One last story worth mentioning concerns the exploits of fifty-five-year-old Cynthia Payne, a national institution and the inspiration for several books, plays and one successful film, *Personal Services*. She earned her notoriety in 1979 when her house on Ambleside Avenue in the London suburb of Streatham was raided by the police. Among the fifty-three people picked up by the police that evening were a member of the House of Lords, an Irish MP, and several members of the clergy, along with a whole squadron of young prostitutes. One of the guests, in his seventies, when questioned by the police said, "I thought it was a Christmas party". The guests had paid Payne with luncheon vouchers as their hostess thought she could avoid trouble with the law this way. It turned out she was wrong; she spent the next eighteen months in jail.

Recently Ms Payne was back in front of the judge. The crimes she was charged with seemed to come straight out of the past: sixty guests of Madame Cynthia, back once more at Ambleside Avenue, were captured *in flagrante*. Most of them were between fifty and sixty years old and were found with young prostitutes. Five men were dressed as women, one as a French maid. According to a detailed police report, substantiated by photographs shown to the judge, the guests were

taken by surprise and caught all over the house –
on the landing, in bedrooms, in all the bathrooms.
One Susan Jameson, it read, "apparently surprised
by the entrance of the police, jumped up knocking
Mr Stanley Freeman into the bathtub". One witness,
Jana Lynn, – thirty-seven with an improbable Scandinavian accent – explained to the judge with a gig-
gle that she "would have sexual relations or whatever for twenty-five pounds", but she drew the line
at "having more than three men in her room in one
night". The trial, which I attended, was deemed by
the British press to be one of the most hilarious of
the century. It ended with the acquittal of Mrs
Payne who celebrated with a lively intimate party in
a suite in one of the big hotels on Park Lane. She
was encouraged not to return.

OI, WHO'S THAT YUPPIE WITH ANDY CAPP'S DOGS?

Greyhounds are smaller than horses. That's about
all I knew when I went to the dog races at Wembley
Stadium one Friday evening. The event is fascinating but also rather mysterious. The dogs are truly
fast, but as an Englishman remarked when I
seemed surprised, that's the point, isn't it. Each
race lasts only about thirty seconds, just long
enough for you to figure out which one is number
4 (in the little black coat) and whether he has won.
The program for the evening's races is enormous
and in hieroglyphics, though in theory written to
help you choose a winner. Here's what it says about
Liverpool Wonder, a dog worth betting on just for
the name: Oct 28 490 6 5.91 4335 5 6 Aubawn
Cutler BCrd3 30.24 + 10 25.8 3/1 A6 30.82 Season
9.6.87. After I discovered that the last set of

numbers was the date when Liverpool Wonder was most recently in heat, I thought it better not to ask any more questions.

Until recently greyhound racing was a working class pastime. Lately though its devotees are changing. One finds more middle class fans at the races these days, recognisable not just by what they are wearing – casual elegance has spread all over London just as in Milan – but also by the stupid questions they ask. A few thirty-year-old City types with their girlfriends started to come, a series of newspaper articles followed, and then more City types and their girls came. Among the many recent pastimes of young well-off Londoners, this has to be one of the most sensible. An evening spent "going to the dogs" is good value (£2 to get in), lively, unusual, and a potential place to pick up a girl (or "to pull a bird" as they say). Working class girls may not wear tights but they are famously healthy and broadminded.

Aided by yuppies and journalists, the greyhound industry has begun to prosper again after several lean years whose low point was the conversion of the dog tracks at White City into a car park. Today the races are held at Wembley Stadium – the dogs run round and round, the footballers run back and forth – , at Wimbledon, Walthamstow and Catford, the latter two in East London. In Walthamstow's four restaurants, they serve four thousand meals every Saturday night, the waitresses dress up like Barbarella and there is enough neon to light up all of Calabria. Wembley races are held three days a week, Mondays, Wednesdays, and Fridays, and attract about sixteen hundred people. Young couples are in abundance. Typically, he drives a Ford Sierra but dresses like a drug dealer and she wears a mini-skirt and bets only on dogs with pretty names. Another track in Hackney has remained the refuge of the working class. The only woman you'll find there is seventy-three, has a wooden leg and works behind the cash register, or so I'm told by someone who has obviously checked things out.

If you want to delve deeper into the world of dog racing, I recommend Wembley, where new devotees mingle with old established fans and bookies look on with affection. The stadium is under renovation. Below the Grandstand Restaurant a new stand is being built and scaffolding blocks the track. To overcome this slight impediment, the management has installed televisions everywhere. Old-age-pensioners stop mid-bite (not a bad idea, given how tough the meat is) and stare mesmerized at the screens. They keep a close eye on the results and the odds and make careful notes in their programs. A shoal of waiters weaves among the tables. The young men carry beer and sickly-looking smoked salmon (not included in the *prix fixe* menu). The young women take bets for the customers. Newcomers prefer getting up and going to the bookies themselves which the waiters detest, but they manage to slalom around them anyway, with their pints of beer.

The restaurant can seat a hundred people. The overflow fills the ground floor around the betting halls. There are twelve races a night, one every fifteen minutes. If you are timid about placing a bet with one of the po-faced bookmakers you can use a tote. You can bet on the winner, the placers or on a series of combinations with mysterious names (Forecast, Each Way, Trio, Straight and Reversed). The minimum bet is 50 pence. Young City chaps, used to working with numbers, catch on fast. Foreigners, unfamiliar with English betting language, appear feeble-minded and drive the bookies crazy.

Among the punters, many know the individual dogs who are running and repeat their names like a litany (Decoy Madonna/Who's Sorry Now – Full Whisper/Ring Rhapsody/Corrigeen Time – Gone West/Easy My Son). The greyhound owners are romantics who love their dogs more than their wives. They take them out for a run in the countryside on Sundays and they rarely get rich. The prize money for each race is seldom more than £100 and it's put up by the bookmakers who do become rich and park their big fancy cars with their splendidly vulgar girlfriends directly in front of Wembley Stadium. One dog that proved worth the investment was Ballyregan Bob, who won thirty-two races in a row in 1985, a record. He was a slow starter and just at the point when it looked like he was giving up, he would bound off as if his turbo engine had just been switched on.

Speak of Ballyregan Bob in any British pub and eyes grow misty. This is proof that not even an invasion of yuppies and their consorts has changed the nature of dog racing. If horse racing is the sport of kings, greyhound racing is the working man's pleasure. Fans swear they'd rather spend an evening at Catford than an afternoon at Ascot. A dog, they point out, doesn't have a jockey on his back who might forget to win and it is no less noble a creature than a horse. Dogs were praised by Shakespeare, Chaucer and Richard II. The Abbess of Sopwell in her *Boke of St Albans* (1486) lauded the greyhound who was "headed lyke a snake, and neckeyed lyke a drake, backed lyke a beam, syded lyke a bream, footed lyke a catte, tallyd lyke a ratte". More recently, the relationship between horses, dogs and the working class produced this more straight-forward exhortation: "Keep off shorts and horses, stick to pints and dogs". This was what a father would tell his sons in the days when they all dressed like Andy Capp, Britain still smelled of coal, and dogs and yuppies kept their distance.

ABROAD, ABROAD!

We've suspected the British tourist was unique for a long time. That he's always been like that, we discovered reading a sample dialogue in a little guidebook, *The Gentlemen's Pocket Companion*, for English gentlemen holidaying in Italy.

> Italian maid: "Does Sir need anything else?"
> English gentleman: "Yes, my dear, snuff the candle and come close to me. Give me a kiss, so I can sleep better."
> Italian maid: "But how can you be ill if you talk about kissing! I'd sooner die than kiss a man in his bed or anywhere else. May the Lord grant you a peaceful night and a good rest."
> English gentleman: "Thank you very much, my good woman."

A British tourist might have fantasized about having such a conversation in the years of the Grand Tour. By the time the Seven Years' War against the French had ended in 1763 and relations improved between Britain and Catholic countries, the Industrial Revolution had created a class of people able to take long trips for pleasure and education. The Grand Tour, the last step in a liberal education, did not just create new tastes in art and architecture, it unleashed in the English romantic fantasies, a passion for the classical and a love of sun, wine, food and – as we have seen – Italian maids. All these were reasons Adam Smith felt the Grand Tour had a deleterious effect on the young and declared that "young people come back ever more debauched, conceited, useless, and unprincipled. Nothing apart from the sad state of British Universities, can possibly give a good name to such an absurd practice as travelling". But no one took any notice of him. Generation after generation, young men of discretion left for the south in search of Truth and Beauty. If they also met up with a handsome young lad or maiden, so much the better.

Two hundred years later, the British still come. And when they travel to Spain or Italy searching for the sun, they like to read what their predecessors wrote. Two books have recently been published on the subject, *The Grand Tour* by Christopher Hibbert and *The Mediterranean Passion* by John Pemble. The latter looks closely at the reasons and manner in which his fellow countrymen travelled to Italy in the Victorian era. First of all, they never came in July or August and, like good tourists everywhere, they looked for places free of other tourists. They feared in equal measure "the burning rays of the sun which turn the sand into a blazing desert" and "the languor of the Southern tribes" (John Ruskin). They were quick to blame economic backwardness on superstition, the heat and religion, and they felt infinitely superior. "If we had no other reason for being pleased about being Protestant, it would be sufficient to consider that our religion prevents us from being as ridiculous as the people here," wrote the Reverend Henry Christmas. Pemble observed that ninety thousand British tourists came to Italy each year at the end of the nineteenth century for one of the following reasons: a pilgrimage, culture, their health, gambling or homosexual encounters. He concluded that even if these visits by Victorian tourists contributed little to an understanding of the Mediterranean, they contributed a great deal to the understanding of the tourists themselves.

Studies about the British summer migrations of today unfortunately don't exist, just a few facts and figures. Eight million – 70% of all those who choose an all-inclusive package holiday – go to Spain. The press and television are under no illusions about what British youth get up to there. Each year in June, when the vanguard takes off from Gatwick on the first charter flights, the Sunday tabloids remind the country of what happens in places like Benidorm on the Costa del Sol, telling tales of drunkenness and brawling. More serious papers limit themselves to describing the wild nights of the secretary from Manchester, hinting that no sooner does she find a few friends and put on her bathing suit than she is taking it off.

A week in Spain, booked at the last moment, can cost as little as £99. The typical Brit, travelling with wife, children and number 45 suntan lotion (it does exist), usually only wants to escape the cool British summer and is quite content with a bit of sun and a cold drink. But a minority of youth, almost always tattooed and always drunk prefers a good fight, particularly with the locals. Every police station on the Spanish coast has its story to tell. Each year there are arrests and injuries and every now and then, a death. In Torremolinas British tourists are referred to as "animals". A cabdriver died of a heart attack in 1988 after being roughed up by a bunch of these yobs.

These are the same young men referred to as hooligans at soccer matches and we all know what they get up to there. In spring 1985 I was in Liverpool after the killing in Brussels stadium and I saw them crying into their banners, their faces still painted, but that was a rare example of remorse after an enormous piece of stupidity. In summer 1988, during the European final in Germany, the world saw only the stupidity. "We attacked the Dutch because they considered themselves better hooligans than us," one explained in all seriousness after the fight near Dusseldorf station. Another English fan, expelled before the game even started, boasted on the ferry on the way back home, "I am Europe's top thug". If he had read the headlines of the tabloid that said "WORLD WAR THREE" when he landed at Dover, he would no doubt have felt flattered.

Only eight hundred thousand British tourists come to Italy each year and they are very different from the ones looking for fights at German football stadiums and on Spanish beaches. Believing that group holidays are working class, these more sophisticated Brits choose Venice, Rome and Tuscany and try not to notice that their compatriots have also chosen Venice, Rome and Tuscany. When they bump into each other in a trattoria that they consider their personal discovery, they are momentarily nonplussed. Restless would-be romantics, they see Italy as a kind of private garden in which to indulge their poetic fantasies. Only after a couple of public transport strikes do they begin to agree with nineteenth-century British authors who characterised the Italians as "the only black spot in a magic land". But as soon as they have crossed back over the Alps, they agree once again with Samuel Johnson's maxim, "A man who has not been in Italy, is always conscious of an inferiority". They like to repeat this in the autumn at a dinner party for the benefit of friends who preferred Kent to Chianti.

The best parts of France for the British are Brittany and Provence, the first because it is close and the second because it has a nice name. Switzerland is popular in the winter and not only because Margaret Thatcher goes there in the summer. No thirty-year-old from the upper classes, unless he is broke, can turn down a week at a ski chalet, during which he'll ski a little and drink a lot and never learn that chalet is pronounced without the final "t". In Greece and Turkey (which is very fashionable at the moment), hundreds of charter flights arrive filled with unpretentious young people who dream only of clear blue water and cheap restaurants. Any book about them would be very short.

Twenty million British, demonstrating a touching faith in British weather, choose British beaches. If they were to choose them for their melancholy surroundings, for the crumbling piers with Indian cupolas or for pebbles on a beach that they can walk on as they wander lost in thought, they would return home content. Instead, though, they choose them for the sun and the sea, find wind and rain and go home disappointed. In fact, the very word "holidaymaker" sounds more like an exhortation: go *make* your holiday. Americans on holiday, more optimistic, call themselves vacationers and they would spend a maximum of two hours in Bognor Regis, Walton-on-the-Naze, or Great Yarmouth, but only if you tie them up very tight.

VIRTUES

DON'T WORRY, IT'S STILL ENGLISH

Few things amuse Britain more than the summit meetings of French-speaking countries, the cries of pain of the Académie Française and the French attempts to get rid of *le weekend, le ferry boat, le duty free* for *la fin de la semaine, le navire transbordeur* and *la boutique franche*. The British claim their language needs no meetings, academies or proclamations for a very simple reason: they've already won the battle. Of the one hundred and seventy-one countries in the world, English is the official language in one hundred and one. Three out of four business letters are in English along with three out of five TV programs, half the scientific papers and journals, and 80% of computer data. Streets and squares all over the planet are full of Art Shops, Multicleans, Drive-ins, Hamburger Restaurants, Flash Copy and Fitness Centres.

The British attribute the success of their language to three factors, two obvious and one less so. The first is the extreme simplicity of their grammar and syntax, at least as far as a base language is concerned. The second is British colonial expansion coupled with American economic expansion. When the first ended, the second began. The third reason for the success of the English language is its great elasticity. In Britain, linguistic protectionism doesn't exist in any form. If people want to take the English language and rough it up to the point where it is unrecognisable, they are free to do so.

One could offer dozens of examples of this great capacity to adapt to new customs and needs. The Japanese have transformed the term "mass communications" into *masukomi*; the word "nonsense" has become *nansensu*. In Hindi, the English phrase "see how the great democratic institutions are developing here in India" has become *Dekho great democratic institutions kaise India main develop ho rahy hain*. In Nigeria the Hausa word for "biscuits" is *biskit*.

Examples of how the British have tolerated the most monstrous distortions of their language in other English-speaking countries – apart from the Americans about whom we will say more later – can be found in Australia and New Zealand. On their side of the world, a motorcyclist becomes a "bikie", a lorry driver is a "truckie" (from the American word for lorry, "truck"). The Australian Rupert Murdoch, owner of *The Times*, brought over "journo", shortened from journalist. At first it sounded like a put-down, especially since it appeared at the same time as the forced move from Fleet Street to Wapping of these "journos" occurred. But it was short, so it was soon adopted.

Some, like the literary editor of *The Times*, Philip Howard, maintain that a pure English, something equivalent to Hochdeutsch or Tuscan Italian, probably doesn't exist any more. Fifty years ago, it was the English spoken in southeast England and taught in good public schools. Thirty years ago it was BBC English, spoken by anchormen in black evening dress as they read the nine o'clock news.

This was also the English spoken by the upper-middle classes (their enunciation was far too good for the true upper classes). In the sixties, language came to be a reflection of other events taking place at the time. The first newsreaders to speak with obvious lower-middle class accents worked for the BBC, pronouncing Africa as "Ufrica" and letting their regional inflexions show. Commercial television, domain of virile women journalists from Manchester, followed suit. The BBC has since regained a certain balance, the upper class continues to mumble, the upper-middle class continues to imitate them, and almost any accent is acceptable: you just need to be rich and successful, and you'll get plenty of dinner party invitations.

This doesn't mean that the choice of word is not important to the British. However, for the foreigner, who inevitably gets it wrong and then must be excused, it becomes an esoteric ritual. In fact, word choice and accents are powerful indicators of social class, although half the people in the country, according to a poll, deny they even have an accent. The other half, of course, is ready to swear that they do.

A few examples. Loo, bathroom, gents, ladies, lavatory, toilet, convenience, lav, water-closet, WC, bog, john, can, heads, latrines, privy, little girls' room, powder room, khasi, and rears are all words for the same place. "Loo", as ugly as it sounds, was the word used by the upper class until it was appropriated by the upper-middle class, at which point the upper class went back to the word "lavatory". The lower-middle class, to show their familiarity with French and to seem more chic, use the word *toilet*, just as they also use *pardon, serviette, perfume* and *gateau*, which leaves others horrified.

The situation is not always so clear. "Pudding", for example, is used by both the upper and the working classes while the middle class prefers "dessert". In the same vein, the plumber may greet you with a "how do you do" like a duke, while a young intellectual might say "how are you doing?" The word "mirror" has won out over the more elegant "looking glass" and only a few upper class exhibitionists still say "wireless" instead of "radio". Sloane Rangers, girls from good families who hang out in London's Sloane Square, gave the nation not only Princess Diana but also a style of speaking. Words like "actually", "awfully", and "really" became their trade marks. Young fogeys refuse to use expressions like "hi" and "see you", remain resolutely faithful to "hello" and "so long", and eschew "have a nice day" completely.

But let's leave accents aside and continue with our well-deserved praise of the English language. One proof of its vitality is the way it has been able easily to absorb certain foreign words, like the German *kindergarten*, the French *chauffeur*, the Spanish *patio*, and the Dutch *koekje*, which became *cookie*, along with technical terms, Americanisms and words brought back from the colonies, like *tandoori*, an Indian method of cooking that comes from the Urdu word *tandoor* for oven. Today of all the languages in the world, English is the richest. You can choose from over half a million words and three hundred thousand technical terms. The British get their revenge for this reverse colonisation by pronouncing foreign words any way they please. This is particularly true of proper names. In London, Beauchamp Place, a little street near Harrods's in Knightsbridge, is pronounced Beechim Place. Don't bother to pronounce it any other way. Not only will taxi drivers have no idea what you are saying, but others will look upon you as a presumptuous show-off.

There is one drawback to the way the language changes so quickly. Words and expressions come and go quickly and once they are passé, no one uses them anymore. Actually, they do continue to be used, but only by Italian English teachers who learned them when they were students in England, back in 1967. A word like "groovy" is now consigned to linguistic archaeology (though we have discovered that for some mysterious reason it is still used in Northern Ireland, only there it means "extremely ugly"). Similar casualties are "smashing", "magic", "epic", "fabulous", and "brilliant", though at the moment a shortened form of the last, "brill", is used. The British themselves will admit to having difficulties with this dizzying process. Patricia Wheatley, who works for the BBC, recently confided that she had a conversation with two people and didn't understand either one of them. One used expressions from before her time and the other used expressions too recent for her to know them. The former, a producer in his forties said things like "Let's cool it" for "Let's stay calm" and "Let's split" for "Let's go", two expressions from the swinging sixties, while the latter, a nineteen-year-old secretary, offering to get coffee for everyone said "It's my crack", the latest expression for "It's my turn".

Words and expressions come and go with amazing speed. Among the "typical expressions of the eighties" that Oliver Pritchett collected in the *Sunday Telegraph* was "inner city". Race riots first exploded in the inner cities of Birmingham and Liverpool. When similar riots occurred in Brixton and Tottenham they were still called inner city riots even though they were on the outskirts of London. Other expressions have been invented by journalists and people in the media, and reveal a certain lack of imagination: "Enterprise economy", a bad attempt by the British to sound American; "rescue package" (Westland helicopters collected quite a few); "inner cities" where it is now impossible not to find "urban deprivation" and of course, "disaffected youth". The situation, according to Prince Charles, could be helped if people turned to "community architecture" (whatever that means – someone ought to ask the Prince).

The tumultuous transformation of the language has brought with it a series of errors that drive the five writers who run *The Spectator* magazine crazy and leave the other fifty-six million citizens completely indifferent. *The Economist* has even published a handbook for its journalists, full of advice and recommendations. For example, writers are reminded that "the alternative" is always between two and not three, four or five choices. One speaks of "the circumstances in which", not "under which"; it is better to use the verb "to suggest" if that is what you mean, rather than "to come up with"; "to compare" requires the preposition "with" if you wish to draw attention to a difference, and "to" if you are stressing similarities. You say "different from" not "different to" or "different than"; "effectively" means "with effect" not "in effect". "Presently" means "soon", not "at present". Use "the reason that", not "the reason why" (in spite of Tennyson's poem); an agreement is always "verbal", but if it is not written down, it should be called an "oral" agreement.

Along with the many errors and inconsistencies of English that the British themselves are prey to, there are Americanisms. So we get "additionally" (and), "corporation" (company), "neighbourhood" (district), "regular" (ordinary), "meet with" (meet), and "riders" (passengers), to mention just a few. Strong transatlantic influences can also be blamed for the problems we have with the past tenses in English.

A good example of "linguistic pollution" and more proof of English's ability to insinuate itself into other languages is the effect it has had on the Italian spoken by Italians living in Britain. After awhile, they begin to make – and unfortunately to write – terrible mistakes. They use *eventualmente* (meaning "possibly" in Italian) as if it meant "eventually". They say *attitudine* (meaning "aptitude") when they mean *atteggiamento* (the Italian for the English word "attitude"). This awful Anglicisation of Italian celebrates its little triumphs in restaurants all over London. Young waiters from Bari and Bologna serve *vegetali* to hungry customers (when they should be serving *verdura*) and in books, magazines and newspapers, they write *memoriale* (from the English word "memorial") when they mean *monumento*. For the English language, of course, these are all considered victories.

GOD SAVE THE FIRM. THE QUEEN CAN TAKE CARE OF HERSELF

In Britain, republicans are scarcer than West Ham supporters and a great deal more pacific. There is a simple reason for this. The monarchy, in Queen Elizabeth II's revised version, is the totem pole around which a contented tribe gathers. For the British, the royal family is a comfy reassuring habit. And over the years, the royal family has done what's been necessary to return the compliment. It has allowed television into the palace and journalists through the doors, and it has kindly provided an endless stream of gossip. Moreover, it has refused to imitate the Dutch or Scandinavian monarchies. The British, who value good form, would never put up with the queen riding a bicycle. This does not mean that the Firm – as Elizabeth calls it – has remained unchanged. Among weddings, children and discord, it's hardly possible. Other things have also changed. The younger generation took to heart the notion that they were just like everyone else. Charles decided to share his thoughts with the public and the popular press attacked him mercilessly. And finally, the queen had to deal with a prime minister who was strong-willed and a woman to boot.

Of the two women, coming from the same generation, the more domestic and beloved was the queen. The more regal was Margaret Thatcher, who liked to use the royal "we" ("We have become a grandmother") and installed a gate at the entrance of 10 Downing Street to match the one at Buckingham Palace. We don't know whether they checked out each other's wrinkles. Certainly, their relationship has been one of the most intriguing mysteries of the century. Though described as "cordial", this cordiality always seemed somewhat forced. In the last years of Thatcher's administration, particularly, there were rumours that the two women did not see eye to eye. The British were amused by this and didn't bother to contradict the rumours.

On the subject of clothing they clearly didn't see eye to eye. Several times, Margaret Thatcher showed up at a ceremony in the presence of the queen, wearing the same dress. After one episode too many, Downing Street sent a discreet note to Buckingham Palace. Would it not be possible, she asked, to let us know in advance what Her Majesty was wearing so that the prime minister could dress accordingly? Buckingham Palace wrote back politely saying that Her Majesty was not in the habit of informing other ladies of her dress.

The episode, told by John Pearson in his book on the British royal family (*The Ultimate Family*) is interesting to the extent that it sheds a bit of light on their silent battle. The two women jointly ruled the country for ten years and grew old together. Elizabeth II was born in April 1926, Margaret Thatcher in October 1925. The queen set foot in number 10, Downing Street only once while Thatcher was in residence. But they did meet weekly at Buckingham Palace. For more than two hundred fifty years, fifty-one prime ministers had gone there to advise the sovereign on matters of state, but never before had there been two women. The ritual is precise. Just before 6 pm, the PM's car leaves Downing Street, turns right into Whitehall, crosses Parliament Square, then heads towards Buckingham Palace. A liveried valet shows the guest to the queen's study, facing the Palace gardens, and announces, "Madame, the prime minister". The conversation lasts one hour and is completely informal.

Between Elizabeth and the Labour leaders James Callaghan and Harold Wilson, there had been mutual sympathy. Wilson once accompanied her on a visit to her mother's, with the queen driving and Wilson at her side. With Margaret Thatcher, leader of the Conservative Party, but impulsive and of more common birth, the situation was different. According to gossip, the lady prime minister was forced to remain standing during an entire meeting shortly after the American intervention in Grenada, a Commonwealth territory. Elizabeth had been kept in the dark about it and this was her way of protesting. In November 1988 the same thing happened again. The prime minister let it be known that she was against a visit by the queen to the Soviet Union and she was forced to apologise – we don't know whether seated or standing – at her weekly meeting at the palace.

All her former prime ministers agree that the queen is very well informed and it is often she who gives advice to her ministers. Harold Wilson wrote, "Her Majesty wanted to be informed of everything that was going on". Sir Alec Douglas-Home said, "After over thirty-five years of reign, the Sovereign knows more than the diplomats who come to see her". They say that the queen recently complained to the Foreign Office that her briefings were too "elementary".

Of the various caps she wears, her favourite is surely Head of the Commonwealth. Her attachment to the former colonies explains why the institution has stood up to the vagaries of the post-war period and to the comings and goings of a host of presidents, generals and dictators. On matters of the Commonwealth, Elizabeth accepts advice from no one. She went to Ghana in 1961 in spite of Harold Macmillan's urging caution. In 1979 after Margaret Thatcher's election, she was advised not to go to a meeting in Lusaka because there was a civil war being waged in nearby Rhodesia. The press mounted a campaign against the trip. The queen listened to everyone, said not a word, and departed. This passion made relations difficult with the only pro-Europe post-war prime minister, the Conservative

Edward Heath. In her Christmas message to the nation in 1972, six days before Britain's entry into the Common Market, Elizabeth ignored the prime minister and informed the British people that entry into the European Union would not alter the "long-lasting and personal bond with our friends overseas". In other words, the Common Market didn't count any more than the Commonwealth – possibly in fact it counted a little less.

Today in her sixties, the queen is no longer young. Her mother has aged more gracefully – at ninety, the queen mother still enjoys eating ice cream and riding a gondola in Venice, which goes a long way towards explaining why she is the most beloved of the royal family. According to royalty watchers, the queen takes no interest in her appearance. Her style is not to have a style. Her dresses are always the same, always designed by Amies and Harnell and kept in the royal wardrobe forever. The rectangular handbag she carried on her forearm was a match for some of Margaret Thatcher's unfortunate wardrobe choices until the prime minister discovered dark suits and fashion. Yet the fact that the queen is unassuming in appearance and decisive of character has won Elizabeth the sympathy of her people. The walkabout, which Diana turned into an art form, was the queen's invention. Pushing Charles into a marriage with a pretty girl above reproach, and Andrew into a marriage as fast as possible were considered strokes of brilliance on her part (in spite of the fact that neither marriage has been successful). The idea that the former nursery school teacher (Diana) has become a superstar doesn't bother her, since it has improved the popularity of the Firm. Only in 1984 at the opening of Parliament when the House of Lords paid more attention to the princess's new hairstyle than to the queen's speech, did the queen show a certain displeasure. Everyone agrees that under her reign the monarchy has become a well-oiled machine. At home, she provides her subjects with a home-grown alternative to American soap opera – all the characters are there, the kindly grandmother, the impish little sister, the wild eldest son who finally settles down and gets married. Abroad, she provides fascinating material for foreigners. The *Boston Globe* wrote that "The British royal family comes out of ceremonies as the Israelis emerge from anti-terrorist operations: with grandeur".

This queen is so capable – an American diplomat called her "street smart" – that it is unlikely she will step down soon. There are many reasons for this. Foremost is that forty years ago Elizabeth swore to her subjects that "her whole life, whether long or short" would be dedicated to their service. Another reason is that in all of British history only once did a living parent pass on the crown to his heir and that was by force. In 1327 rebellious nobles forced Edward II to cede his throne to his fifteen-year old son who became Edward III. A third reason is that if she abdicated, she would become queen mother, but there is already a queen mother who is in fine health. The only possible reason to abdicate, according to malicious tongues, would have been if Margaret Thatcher had won again in 1992. To steal her thunder, Elizabeth might just have forgotten about pledges, history, and mother, and stepped down.

But as we know, history chose a different route. The queen therefore is destined to stay on and everyone around her will continue to do what they have been doing all along. The British will continue to admire her silently as the popular press continues to make up malicious stories about her family, an activity at which they are considered unbeatable. Here is a sample of the news that was on offer on a recent Sunday morning: Charles was tired of his wife and preferred the company of an Italian countess; Sarah had been seen stuffing herself with strawberry jam and since Diana had loved to eat strawberry jam when she was pregnant, Sarah must be pregnant; Sarah declared she was the best hockey player at her school but slept through her Latin lessons; Charles was under the influence of an eighty-year-old Jungian analyst who forced him to walk through the desert; Charles wanted to have a black man among the guards at Buckingham Palace; and Charles was in Italy alone, because his wife preferred English rock to Italian baroque.

When they are tired of innuendo or unable to come up with anything new, British journalists like to give the royal family lessons in decorum. Not just the so-called quality press, which might occasionally say something worth listening to, but also the gutter press, which seems to be in the grip of a kind of schizophrenia. On their front pages they make heavy-handed references to the married life of poor Princess Diana; on the editorial pages, they take on a paternalistic tone, admonishing members of the royal family to stop behaving like characters in a soap opera. The youngest members of the royal family come in for the heaviest criticism. Heading the list for years have been the Princess of Wales and the Duchess of York, who until 1986 was Miss Sarah Ferguson. Charles, more than criticised, is a source of wonder and bewilderment, especially when he talks to the press about things like modern architecture, the environment and race relations, rather than sitting back and smiling as he waits to become Charles III, the sixty-third English monarch.

The accusations aimed at Diana and Sarah range from the generic to the hysterical. The princess and her sister-in-law were recently the subject of an endless editorial in *The Sunday Times* that said, among other things, "Charles and Andrew have married two beautiful and fascinating women. But all too often their Sloane Ranger selves take over and they do not behave according to their rank, with disgraceful results". Translation: Diana shouldn't poke her friends in the bottom with the tip of her umbrella to get their attention (which is what happened at Ascot; the bottom in question belonged to Philip Dunne, a young banker). Sarah shouldn't laugh unrestrainedly in public and run around like a clown (as she did during a pantomime "It's a Knock-out", organised by Prince Edward as a benefit, and then again at Wimbledon). Diana should not sit with her husband in their Aston Martin showing off her legs. She shouldn't drive around London alone at night and then speed away when she's spotted, running the risk of causing an accident. Diana and Sarah should not dress up as policewomen in order to sneak into discotheques (as happened at Annabel's in Mayfair). Diana should at least pretend to like classical music as much as James Bond films.

So far, these are friendly observations. Less friendly ones followed, especially about their marriages. Not long ago, the usually well-informed gossip columnist Nigel Dempster wrote that Princess Diana had spent a weekend in the country house of a young friend of the family without his parents or her husband present and in an apocalyptic tone, he concluded "There is fear and despair among the three thousand people closely related to the Royal Family". In 1987, law professors began to discuss the implications of a royal divorce for the first time in the media. On Prince Charles's fortieth birthday in the autumn of 1988, books began to appear, inevitably irreverent and often serialised in the Sunday papers ("A Match of Opposites. He no longer understands her and doesn't much like her either," were the headlines in *The Sunday Times*). Everywhere, you find articles devoted to the theme of how different the two are, what opposite tastes they have – he likes watercolours, meditation and vegetarian cuisine; she likes shopping, Sony Walkmen, and holidays by the sea. When Diana left her husband behind for the first time at the Scottish royal residence of Balmoral, according to Anthony Holden who wrote *Charles: A Biography*, she summed the place up in two words: "Boring. Raining". Only a few small voices have been raised against this barrage of words by publishers and the press. Norman Stone, a professor of modern history at Oxford, has raged against the excessive "Dallas-ization" of the monarchy and advised the royal family to withdraw a bit into the shadows, which, according to Walter Bagehot, "would help to preserve the magic". Since despite his name, Professor Stone has no connection to the Rolling Stones, nobody has listened to him.

DREAMS OF THE COUNTRYSIDE

There is a strip in England which journalists have dubbed "The Golden Belt", an Americanisation which of course no one else uses. It is a strip that begins in Cornwall, then cuts diagonally northeast and ends in Norfolk. It crosses Devon, Dorset, Somerset, Oxfordshire, Cambridgeshire and Suffolk. In the rest of the country the population has remained stable in the last ten years, but in this strip it has grown by 10%. In the last quarter century, the population of counties like Dorset and Wiltshire has grown by a third, and the number of dwellings by two-thirds. Since this Golden Belt, the subject of watercolours and day dreams for Londoners, is mainly rural, clearly something curious is happening. After years of talking about the countryside, it looks as if many English have decided that perhaps the time is right to see what it is actually like.

This is no small phenomenon. The "new rurals", according to Professor Howard Newby of the University of Essex, are being studied carefully because they are the advance guard of a new movement. What seems to be happening is this. For the first time since the Industrial Revolution, technology has made it possible for rural areas to compete with big cities. In other words, phones, faxes, decent roads, frequent train service and round-the-clock deliveries have made it possible to live in East Anglia while working for a company in London. Professionals and artists, writers and journalists, consultants and cottage industries have all discovered this and are willing to let themselves be photographed for the Sunday supplements, working on their computers in the garden, with their smiling wives at their side lighting the barbecue.

If we keep in mind that for many English the countryside is more of an idealised place than a real one, this change becomes even more intriguing. Every English man and woman lives in the country, at least in his or her dreams. They fantasize about open fires – against the law in London – , decorate their city flats like country cottages and admire the flowers, fields and cows from afar in the glossy pages of a magazine, thereby avoiding the mud and marshes.

This "rural obsession" has coincided with lean times for English farmers, who are therefore not entirely opposed to the arrival of new colonists with money and enthusiasm. The problems of farmers are relatively new. In the seventies the countryside enjoyed good health. Entry into the European Union was favourable for many producers and those who were considering abandoning farming, thought twice. But in the last few years, a succession of poor harvests hit two staple crops, wheat and barley, particularly hard and the revision of the Common Agricultural Policy in Brussels in 1988 demanded further sacrifices. In the last ten years, there has been an annual reduction in the agricultural labour force of 2%. There are few rural districts now where agricultural workers make up more than 25% of the total population. In all there are only two hundred and sixty thousand farms today, 70% of which are run by their owners and they employ six hundred and eighty thousand. The government is concerned and is encouraging other use of the land, like developing agri-tourism or selling the buildings to developers.

While agriculture was in trouble (though, one must not exaggerate: like everyone else in Europe, British farmers know how to milk the European Union), cottage industries and service industries were sprouting up in the countryside. The result is that overall unemployment in many rural areas has practically disappeared; in fact graduates are in great demand, something Margaret Thatcher never dared to hope for. East Anglia, a flat area that looks a bit like parts of northern Italy, is the only region in the country in which the figures for manufactured goods grew between 1975 and 1985, which is a bit of a miracle. Even more miraculous is the number of workers willing to leave London and Birmingham for the country. No sooner does management offer a transfer than the employees have packed their bags, happy to move to sleepy little towns in Suffolk where they can spend Sunday strolling around the market square and talking about summers that never come.

Since the new arrivals have descended en masse on these sleepy little towns, however, they are no longer so sleepy. At Diss in Norfolk the population has doubled and there are now nine estate agents on the high street ready to take advantage of the boom while it lasts. They are often the ones responsible for the rows of executive houses, perched on man-made slopes in unlandscaped gardens, big, cold, and expensive. Elderly gentlemen, concerned about "the view from one's window", to use the expression of a sympathetic Conservative Minister of the Environment, must look with horror at the mania for development that has reached all the way to the southern counties. In East Sussex and Gloucestershire, the number of cubic metres under construction has grown by 60% in the last ten years. *The Sunday Telegraph*, the Sunday paper most likely to lament these changes, wrote disconsolately that "it is now impossible to find a hilltop where no new ugly buildings are being planned; there is no place in England where the night sky is not spoiled by the orange lights of the expanding town".

The ones who don't feel up to colonising the countryside, stay in London, close their eyes and dream. The ones that have the money – and many do after ten years of Thatcher – buy a weekend cottage. Many long-time rural families can't get over the numbers of new arrivals, the passion for country life of the newly rich and the sums of money they are willing to spend to be part of it. In some regions like the famous Cotswolds, the ramshackle old houses that gave such charm to the English countryside have all been sold to city folk. This neo-bucolic exercise produces a traffic jam every Friday evening in the centre of Bourton-on-the-Water as the new landowners come down to spend the weekend in their country cottages. Increasingly their gardens, which the local gentry think should be left as natural as possible, are turning into neat little plots, looked after by a part-time gardener and the young mistress of the house who tells her friends how she reads Wordsworth to the hydrangeas.

In 1945 Evelyn Waugh wrote *Brideshead Revisited* as the swan song of the countryside and the way of life it represented. He could not have anticipated the new arrivals and for this he can be forgiven. Country houses, in fact, did suffer during Margaret Thatcher's administration, but less than is believed and not from decisions she made, as she limited herself to imposing heavy death duties. The high cost of maintenance and the lack of servants are facts of life, but a boom in the antiques market has turned every old house into a potential treasure trove. Selling the contents of a room – a few oil paintings, six chairs, two tables and some knick-knacks – can net the owner as much as he might have made on the entire house fifteen years ago. Another demonstration of the changing times is the extraordinary amount of work now being done on many of the stately homes. Today it is tennis courts and conservatories, while only a few years ago, if anything was done at all, it was limited to making sure the roof didn't fall in.

It's not just the property market which has profited from this rebirth of the countryside. Brand new illustrated magazines have started publication offering bucolic dreams for just a pound or two. *Country Living*, for example, paints the reader a romantic picture of the countryside more concerned with the fabric of the curtains than with the health of chickens. The magazine, which sells more than one hundred and fifty thousand copies a month, heralds in full colour on glossy paper the arrival of a post-urban society, and according to its editor Deirdre McSharry, it has a definite role to play. "I can't pretend to have mud on my Gucci boots, but I do believe that the countryside belongs to all of us, wherever we live. The countryside is a state of mind as much as a geographical location. It is far too important to leave it to the farmers and politicians." This idea, which would be interesting to run by the farmers, could be the slogan of another publication, *Country Homes and Interiors*. According to the magazine, its readers have no interest in geese and pigs; what they want are "blazing log fires and long walks". Another ecologically-inspired magazine, *Landscape*, launched in 1987, has recently merged with *Country Times*, one of the favourite pieces of reading matter of the hunting and shooting set. It will be interesting to see how the new merged magazine treats such advertisements as those run by the League Against Cruel Sports which *Landscape* used to accept enthusiastically in its early months of publication.

The ones who aren't readers or hunters, who live in flats in the city but can't give up the dream, decorate. The price of country furniture in recent years has sky-rocketed and there are people who end up paying £5000 for an eighteenth-century gate-leg table after discussing its single drawer, the curve of its legs and the lamentable state of its hinges with a smiling salesman. Oak often replaces mahogany in London dining rooms and on weekends, young people in their barbours – the mythic all-weather coats invented by John Barbour in 1890 and today the uniform of gentlefolk in the country – scour the countryside around Oxford looking for furniture makers specialising in imitation Windsor chairs because they've bought an original table but can't afford the chairs to match. At Stow-on-the-Wold in Gloucestershire, an industry has been created based on the bucolic fantasies of the newly rich. The young owner of this small business works in an office lit by two candles – no neon in the countryside – and combs the area in a Range Rover equipped with mobile phone and video recorder in case he discovers a superb piece of country furniture – say, a long Jacobean refectory table, or a double gate-legged Charles II table with twelve matching chairs. He can then immediately call his customers and tell them he's sending them a video and the paperwork. "This may not be America but it sure seems close," we remark to the man with the video. "Not really," says he, "the Americans pay a lot more."

WHAT LIES BEHIND THE WALLPAPER?

"Merridale Lane is one of those corners of Surrey where the inhabitants wage relentless battle against the stigma of suburbia. Trees, fertilised and cajoled into being in every front garden, half obscure the pokey 'Character dwellings' which crouch behind them. The rusticity of the environment is enhanced by the wooden owls that keep guard over the names of the houses, and by crumbling dwarfs indefatigably poised over goldfish ponds. The inhabitants of Merridale Lane do not paint their dwarfs, suspecting this to be suburban vice, nor, for the same reason, do they varnish the owls: but wait patiently for the years to endow these treasures with an appearance of weathered antiquity, until one day even the beams on the garage may boast of beetle and woodworm."

John Le Carré, *Call for the Dead*

In a street in London not far from Shepherd's Bush, there lives a middle-aged man with his family, to all appearances normal, who spent three years working on his house to take it back to its original state. He built window sills, redid the brickwork and changed the drains. When he finished his work he set up a spotlight in his garden and organised a *sons et lumières* for his neighbours. Then he had a nervous breakdown. The house, in spite of three years of handiwork, is not very different looking from the others around it, at least on the surface, but it is nevertheless a source of pride to the owner who is convinced he has increased the value of his house and is pleased to have demonstrated his talents as carpenter, plumber and restorer. It is likely that each evening when he returns home he looks at his drainpipes standing out against the evening sky, so much finer than his neighbours', and congratulates himself.

The obsession the British have for property is legendary, fascinating and commendable, and it explains a great deal about them. Numerous clues suggest that the house has deep roots in the national psyche: the abundance of offers in the Sunday supplements for hideous home improvements, the £7.5 million spent every year at DIY (Do It Yourself) establishments, the popularity of mortgages – someone calculated that "mortgage" is one of the most frequently pronounced words in modern language – and the fact that when a body is found in a room after a murder, the press reports the value of the house ("The woman's body was found in the bathroom of a £250,000 Camden house), as if to say she may be dead but she didn't live too badly beforehand. This passion for property also explains the more tranquil appearance of Britain as compared to Italy. The two countries are pretty much on a par in terms of wealth, but while the British spend their savings on an extension in the back, we Italians buy a car and park it in the front.

There are twenty-two million houses in Britain, and many date back a ways. Three and a half million dwellings were built before 1880, three million between 1881 and 1918. Four and a half million went up between the two wars and seven million were built between 1945 and 1970. Only 15% of dwellings are less than fifteen-years-old while in Italy 60% of the housing was built after 1960. The fact that they eat, sleep and watch TV in older buildings does not bother the British at all. They don't care much for the new and they have gone through revivals of every sort (neo-classic, neo-Tudor, neo-Georgian, neo-baroque, neo-gothic, even neo-Byzantine) to block the way of modern architecture. When they've ceded the pass, as we will see, they've regretted it.

The passion for little detached houses – the kind which made Roland Barthes so indignant and which are so fascinating to see from the air – has a psychological, more than an historical explanation. We may not agree with Oliver Wendell Holmes when he wrote that "the trouble with modern houses is that they have no room for a ghost," but we must admit that the British do like to be alone and that, with its small windows, gardens front and back, and hedges all around, only a little house can guarantee them the privacy they want. Only in Britain where borders hold a deep fascination, can hedges become the source of inspiration for men of letters and scholars alike. John Evelyn, the great seventeenth-century diarist, wondered if "there was anything more marvellous and relaxing under the sun, than an unpassable hedge". Lord Keynes, the economist, wrote just before the last world war that Britain's wealth was in its hedges and a country with hedges like theirs could certainly afford a long and costly war. He seems to have been right.

For a people who want to have neighbours on each side only for the pleasure of ignoring them, difficulties arose in the fifties when it was necessary to replace the two hundred thousand dwellings destroyed by the Luftwaffe, an event which coincided with the repeal of a law established by Queen Victoria that declared that no house could be taller than a fireman's ladder nor wider than the street. With the sky the limit, government money in their pockets, and Le Corbusier's ideas in their head, a group of "functionalist" architects proceeded to build parallelogram-shaped tower blocks, "living machines" as they liked to call them. The first one, which gave rise to the term "concrete jungle", was the Alton West Estate at Roehampton, a section of Richmond Park on the outskirts of London. It was designed for one thousand eight hundred and fifty families. In 1964 Labour leader Harold Wilson, keeping an election promise to build half a million new houses a year, gave orders to the local authorities to carry on house building, full speed ahead. The result was not little Victorian cottages with flowers in window boxes. It was more concrete tenements, connected by aerial bridges, stairs and underground passages, with lifts that were too small, no place to park, and a lack of responsible management (the generation of ex-Navy officers, active in the fifties, had by then retired). Problems started before construction was even finished. Leaks and cracks appeared in the walls, lifts were constantly out of order, corridors and stairs were home to vandals and soon reeked of the vomit and urine of drunks. Even the worthy aim of the designers, that these buildings would promote good relations among families, turned out to be an illusion. The tower blocks proved no different from the little houses: even when they lived on the same floor, people still ignored their neighbours.

The collapse of Ronan Point in Canning Town signalled the end of the experiment in London. The explosion that demolished a building was caused by an oven lit by an elderly resident on the eighteenth floor, at six in the morning of May 16th, 1968. Five people were killed, eighteen were injured and the episode was etched on the national conscience. Only recently have people begun to talk again of the merits of a twentieth-floor flat, and the sales of a few penthouses in a complex at World's End in Chelsea would seem to confirm that interest. Still, a passion for lifts and rooms with views remains essentially the domain of a few lucky intellectuals. Real British people continue to prefer a "two up, two down" with bay windows, white fixtures and a bathroom on the landing. Prince Charles, every time he opens his mouth and says something about architecture, supports them.

This passion for houses, not surprisingly, encourages people to buy, rather than rent. On the eve of the first world war, nine out of ten families paid their shillings over to a landlord for rent. Today only three families out of ten do this. One pays rent to a private landlord, protected by various Rent Acts. The other two rent from the local housing authorities and hope to buy their flats, encouraged by a government that is convinced a person turns Conservative the moment he owns property and starts thinking about new wallpaper.

Wallpaper is not the only thing that people think about the minute they sign the papers. We have already noted the millions spent on DIY. We might add that each year in Britain six hundred and fifty thousand modifications and home extensions are in the works. This is possible because as long as a house is not listed, the owner can do what he or she pleases without asking permission. The results of this laissez-faire policy are especially noticeable in working class housing estates where new homeowners want to distinguish themselves from council-house tenants. To do so, they install metal fixtures, stone cladding and fake Georgian doors ("Kentucky Fried Georgian front doors" as they are disparagingly called). In some cases the local council has been forced to resort to a "General Development Order" to try to prevent unrestrained DIY-ers. This is what happened in the London borough of Wandsworth where the uniform character of two housing estates, Totterdown Fields and Dover House Estate, two of the best examples of turn of the century housing, was under threat.

Sometimes, though, one has no alternative but to turn to the professionals. A large insurance company did a study that revealed that 20% of the British who buy houses find they have to do major repairs within the first ten years of ownership. This happens because the conversion industry is expert at hiding flaws in old buildings, even from the building inspectors of the mortgage lenders. Foreigners are particularly vulnerable from this point of view since they often don't know what they are getting into. An employee of the Italian Cultural Institute recently had to sell his Holland Park flat shortly after he bought it when the ceiling quietly collapsed.

When they are not converting, repairing or adding to their houses, the British redecorate. How they do this depends, of course, on their social class. The aristocracy proceeds without much of a plan. They don't buy furniture because they inherit it, they happily mix various styles together in the same room, they don't bother much about bathrooms and are genuinely surprised if a guest notices their furnishings. "Fellow noticed my chairs," remarked the Earl of Derby after a visitor left. The wealthy upper-middle class, or rather, the *nouveau riche*, spends a good deal of money and effort – copying ideas from magazines and from the homes of their upper class friends – vainly trying to copy the unstudied look of the houses of the aristocracy. Since they can't get it right, they grow nervous and turn to friends for approval. Jilly Cooper, in her saga about British social classes, tells of a well-to-do woman who invites an upper class friend over to see her newly redecorated flat. She is mortified when the friend brusquely asks, "Whatever for?".

The middle class is also true to stereotype. They buy matching sets of furniture, put down flowered carpets and fill their houses with flowers which they make a point of calling "fresh flowers" to distinguish them from artificial flowers. Their wallpaper of choice used to be a red flocked pattern on a gold background. Now it is found only in Indian restaurants in the suburbs. The middle class, the most ferociously conservative of all the classes, likes revival styles and it prefers certain eras more than others. Fake Tudor for example, with its dark exposed wooden beams, has always been popular. There are various explanations for such devotion. Some hold that the British like to go back to the period they know best, the one that shaped the national character: the time of Henry VIII, Elizabeth I, and Shakespeare. Others maintain that Britain was the first industrialised country and the first to suffer the consequences. Therefore, for more than a century, people have thought with nostalgia of an idyllic rural past and this they prefer to do under exposed wooden beams.

The same cannot be said of the new class of rich – from estate agents to rock stars – who build ugly houses on the outskirts of London filled with waterbeds, jacuzzis, burglar alarms and automatic doors, which fortunately cannot be seen since they are all hidden behind huge walls around the property. The working class, corrupted by advertisements in the papers, goes for plush toilet seat covers, aluminium tables, Manet prints and souvenirs from their holidays in Spain, microwaves the size of TVs and TVs the size of aquariums. Lined up on their pine bookcases are a few novels forced on them by a particularly aggressive book club and an illustrated book on the royal family. Since it is against the law to burn real wood, they have a fake-log electric fire in the fireplace that can be turned on with a switch.

These electric logs have replaced the flocked wallpaper lately as the symbol of the little houses of suburban Britain. However, there are also lords who have fake electric log fires that they turn on when it gets chilly. That, however, doesn't count. At home or abroad, a lord can do what he wants.

AN ITALIAN IN BRITAIN
(CONCLUSION)

There is no doubt that Britain is richer and more confident today than it was in the early eighties, when its new role in the world was not yet defined. Margaret Thatcher was a necessary purgative for the country, something even her detractors will admit. She wasn't always popular, since no one, neither nations nor children, likes purgatives. But thanks to her no-nonsense approach, the United Kingdom saw that as the new millennium drew near, it was not enough to have once been a great world power. What it needed to do now was become a medium-sized European power. Over the last years, sometimes with difficulty, Britain has awakened from the victory-induced somnolence it fell into after the second world war. Like the nobility, the nation realised that it was no longer able to live off its rents; it had to work for a living. The fact that sometimes it doesn't seem to know where to start is another story.

Discussions about the decline of the country – or the end of the decline of the country for some – fascinate the British. You will find weekly magazines dedicating entire issues to the question, "Are we in decline?". Both the well-informed and the less informed attempt to answer the question, for it is a question they take seriously. Every taxi driver is ready to discuss the rate of growth, industrial production and unemployment rate, and their comments are not much less knowledgeable than any politician. According to a recent poll, 80% of the population believes that in the last forty years respect for law and order, sexual morality, the correct usage of the English language, and professional ethics have declined. The majority also admit that there have been improvements in economic and industrial efficiency, in the integrity of politicians and in social integration. We won't comment on the integrity of British politicians. It would be too cruel to Italian readers brought up with Italian politicians. It is harder to agree about social integration. If the British car industry were in as good shape as the British class system, Europeans would be driving Vauxalls instead of Volkswagens.

The transformations, the upheavals, and the fact of having had a woman as prime minister – this is surely divine intervention in such a male-dominated country – have not changed the basic nature of the country. Even today the British possess qualities that are completely foreign to us. For one, they respect the State in any form it takes, whether it's the police or a public litter basket. In Britain people have dirty houses and clean streets, whereas in Italy, families maintain a spotless house but may throw their trash out the car window.

The passion the British feel for all things done for the common good brings its rewards. The state hires top-notch people and they are paid (more or less) what they are worth. There is less red tape which means you can usually prove your identity with just an envelope with your name and address on it. Laws were drafted for gentlemen and are therefore very easy to take advantage of (rogues and scoundrels, categories in the process of expansion, have been aware of this for some time, as recent scandals in the City and in the housing market demonstrate).

Frugality and stoicism are two more national characteristics that have not changed over the years. The British will suffer anything – rain, queues, war – and are satisfied with very little: British homes are often decorated with a touching simplicity. The Victorian writer and economist Walter Bagehot, possibly with this in mind, wrote that the British were a bit thick and that was their salvation. It's an interesting observation. Just look what sort of State we Italians, who think we are clever, have landed ourselves with.

Another splendid gift of the British is their hypocrisy. In all walks of life and in every social class they deliberately hide their feelings. For most people – with the possible exception of intellectuals, who have other faults – the observation of rites and conventions is an art that brings out the actor dormant in each of them. Forms of courtesy in the English language are fascinating examples of this phenomenon. The British operator will ask, "How can I help you?". Her Italian counterpart will hiss a brusque "Tell me," the implication being that you have disturbed her (or him).

For these courteous and well-mannered people the trouble begins when courtesy and good manners end. When they drink too much, when they get angry and when they let themselves be caught up in fanaticism, the British become unrecognisable. This may have helped them win wars in the past. But today drunks, thugs, and fanatics go to football matches with consequences we know only too well. It is mostly (but not only) the working class who is guilty of such excesses. As for the middle class, Orwell once wrote that if it were to commit a crime, it would choose murder by poison. Today they are expanding their repertoire: child molesting and sex crimes are multiplying. The arch-conservative Peregrine Worsthorne, editor of *The Sunday Telegraph,* wrote not long ago that he blamed Margaret Thatcher. The woman, in his mind, liberated "homo britannicus" from many inhibitions without considering that he might not use his new-found freedom for the good. Others have remarked on the pathetic look of gratitude and surprise on the faces of pedestrians these days when a car stops to let them cross the street. This used never to happen. In the past, a pedestrian crossed the street confidently and with head held high, secure in the knowledge that he was merely exercising his or her rights. It is one small sign of a larger malaise. The country is less polite, words like "solidarity" and "compassion" are no longer in fashion, and people – rightly or wrongly – feel vulnerable.

Encouraged by Mrs Thatcher – not always gently but always with conviction – to come out, this "New Britain" is genuinely incomprehensible to many. The most bewildered are old style Conservatives of the sort to take blankets and boxes of biscuits round to their tenants at Christmas, who genuinely were concerned about the misery of others. Today, in the era of Concorde, a mode of transportation for which these same gentlemen have too much luggage and not enough money, they are completely lost and, thirteen years after Thatcher's accession to the throne, are left trying to figure out what happened. Even more confused is Labour's traditional left wing, which has been preaching to the poor and angry for more than twenty years and is now seeing voters turn their backs on ideology in favour of a VCR. The only clear winner from the eighties is the middle class which seems happy to have more money to spend in the chain stores of the high streets. There are some who worry that Britain will end up like the United States, a model which the new Conservatives, John Major less than Margaret Thatcher, seem inspired by. This, given all we have seen, is not likely to happen. The people on this island are too arrogant to imitate anyone else. They are also too lazy and self-satisfied. The mail arrives on time, the beer is good and the government not too bad.

Today Britain – and this has been its biggest victory – is not only a country with a great past. It is also a nation with a pretty good present. It has finally stopped being the garden of eccentrics that we all liked to visit, at least for a weekend, thinking we understood it pretty well and laughing when we did not. We shouldn't feel guilty about this. The British deserve to be examined in haste and judged without pity. They've been doing it to everyone else for centuries. But they are more fascinating than they would like and that is unforgivable.

DOING AN ITALIAN JOB ON THE ENGLISH
by Stephanie Calman, *The Times*, August 14, 1991

*The first flat Giuseppe Severgnini rented in London was in
a basement in Notting Hill. He had not been there long
when a bunch of people turned up from Chicago, introducing themselves as the Jimi Hendrix fan club. Apparently
he was occupying their idol's last home. For a writer, it was
an auspicious start.*

*Signor Severgnini (known to his readers as Beppe)
had envied British journalists long before being posted
here as a special correspondent for* Il Giornale, *an Italian
daily newspaper, in the 1980s. "The sheer variety of your
sex scandals is quite wonderful," he says appreciatively.
"Italian politicians are the most boring in the world. And
if you do see them with a gorgeous brunette in intimate
circumstances, you don't report it: it would only gain them
more votes."*

*Signor Severgnini's first interview here was with
Christine Keeler. Shortly afterwards, he left the Hendrix
shrine for a covetable flat in Kensington Church Walk
and set about observing the wild life in earnest. Bold
expeditions were made to derelict inner cities, gentlemen's
clubs, pubs and racetracks. He observed the natives eating,
talking, dressing and falling down drunk, and has now
gathered his findings into a book titled* Inglesi. *In returning
here to publicise – or defend – it, he takes his courage in
his hands. The Italians loved it, but then it was not about
them.*

"The British are not very communicative. They love tradition and read a lot, but don't wash too much." So runs one of many provocative Severgnini statements which hide among the thoughtful, meticulous reportage. After digesting them, it comes as a surprise to meet a lively but not loud, charming but not flirtatious man in a sober grey suit and glasses. At 34, Signor Severgnini disingenuously cultivates the demeanour of one of his favourite English tribes, the young fogeys. He comments that "the British eat worse than they would like to, but much better than we think they do". If he is anything to go by, the Italians dress worse than we think they do, but better than he says they do. However, he is quick to establish his dubious status as an untypical Italian, citing by way of comparison the Milanese banker who turned up for work in the City in a patterned jacket and brown shoes. "They asked him if he was going shooting."

We are eating lunch at Chelsea Harbour, the sort of expensive, sterile development Signor Severgnini might well have documented. Our exact location is Deals restaurant (co-owner, Viscount Linley), a ranch-style room with soul music on the speakers and farming implements on the walls. The menu offers Korean, Thai and burger food under such headings as "Raw Deals" and "No Big Deals". What is his assessment?

"Why an English viscount would open a western diner in the middle of a post-modern marina designed by architects in blindfold is beyond me," he says. He cannot pronounce "viscount", but makes a wonderful lunch companion. Looking out at the view of the railway line, he imagines passing travellers must be tempted to throw things. Possibly, he says, that might account for the farming implements. None the less he is grateful for the invitation "to see the remains of an ancient civilisation: the 1980s".

We had set off from the Reform club and come here, around London in 80 delays, in keeping with Signor

238

Severgnini's career, which is a testament to the benefits of straying from the beaten track. After just two weeks on Il Giornale's foreign desk as a graduate trainee, he rode across Poland on a motor bike in 1982 at the time of martial law. The next ten years saw him posted to South Africa, the Middle East and most of Eastern Europe, including Moscow, to which he has recently returned. He is, he says, prepared to endure the numbing tedium of central committee briefings in order to gather the social nuggets which his readers like.

"Lately there's been a spate of thefts of red flags in Moscow," he confides delightedly. "The new craze this summer is for red trousers, and there's nothing else to make them out of."

His favourite thing about China – which ranks equal to Britain in most-demanding postings – is the Chinese version of Monopoly. "It comes with a card inside which says 'Warning to children: this game is a capitalist ploy'."

And what is his favourite thing about England? Coming from a country where people are "too lively and too sincere", he claims to treasure reticence. "Ask an Italian how he feels, and you'll get a history of his digestive problems. A Brit will say 'very well, thank you' or, if he is dying, 'not too bad'."

From the candlelit east London mansions of the new Georgians to Newcastle in an Austin Montego, Signor Severgnini has covered the (post-modern) waterfront. He has a crazy fantasy that one day the English will fit their bathrooms with mixer taps "instead of one scorching, one freezing", and start using their bidets. Until then, he will continue to collect English words for lavatory – 29 so far – and would like to welcome his proud, rained-upon English friends into the European Community.

"Europeans think the British don't want to join them because they feel superior. It's actually because they're terrified of anything new. Look, you've survived losing the *pound note and televising the Commons. Going into Europe, you'll be like a kid going to the dentist. We'll drag you screaming and kicking – and afterwards you'll say 'Oh, was that it?'."*

In the meantime, he is proud to display those of our qualities which have rubbed off. "I'm quite good at lying now, I can be polite to people I hate. And", he adds, arms folded, "I only speak with my hands at weekends."

TWELVE YEARS
(1991-2003)

THE JOYS OF SPYING

In the autumn of 1991, BBC Radio 4 produced a series of programs entitled "As Others See Us". This was my contribution. Polite protests followed.

In 1984, I was twenty-seven and was sent to England to head the London bureau of my paper. I knew that it would not be easy. In the first place, there wasn't any bureau to head and I had to share a house in Clapham with an English sculptress and an Egyptian rug repairer. A few months later I moved to a basement flat in Notting Hill, with a view out onto someone else's dustbins. I quickly got used to my new situation and eventually began to enjoy it. When I saw lots of plastic bags with the logo of a nearby supermarket, I knew there was going to be a party. When I found lots of empty bottles, I knew there had been a party. I was never invited but I felt like one of the family.

However, getting used to you, the English, turned out to be more difficult than just getting used to your trash. I came full of preconceived ideas (England is full of people who get embarrassed easily, read a lot and bathe very little) and realised after a few days that these ideas were actually correct. The blow was so great that for at least six months, further research became impossible.

Then it became fun. The first thing I realised was that you are great actors and I shouldn't take anything at face value (that was certainly true about things you said. It was hard for me to accept that when someone said "Let's have lunch together sometime", it was really only an inflated good-bye and no one ever meant to invite me to lunch). In particular I noticed that you like to play roles, often ones assigned to you at birth. Unless I am mistaken, you call this "the class system". From the start, I found this very entertaining.

My landlords and their dustbins taught me other important lessons. The young mistress was definitely upper class. She called my basement flat a "garden flat" and when she put out her trash in front of my window she never said a word. However, according to her upper-middle class husband who worked in the City, I lived in the "lower ground floor flat". When he came down to put out the trash, he smiled and talked about the weather. The nanny, a working class girl from Liverpool, with a miniskirt and an accent I'll never forget, carried out the same chore, cursing her job, her employers' dinner parties and the "bloody stairs going down to the basement". And, of course, that is exactly what it was.

This was my introduction to the class system. The same flat – my flat – meant three different things to three different people, simply because of their backgrounds. The same chore – putting the same trash in dustbins in front of my window – revealed something about each of them. When I was finally invited upstairs, I realised that "the class game" was adaptable to any situation. The upper class wife liked furniture but it was not a subject she would talk about. The upper-middle class husband had little interest in tables and chairs but did like to talk about them, confiding how much he had paid for each one. The nanny had no interest in furniture at all except insofar as a table could support the TV.

Ever since those happy days in Notting Hill, I came to realise that the English and the class system were unlike the French and sex (they don't do it any more than anyone else, they just talk about it more). I've always thought that your obsession with the system was genuine, for the simple reason that you enjoy it. Perhaps because, as George Bernard Shaw once observed, its rituals draw on your talent for recitation. Or maybe because its existence is reassuring to your conservative nature. In a rapidly changing world, it must be nice to have some things that stay the same.

Take the Great Mystery of Rinsing Dishes, as we on the continent call it. Basically, no one in this country rinses their dishes after washing them. Not the upper class in their country houses, not the middle classes in their semi-detached, and certainly not the working class, who consider rinsing a decidedly European habit. No one has been able to explain to me why you insist on flavouring your meals with washing up liquid. I often rinse my plate myself before dinner with friends but I can feel the hostility around me. I wonder when it will occur to you that washing a dish without rinsing it afterwards is bizarre and actually not very good for you. Perhaps when your children stand up and start to blow bubbles as they leave the dinner table.

After a few years in England I too have begun to feel the attraction of it all. People here love to complain but opinion polls reveal that this is the most contented country in Europe. The good life, I happen to think, is here. The upper class is proud of its genuine or feigned eccentricity. The middle class seems content with the insincerity that underlies its social life. The working class is happy to sit in front of the television or to contemplate a bare-chested Page Three girl in the popular press. No one, of course, admits any of this. But that's what makes Britain so fascinating for a writer. Spying on you, while you pretend to hide, is a pleasure. Brit-watching is as interesting as bird watching. You don't even need binoculars. You only need to be alert and careful not to make too much noise. If either is startled, bird or Brit, the game's over.

AN ITALIAN IN LONDON

This was my farewell piece when I left my stint at The Economist. *It was published January 8, 1994.*

> "When after months of travel, one returns to England, he can taste, smell and feel the difference in the atmosphere, physical and moral – the curious damp, blunt, good-humoured, happy-go-lucky, old-established, slow-seeming formlessness of everything."

So John Galsworthy saw his country – above all 'cosy' and glorying in its ability to muddle through. Foreigners see things rather differently. I have watched modern Britain not only from the comfortable heights of The Economist's building in St James's Street, but also from the challenging lows of a basement flat in Notting Hill, and have travelled through most of the rest of the country. My views may irritate but that, at least in part, is my intention. Italians are not keen fans of cosiness.

In 1984, with Thatcherism in full bloom and Labour in mourning, I arrived in London as my newspaper's correspondent and watched Margaret Thatcher try hard to change the nation. Britain's peculiar and – to any foreigner – highly visible class system was only one piece of tradition she tried (and failed) to reform. Even those who cannot stand her admit as much. What her opponents believe, though, is that her ruthless remedies were, at the end of the day, unnecessary. Many British people (and most of my friends) do not seem entirely convinced that the country was going to the dogs at the end of the 1970s, and believe (though they are loath to voice their feelings aloud) that being one of the oldest democracies of the world and having had the largest empire, the British are somewhat special. And special people will always find a way out, one way or another.

They are wrong. Thatcherism has been like a trumpet call blared in the ears of those who were asleep in a sinking ship: it is hardly surprising that the people who were woken up that way are ungrateful. Pre-Thatcherite Britain – the one I got to know as a student in the 1970s – was not a nation like other nations. It was more like a church, in which all institutions, from industries and trade unions to the judiciary and the police, from universities to the civil-service bureaucracy, were sacred and perennial. They were supposed to work well, but often they didn't.

Such ingrained conservatism could be a blessing if carefully monitored. Any sensible Italian envies the British love and respect for tradition. The trouble is that very often the British love of what is ancient and well known turns into fear of what is new and unknown. The class system itself survives because it has always been there. People in Britain, apparently, do not want to experience the unsettling feeling associated with change.

It is not, therefore, surprising that Mrs Thatcher frightened so many. She wanted a quiet and contented nation to be restless and busy. She made a lot of mistakes, I believe: some were only a matter of tone and presentation, some of substance. But the refusal of the harsher side of Thatcherism is no excuse for resuming the bad old ways. The danger is always lurking. Siren songs can be heard on the left and on the right. Even John Major's "back to basics" theme sounds ominously reassuring.

Britain does not need tranquillity – which would be immediately converted into genteel decay. It needs more shaking up. In spite of the recession, a few things have improved. Money is no more a dirty word, and people gingerly ask you to pay up for whatever you do and wherever you do it (parking your car, visiting a sheep farm, asking the Central Office of Information for a copy of a government handbook). The north of England, where I have travelled extensively both in the mid-1980s and in 1993, has stopped moaning and has rolled up its sleeves, displaying some of the grit and determination which astounded the world one hundred and fifty years ago.

There are other areas where I was glad to see that the country has picked up. Take race relations, where Britain can teach a thing or two to France and Germany, or personal freedoms, which in Britain are still widely respected (there are signs that even the very British, and most amusing, obsession with secrecy is easing). Take the relatively straightforward tax system, which any Italian, burdened by a couple of hundred tributes, looks at with misty eyes. Consider privatisation, which Britain has mastered more than any other country (sometimes stepping into the traps that we can now avoid). Or look at the state of British industry. It still has a long way to go but, compared with the 1970s and early 1980s, is now lively, competitive and in rude health (just think of the turn-around in the Japanese-assisted car industry).

For some mysterious reason, though, most of my British friends seem to find all this irrelevant. They prefer to remember the country's past glory, rather than its worthy present. The British prefer to praise things when they are either dead or dying (from the House of Lords to red phone boxes). They love to talk about decline and one is never sure what they mean by the word. The favourite poet of middle class England is the gloomy Philip Larkin.

Of course, there are things that need sorting out, as *The Economist* never stops reminding its readers. From overly bureaucratic police forces to an aging judiciary, from juvenile crime to poor education, from feeble local government to a growing underclass. But I can easily name a hundred things that the British should be proud of, but aren't. These range from their commerce to their performing arts, from bits of their service industry to most of their press, from broadcasting to science, from their military to their truly unique, even mystifying, sense of humour.

The British are good at living next to each other, and at pulling together when need be. Government in Britain is better than almost anywhere else. Although the present government's policies are sometimes ill-conceived (and most of the time half-hearted), the machinery of British government is still reasonably efficient and clean. What John Gunther, an American journalist and traveller, wrote in the 1930s still rings true: "The standard of public life in England is the highest in the world; honour and idealism play a part in politics that the suspicious foreigner finds it difficult to understand".

Political scandals in Britain are also few and far between. Most of the time they involve a young woman (some of the time a young man) and are almost touching in their display of forgivable human fallibility. Italian scandals are nastier, more sordid and definitely most boring. They always revolve around the same commodity: money. I remember my colleagues at the *The Economist* being spellbound as they watched on television former chancellor Norman Lamont's bitter resignation speech in the House of Commons. They obviously saw it as high political drama. For me, used to the appalling mess in Italy, it was democracy at its best. A minister, who lost his job, speaks up in Parliament to defend his record and settle a few scores. I remember envying them, like a cynical grown-up envies the excitement of a group of children.

The nation's foundations, in other words, are sound. Never mind the weak state of the monarchy or the Church of England (Britain would do all right without either a monarchy or a state religion). British nationalism – when it is sober and is not paraded around football stadiums – is healthy, an expression of Britons' genuine affection for their country rather than an ugly or aggressive expression of contempt towards others.

The British do not seem to have any inhibitions about being British. The country's geography, undoubtedly, helps. So does history. Britain has no big chunk of its past it needs to forget – unlike Japan,

Germany or Italy. As there is no British Vichy and no British Vietnam, Britain has also fewer hang-ups than either France or the United States. In twentieth-century Britain there has been no scuttling around censoring monuments and covering memorials. The bits of history the British want to remove (from the bombing of Dresden, to some colonial heavy-handedness, to their treatment of the Irish), they do so painlessly, in a careless sort of way.

The British still display two other characteristics I noticed on my first visit in 1972: stoicism and thrift. They still put up with anything: rain, queues and bombs in London, and they do not need much, judging by the same plain decors of most British homes (and by the atrocious home-improvement offers in the Sunday newspapers' colour supplements, a source of amazement for every foreigner). Walter Bagehot wrote that the British have a redeeming feature: they are dull. It is an interesting observation. Just look what of State we Italians – who think we are clever – have produced.

And yet the British themselves seem unable to appreciate any of the achievements of modern Britain, and prefer to dwell on the embarrassments, mistakes and cock-ups (of which, to be fair, there is no shortage). It is a form of masochism which brings people to enjoy sporting defeats more than victories. Knocked-out Frank Bruno, not his conqueror Lennox Lewis, is the modern British hero. Not once was I told how good British theatre or the BBC World Service still are, or how impressive Marks & Spencer and British Airway have become.

There are many more examples of the British failing to appreciate what they do well and concentrating instead on what they do badly. The nation whose supremacy in the nineteenth century spanned so many fields – "with the notable exceptions of abstract philosophy, music, cuisine, and love-making", as Luigi Barzini, my countryman, once noted – has managed to excel again. This time, though, its triumph is a sour one. The British have managed to turn grumbling into an art form, and are kilometres ahead of anyone else at it.

Then, there is Europe. Whenever I am in Britain, the British are busy quarrelling about it. When I first came as a student, in the early 1970s, the country was arguing about its belated entry into the Common Market, where it should have been in the first place, using its skills and experience to lead the continent. When I came back to London as a journalist in the mid-1980s, Mrs Thatcher was fighting furiously about the common agricultural policy and Britain's contribution to the budget. On this visit it was Mr Major wrangling over Maastricht.

I found Britain's Maastricht debate both sad and hilarious. The Maastricht saga could have been avoided if someone had stood up and said loud and clear that there really was no choice. The British are right to be wary of yet another vast and vague continental design. But Maastricht had to be accepted, as Britain in Europe or in limbo. If it leaves, or takes a back seat, the country will gently decline, just as the Republic of Venice or Portugal have declined (they too were proud imperial powers based on commerce).

The fact that Britain is now firmly inside the European Union, of course, does not mean that the British are Europeans. When asked, they will say they are, as an Italian, Spaniard, Dutch or German would. But Britons always have to ponder before replying – unlike anyone else in Europe.

Their answer will follow "a long thoughtful pause in which all the other continents are mentally evoked and regretfully discarded" (Barzini again). Now, admittedly, that "long thoughtful pause" has become shorter. But it is still there.

THE MUSIC OF TONY BLAIR

Ten years ago, the British Left was symbolised by a miner from Yorkshire. If this miner had found himself in a pub sitting across from someone like Tony Blair, an elegant good-looking forty-something Oxford graduate in favour of privatisation, he would have chased Blair out the door. Or if the Yorkshire miner had been feeling a bit more generous, he'd have tried to get Blair drunk and he might well have succeeded (the future prime minister didn't drink or smoke at Oxford – neither cigarettes nor any other kind à la Bill Clinton – and he didn't chase girls). A few months later, however, our Yorkshire miner, along with a million other British citizens, would cast his vote for him and put Labour back into Downing Street after an absence of eighteen years. The last Labour prime minister James Callaghan was swept out by the Thatcher hurricane. When he was in charge, he remarked that history would remember him for having introduced cat's eyes in the middle of the roads. And so it has been.

To get Blair, the British Labour Party had to go through four leaders (Callaghan, Foot, Kinnock, Smith) and lose four consecutive elections (1979, 1983,1987,1992). In Italy, the Left also won after a memorable series of defeats but narrowly. It did it by bringing together Liberals and Marxists, Catholics and Greens and the idea, thanks to consistent help from their opponents, worked. Now, if the Olive Tree coalition doesn't take advantage of the situation by finding its own Tony Blair among its ranks, it is wasting an opportunity. Its opponents will find him instead. Certain ideas don't belong just to the Left or the Right these days. They are inevitable and belong to whomever grabs them first.

Let's begin by saying that Blair's New Left is not an ideology; at best, it is vaguely idealistic and that does it no harm. It is passionate about the future, to the extent of trivialising it somewhat. It is also openly pro-technology (a computer for every child), sincerely liberal, moderately in favour of free trade, and only lukewarm about public assistance. It has no patience with the romantic side of the old Left. In a knock-out blow to the Marxist wing of the Party, Blair used the sharpest weapon a politician can use: words. Instead of accepting the traditional divide between the moderates (Labour's right) and the militants (the pure hard-core, more hard-core than pure these days), Blair brought in something new: Modernisers (us) against Traditionalists (you). This last definition threw the old Left into an uproar and they protested vigorously. But there was nothing they could do. The new label stuck.

Still Blair was aware that the future and an open economy (free markets, competition, privatisation) were sources of anxiety for many people. Therefore it was necessary to explain that some changes were opportune and if they were met with the right attitude, would be to everyone's advantage. Britain would become competitive and wealthy only if it produced goods and services that consumers wanted at a price they were willing to pay. To compete with the rest of the world, innovation, productivity and quality were needed. A pliable labour force was essential, explained Blair, and the trade unions needed to understand this. "Showing special favour to the trade unions is not among the functions of a Labour government." The future prime minister then smoothly concluded by saying that many of these ideas came from Margaret Thatcher – considered the anti-Christ by the Labour Party until the day before.

The Conservatives grew nervous listening to these speeches. And occasionally, they also copied them. A few years earlier, the employment minister David Hunt had been attacked for having adopted word for word, Labour Party slogans on employment. The Tories detested Blair from the moment he had appeared on the horizon in 1983 (the year of his election into Parliament). They feared his youth and his lack of a past (how could they accuse Blair of being an ex-Marxist when his greatest sin seems to have been that he played in a rock band called Ugly Rumours?). More astute Conservatives recognised the attraction Blair held for the middle class, grown tired of the dishevelled appearance of Michael Foot (beaten in 1983) and the verbal gymnastics of the Welshman, Neil Kinnock (defeated in 1987 and 1992). There was the risk that the new Labour Party leader would charm the southeast, that is, recapture the lower-middle class (small businessmen, teachers, middle managers) that Margaret Thatcher had lured away from them in the eighties and then turned over to John Major.

Blair's program is to build a "prosperous and fair Britain". Banal, you might say. What leader would want to build a poor and unjust country? But Blair's talent lies in putting obvious ideas in an attractive package. When he realised that the word "social democracy" was passé, he came up with the "stakeholder society", a society where everyone feels like they own a share. This was the British version of the civil society that America was talking about not long ago, inspired by Robert Putnam and Francis Fukuyama. And it worked. If Blair had proposed a theme entitled "Social democracy: Does it have a future?" we might not be talking about him here.

Many attempts have been made to understand the man, a strange mixture of mellowness and resoluteness, youth and wisdom, tactics and strategies. I'll give you one. It is from an article in the *New Yorker* by Julian Barnes who made a list of the words Blair had emphasised in a draft of his acceptance speech for the leadership of the Labour Party. Here they are in the order they were used.

> Responsibility/trust/trust/service/dedication/ dignity/pride/trust/mission/renewal/mission/ hope/change/responsibility/mission/spirit/community/community/pride/pride/socialism/change/ wrong/right/wrong/right/wrong/right/community/passion/reason/change/change/change/ solidarity/community/anew/afresh/inspire/ crusade/change/progress/confidence/serve/ serve/serve

[By courtesy of Julian Barnes]

I hope you agree. A politician who says such things is either hypocritical and rhetorical, or he is interesting. Tony Blair is no rhetorician. Neither is he the most hypocritical of politicians. Therefore, it is just possible that he is interesting.

(1996)

THE POLITICS OF THE SPICE GIRLS

The Spice Girls praised Margaret Thatcher in an interview with *The Spectator*, a conservative weekly read by young fogeys and retired army officers, people whose only desire if they ever came face to face with the Spice Girls, would be to spank them.

The interview does not imply that the girls understand politics. But it does show they have a good nose for provocation. Exhuming Thatcher might seem bizarre. Baroness Thatcher's power has diminished over time and there's no going back. She is now part of history. Her ideas, which ten years ago produced endless bile among London's young club-goers, today have the cachet of fable. When Emma, "Baby Spice", was born in 1978, Margaret Thatcher was already leading the Conservatives. The following year, she won her way into 10 Downing Street swinging her purse beside her. Mel B and Mel C, with forty-one years between the two of them, cannot remember the explosive effect of Margaret Thatcher's sermons on the British establishment. In the cradles of the United Kingdom in those days, other things were discussed.

Still, the Spice Girls are on to something: the lady with the armour-plated permanent wave showed the insolence of Tina Turner even if her skirts were longer, and she did a lot for the cause of British women (even if feminists don't like to admit it). The Spice Girls' chaotic internet sites are full of unintentional post-Thatcher declarations. If the Iron Lady, during a party congress, had exposed her bra and worn platform shoes (neither likely), she would have been a proto-Spice Girl. The concepts and the boldness were there.

Mel B "Scary Spice" admonishes fans to "Be provocative!" (and Maggie certainly was). Geri "Ginger Spice"'s motto is "If you have something to say, SAY IT!" (and Thatcher was never silent). Emma "Baby Spice" advises you to "Listen to your mother's advice; she's your best friend" (this is pure Thatcher domestic policy, imported from Grantham, Lincolnshire). Victoria "Posh Spice" counsels "If you kiss a boy, make sure you leave a hicky" (I'm sure the mythical Dennis Thatcher could tell a few good stories on this subject). Finally Mel C "Sporty Spice" says "You've got to beat men at their own games. Never let up". And Maggie never let up and she never lost an election. Her own colleagues had to bring her down, the way you do with a wounded lioness.

You must admit, their provocative and insolent advice is like a mini-Thatcher manifesto. At the end of Conservative rule, in the days that precede Tony Blair's triumph, their advice sounds odd. Here is another piece of Spice Girls' wisdom: being in the opposition pays off. It paid off for Paul Weller's Style Council in the eighties when the group turned concerts into anti-Thatcher rallies and it will continue to pay off in the future. Towing Pretty Boy Tony's line would reduce the rogues of Brit-pop to banal agit-prop. The rascals in question know this much: certain kinds of music, like certain kinds of satire, must keep a certain distance from power.

This is a lesson we would do well to learn in Italy. But who have we got to bring back in place of the mythical Thatcher? What depressed dejected monument could music provocatively revive? Is there room for Craxi-rock (with north African influences)? Or for Pertini-pop? Personally I'd like to see a vintage Saragat, toasting with Zucchero, the Italian bluesman. But I fear it wouldn't be the same. Thatcher is Thatcher, and the English are the English.

(1997)

A few flowers, a half-deserted museum, unsold souvenirs. No flags at half mast, no commemoration. Lacklustre remembrances in the papers. An apathetic anniversary marking the death of the Princess of Wales.

She has been gone two years now yet on the day she died everyone thought that it would be a simple transition from the Paris tunnel to the heaven of popular mythology where Marilyn Monroe, James Dean and John Lennon awaited her. It didn't turn out that way. Diana's legend seems to have evaporated in no time at all. Not even her mother-in-law, who was not a huge fan, could have imagined for such a collective dismissal.

What happened? Two things, probably. The first is obvious. Diana didn't have a record of achievements to help us remember her – as Marilyn Monroe had with films or John Lennon with music. She was not a film star or a pop star. She was queen of the gossip columns and gossip columns don't last (may those who measure their value by the number of their television appearances and mentions in the press remember this).

Something, though, did happen. To understand what it was, we must go back to the day of her funeral. Remember, the event was not at all English. There were tears, there was weeping, there were presents and flowers and more weeping and promises never ever to forget her. The composure of the guests at the funeral, something the British excel at, was in stark contrast to the people outside the cathedral, emotional, nerves frayed, exhausted.

London was not London that day either, it was Rome or Naples and it wore its heart on its sleeve like Milan. It was an unrecognisable city, touching and sharing. It was proof of the slow but sure thawing of the English (a phenomenon that has some enthusiastic and others worried). On the other side of the channel they've been talking about it now for a few years: how summers resemble summer now and not just a single day in July that catches you by surprise, before it disappears again for another twelve months; how restaurants are finally learning to cook (not all, not yet), how friends are fighting and couples are breaking up instead of silently putting up with each other for years, punishing each other with adjectives.

This thawing, or rather this "Italianisation", is brought up whenever the English show signs of living in a more instinctive way (the Welsh and the Scots already do this). Enough with hiding your feelings as if they were a nasty rash, enough stoicism and silent suffering. If you are happy, laugh. If you are in pain, cry. Like Italians.

Unfortunately we Italians have other traits: we shed lots of tears, but we have short memories. Our forgotten heroes are innumerable. We are so ready to embrace the new that we forget the old. Our history and politics, culture and entertainment are full of things forgotten.

Diana l'italiana, Diana the Italian, has come to the end of her extraordinary road. There is a melancholy consistency in the way the English are forgetting her. They used to be a cold-blooded people with long memories. Now they are becoming warm-blooded people with short memories. Welcome to Europe, you might say.

(1999)

On the fourteenth floor of *The Economist* Building
at 25 St. James's Street, there is a dining room with
huge windows that overlooks London, a horizontal
city. Foreign politicians and bankers are invited for
lunch here, and, soothed by the food prepared by
Raphael, the Spanish chef, reveal the secrets of the
world. These people are interesting; nevertheless
they always have the same jobs: politics, economics,
banking. Therefore when my colleagues at *The
Economist* heard that I had met Gianluca Vialli, the
Chelsea coach and footballer, they lit up. "Bring
him over!" So, on Thursday, we arrive. The guest in
blue pinstripes, me, his escort, in a grey suit.

Naturally we are the only ones dressed English
style. The English are all dressed Italian style (wide
jackets, comfortable shoes). One is dressed like a
footballer. He's the Europe editor who has hurt his
knee playing football with some teenagers and is
only able to wear shorts and trainers. Two female
colleagues, one an expert on mass media and the
other responsible for the American survey are
dressed elegantly and talk knowledgeably about
football. Vialli looks at me. "Typical," he says.

Still I notice a slight lack of ease. The journalists,
who are comfortable talking to prime ministers, are
almost shy around a famous footballer (he has
turned Chelsea around and endeared himself to
Londoners). He is aware – in part because I tell
him every five minutes – that he is the first footballer to be a guest at *The Economist* in its one hundred and fifty-six-year-history. Gianluca Vialli doesn't
eat much but he understands their questions and
laughs at their witty remarks. He replies in a dry
idiomatic English. He says he learned it from one

of my books. I'm sure this isn't true but I admire the opportunism of his lie.

I look at him as he faces the assault of these unusual fans. The pinstripe suit under the shaved head ("I go to Leboeuf's hairdresser," he says, naming a bald French team mate) is somewhat disquieting. It's as if Lord Astor were to show up dressed as a defender, with his calves bare. The cuffs and open collar show little familiarity with the shirts of Jermyn Street. In the changing rooms of a stadium, his blue overcoat with its velvet collar would make him unforgettable; up here it's a sign of good will and is appreciated as such. His enormous black shoes, English I presume, are vaguely clown-like. But no more than my striped shirt.

Gianluca Vialli answers the questions easily and his modesty – probably calculated – makes him seem charming. The English admire those who perform as long as they do it well. Artifice does not bother them. Up here they call it – correctly – courtesy. When they ask him which of his teams he feels closest to, he replies "Sampdoria" and explains, "I was twenty then, it was like being at school. You never forget your schoolmates". When he speaks of Ken Bates, the unpredictable president of Chelsea, his eyes light up. "Ken calls me 'old bugger'. Sometimes 'bald old bugger'." My English colleagues look at me with admiration. An Italian who not only knows profanity but knows how to pronounce it too. Where did he learn that? In Cremona, I say.

As lunch continues and my companions relax, I have proof of something I had previously thought might be true. Vialli functions well in England because he is a mixture of cunning and ingenuity, courtesy and toughness. A country that could send the ephebic Tony Blair to 10 Downing Street can't help but like Vialli. This coach-player-trainer brings back fond memories of the rough-edged coaches of days gone by. The fact that he is Italian is secondary. Chelsea is a United Nations of football with eleven different nationalities represented. It's a London team and along with Arsenal and Arsene Wenger, is one of the most fascinating aspects of this city: it is open to all that's new as long as it is serious, fun and it works.

Vialli is both serious and amusing. And he is a hard worker. In his first season as coach he won the League Cup and the Cup Winner's Cup. This year again he made it to the European Cup Final. He may not win the championship but he has a good chance of coming in second, by beating the league champions. Three years ago, his first English season was a bit of a disaster between misfortunes and disagreements with Ruud Gullit, but Vialli came back, first as a player and then as coach, and around here, they like comebacks. His success with the English might be explained like this: he is a tough European, but not without emotion. He is a foreigner who comes and doesn't complain about the weather or the food. Indeed, he says he is happy and grateful to be here.

Luca Vialli is completely integrated in the city. He tells about the first time he went to Sainsbury's. He stayed for three hours, happy to be just an ordinary person. When we met this morning at his flat in Eaton Square, hidden among the houses of the Establishment, Vialli told me enthusiastically that sometimes he reserves a ticket to a film by phone, goes and watches the film, box of popcorn in hand and afterwards leaves and grabs a taxi just around the corner. These are the small urban miracles well-known to everyone who loves London.

Tell this to a tabloid and they will be on your side forever (until the day you get involved in a particularly juicy scandal).

There are also things about England that Vialli says he likes less. But, they happen to be the very things the English would like to change. For one, he doesn't like the rapaciousness of the popular press. Vialli also doesn't like the snobbery and he's not crazy about the aristocracy. He finds excessive the reserve and self-consciousness that leads two friends to talk about the weather. He is puzzled by the houses ("Perhaps it is all façade") and irritated sometimes by the slovenliness ("Why do some English go around with holes in their shoes?" he asks. "To make you think they have more important things to do", I reply).

Vialli is probably the best known Italian in the new meritocratic Britain, curious about Europe. Only Romano Prodi might vie for the number one spot but he needs to win something first and Brussels is a difficult field. Vialli and Prodi, along with diverse personalities like Gianfranco Zola and Roberto Benigni have helped change the stereotype of the Italian as nice but unreliable; the British have learned that hidden behind the benign smile are teeth of steel. I think Luca Vialli is aware of his role as a "new Italian" and has accepted it. He knows that in Britain they weigh you and judge you. Then if you don't shock them, they accept you.

When he talks about Italy, Vialli alternates between criticism and praise. The Italian teams, he says, are better organised and more professional, the English more enthusiastic and amateurish ("The other night after the game we came back from Middlesbrough by bus and didn't get home till three in the morning. In Italy they would have rented a plane."). But he adds, "I'm not sure I would want English football to take this step forward, it wouldn't be as much fun". Faced with an attentive audience happy not to talk about the euro or Kosovo for two hours, Vialli explains, "Young Italian footballers are taught that winning is all important. It's obvious then that they throw themselves on the ground in the hopes of getting a penalty called. The English are right when they chant "Same I-ties, Always Cheating" at stadiums. Then, he starts to hum it to the sound of Big Ben striking. *The Economist* listens, rapt.

The conversation continues till it's time to say goodbye. They give him a parting gift, a red *Economist* umbrella. Luca Vialli, class of 1964, with a degree in geometry from the Vacchelli Institute in Cremona, has eaten little but has a satisfied air. My colleagues, who ask for autographs for their children, seem even more pleased than he. In the lift, he tells how when he first arrived in London three years ago, he hardly knew the difference between John Major and Tony Blair. Now he loves the American TV series *Friends* like all true English people. He is thinking, he says, about writing *Learn English with Luca.* I tell him to forget it. I say that in five years he'll be coaching an Italian team and in twenty, he'll buy it. He smiles.

(1999)

I MET HARRY POTTER'S GRANNY

To try to get to grips with a first printing of five million copies, I asked my seven-year-old son Antonio why he wanted to read *Harry Potter* every night instead of watching violent animated cartoons. He replied as follows:

1. Because it's a book full of magic.
2. Because it is about school but the school is magic too.
3. Because it is full of disgusting things like caramels that taste like vomit.
4. Because there are bad aunts and uncles and a book without any bad guys is worthless.

Even a "muggle" like me (i.e. a normal person without any magical powers) can understand a review like that. Harry Potter is the Mary Poppins of the new millennium. The story works because normal things happen in abnormal places. And it draws you in because it has some really good villains who represent the "obstacle factor" which all stories need (Vladimir Propp, *The morphology of fairy tales*, Moscow, 1968). These explanations cover points 1, 2, and 4. That leaves point 3: disgusting things. But I imagine that can be explained too.

Some of these things really are disgusting and some of the characters make Pokémon seem attractive, which is saying a lot. The villain of villains, called Voldemort, killed the hero's parents, a detail which should result in his expulsion from any children's book. And his schoolmate Draco Malfoy is formidably unpleasant. We've all known someone like him even if they rarely have names as good as Draco Malfoy.

Within this complicated world, children and teenagers are in their element. Adults are less so but they can always get help. And in the end they love it too – it's a bit like mastering a new language (it also happens with opera and politics). As I was writing I found myself calling out, "Who the devil is Gilderoy Lockhart?". A voice from the other room answered, "He's not a devil, he's a writer like you".

So in the end I grew fond of old Lockhart who wrote books and then made his students at the School buy them – something that happens I think in normal universities as well.

The author, J.K. Rowling, is good at building a second level of meaning, full of allusions to the life of adults and articulated in comments, some wise ("Man has the ability to always choose the worst for himself") and some surprising ("For a well-organised mind, death is but one more adventure", says Albus Dumbledore). Not everyone, of course, has a child as an excuse to read the books. In America I know Potter fans who run newspapers, manage companies, and work for Microsoft (that last one, I can understand. Bill Gates, without any need of tricks or spells, is a *Harry Potter* character).

Want to hear my excuses? First, it's my duty to read to my son. And second, the *Harry Potter* books remind me of my first English study holiday in Eastbourne on the Channel. I was fifteen. In the house I stayed in there was orange carpeting, pile rugs in the loo, and nylon sheets that gave off sparks. There was a padlock on the fridge door and they had made the bidet disappear. They had dinner at lunchtime and they had lunch at dinnertime. The owner of the house was named Mrs Potter. I think she was Harry Potter's granny. In fact, I'm nearly positive.

(2000)

IN SEARCH OF AN ELECTION

The Economist, *in the spring of 2001, asked me to write about the forthcoming general election. I went back to Liverpool. Here's what I found.*

When it opened in 1914, the Adelphi was one of the greatest hotels in the world. With solid marble walls, indoor swimming pool, full central heating in all rooms, it was Liverpool's arrival and departure point for passengers on the great liners to America. It was here that Harold Wilson – a local MP, and a predecessor of Tony Blair's – used to spend election nights. Room 101, apparently.

I spread the news, to little excitement. People are busy, around here, tonight. There is the graduation ball for Hope University, a convention of church-bell players and a Welsh football team that decided there was no point in waiting for the match in order to celebrate, so they sing and hug each other in the lobby. Not only are these people ignorant of Harold Wilson's sojourn in the hotel, but most seem oblivious to the fact that a general election is only days away.

Merseyside is solid Labour territory, mostly of the old kind. The last Tory MP, Anthony Steen, was elected in 1979, and founded Thatcher's, a tea-room where one could sit and eat apple pie under a portrait of the then-prime minister. "He would come to the house with a thunderous voice, asking for our vote. The children were terrified," recalls Fleur Packman, a retired teacher who has kind words for Jane Kennedy, the sitting Labour MP. But now it is all too quiet, Ms Packman complains. "I haven't seen nor heard anybody. I am waiting. If they want my vote, they'll have to come and get me, you know."

The first time I was in Liverpool, Derek Hatton's Trotskyite militants were running the city council in the 1980s. Mr Hatton, for all his faults (a vast selection indeed), inflamed Liverpudlians, who love a good argument. "Scouse are like Neapolitans. Great sense of humour, laid-back attitude, maybe not the hardest-working people in the world," says Alberto Bertali, an Italian who runs a big factory making household appliances, loves the city and wouldn't want to live anywhere else.

A real Neapolitan – Alfredo Oliva, an architect who moved to Liverpool "per amore" and now walks around camouflaged in an Italian flag as the cook of the Adelphi's pizzeria – disagrees. "Until today, I didn't even know there was an election coming up. In Naples, and all over Italy, people are at each other's throat, before a big vote. That's good. That's how you make up your mind."

Maybe people in this city have made up their minds already, and that's why they don't bother with politics. They prefer to walk around in the drizzle, pretending it is spring. Boys in bright red Liverpool FC jerseys; girls in what looks like their underwear, but turns out to be an evening dress. Their Labour MPs enjoy huge majorities. Jane Kennedy, in Liverpool Weavertree, has almost 20,000. Peter Kilfoyle, in inner-city Liverpool Walton (home of the two football clubs, Everton and Liverpool), 27,000. Louise Ellman, in Liverpool Riverside, which includes poor and volatile Toxteth, 22,000. Bob Wareing, in Liverpool West Derby, 26,000.

Stan Jones, the organiser for the local Labour Party, asks whom I would like to meet. I go for Ms Ellman and Mr Wareing. Ms Ellman is a nice lady with piercing green eyes, and no illusion. Her constituency has one of the lowest turnouts in the country. "Young people are not interested, they don't feel connected. Four out of five are not going to vote. Older people talk to me about their everyday problems. One lady told me: 'If you don't fix my shower, I won't vote for you'."

Next morning I drive to the Dovecot Labour Club in Bob Wareing's constituency. It looks like a police station in Northern Ireland. Same red bricks, same small windows; bigger gates, though, and more graffiti. It is the sort of place where, once in a century, you could meet Tony Blair holding a pint.

Wally Edwards, a former aide to Harold Wilson, is expecting me. He is happy to talk about his days in the navy, and his encounter with the future prime minister, in 1945, in the Shefton Arms pub. He tells me he's got two daughters married to Italians, who live in Tuscany. "What do they think about Silvio Berlusconi becoming prime minister?" I ask. "Not happy," Wally says. "But I told them: 'Come on, girls. At least you had got a couple of nice hammers-and-sickles on your Italian ballot papers.' Some working-class element, I mean."

Mr Edwards says he "is not much of a Blairite". But he works for the common cause. This morning, he must brief a group of volunteers who are about to deliver leaflets in the area. They leave the Labour Club with a shoulder bag that says: "Taking the Lead in Europe". I ask them if Europe is a big issue, in this campaign. "No, it isn't. But the bags were left over from the European election."

I am assigned to a small commando group formed by a mother with two children, Amy and Zac, aged seven and four, who dash from row-house to row-house dropping leaflets through letter-boxes. Amy says, "I keep fit with Labour". I must do well, as Mr Edwards and three old-timers decide it is time for me to meet their MP.

While we drive, they are in a good mood. "You seem to enjoy putting leaflets into letter-boxes," I say. They laugh: "It is not so much putting ours in that we like. It is taking the Lib Dems' out. You know, sometimes they stick out". Good, I think. Four pensioners, two children. At least six people in Britain are having fun in this election campaign.

DIANA, AGAIN

We never really understood Diana. She was baffling when, like a schoolgirl saved by the bell, she married a man whose heart was otherwise engaged. She was beyond comprehension when she silently put up with it. She was bewildering when she spoke through her biographer, friends, lovers and advisors. She was bewitching when she suddenly blossomed into a beauty, like the rose that hadn't been there the evening before. She was beyond reach, even for those who knew her well. Some said she was shrewd and vindictive, others remembered her as sensitive and vulnerable. Maybe she was a little of all that, sensitive and shrewd, vulnerable and a bit vindictive. She wouldn't be the first.

These are the mysteries of Diana. Her death in Paris was simply the ugly finale to a badly written screenplay. The morning of Sunday, August 30th, 1997, the princess and Dodi Fayed were on a boat on the Costa Smeralda and they talked of moving to the French villa owned by the Duke and Duchess of Windsor. Fifteen hours later they met their deaths in a black Mercedes S-280, license plate number 688 LTV 75, pursued by a pack of photographers and driven by a drunk driver, high on drugs.

After that, you could read and hear everything: that Dodi was an enemy of the state, that Diana was pregnant, of religious wars, and of manoeuvres by the secret services (British, American, Israeli, French). Some of the rumours were tragically ridiculous (thirteen minutes after her death, the first internet website appeared entitled "Diana and the conspiracy"; three months later there were thirty-one thousand websites). Some claimed that it had all been orchestrated by a rival car company in an attempt to discredit Mercedes. Others, that Gianni Versace had returned to escort a good client to heaven. The most bizarre theory was that Diana and Dodi were not dead at all but had been picked up by a truck which took them to a secret location where they were living happily ever after. Diana as Elvis: it was inevitable.

As we have said – and we shall see – the mystery of Diana lies not in her death, as disturbing as it was. It lies in her complicated life. It was the trail of a star that for a moment shone brightly and then was quickly forgotten. You will read and hear many commemorations on the anniversary of her death. But watch. Only a few weeks later and the princess will be forgotten again. Diana was not Marilyn – she couldn't act or sing. Lady Di was the reluctant queen of the gossip columns. And gossip columns are furnaces, not refrigerators. They don't preserve, they consume.

The public parabola of Diana Spencer (born in 1961) lasted just sixteen years, from her marriage in 1981 to her death in 1997. During that time she had two sons, a few friends, a couple of acknow-ledged lovers, a talkative brother, an overly reserved husband, many fans and several detractors, innu-merable biographers, and some good causes (like her campaign against landmines which was a genu-ine attempt to use her notoriety for something useful). And, of course, a beautiful shy smile, those lowered eyes on TV, shoulders as fascinating as her legs (and those legs were no joke), some delightful outfits (as well as some dreadful ones), and at least two brilliant haircuts. Because Diana was one of the few women who knew how to control her hairdresser. We can add that too to her mysteries.

Let's start with her marriage. The text goes something like this: a few days after her engagement, the then twenty-year-old Diana discovers that the relationship between her future husband and Camilla Parker-Bowles is still going on. She marries him anyway. Was it for reasons of state, a sense of responsibility, impotence, interest, ingenuity or confidence in herself? It's hard to say. Diana – like certain football teams and many political parties – is not a subject of reflection: she's the object of intense passions. Her biographers are either fans or detractors. Certainly among the former is Andrew Morton, the author of *Diana: Her True Story* (1992). Morton quotes Sarah Spencer saying something that was meant to warn her sister that it was too late to turn back now : "Bad business, Duch" (her nickname for Diana). "They've already printed your face on the napkins."

Naive, then? Probably. Diana's education came later. The Spencer family – dukes who had moved between home and royal palaces for generations – had provided her only with high-ranking friends and the usual Swiss finishing school, one of the ways that good English girls complicate their lives. And Diana was certainly a good girl. She had the usual normal dreams of having an apartment in London with girlfriends, of holidays and of looking at herself in the mirror with pleasure and watching herself grow up. A beauty? Not when she married. "There are all the ingredients here for a fairy tale," enthused the euphoric Archbishop of Canterbury, celebrating the marriage. But let's be honest. As a protagonist, Snow White was sexier and Cinderella more interesting politically.

Diana changed after ten years of marriage. Suddenly she seemed more beautiful, more confident, more self-aware. The result (or advantage) of a husband who betrayed her, said many of her supporters. Her detractors – who also were many – countered by saying that this self-awareness turned into an obsession with her image. An obsession that brought eating disorders and a messy love life. Her admirers insisted it would never have happened if Charles hadn't ignored and humiliated her, leaving her on her own with the children. Out of this trauma was born the sexually bold Diana; Diana, patron saint of the popular press; Diana, moved by worthy causes but unable to give up the show; Diana, torn between Hollywood and Mother Teresa; Diana, who took up with Dodi, born in 1956 and the son of Mohammed Al Fayad, a man deeply unpopular with the British establishment; Diana, the heroine of six hundred books in her own lifetime.

The most interesting book, however, appeared after her death. Published in 1998, it was entitled *Death of a Princess* and was written by Thomas Sancton and Scott MacLeod, two American journalists who worked for *Time Magazine*. A meticulous study that doesn't in the end provide "answers to all the questions about the tragic end of Lady Di and Dodi Fayad" as the cover promises. But it does ask the right questions and explains many things.

Sancton and MacLeod admit that Diana's death raises questions (the white Fiat Uno struck by the Mercedes, for example, has never been found), but they don't believe in a conspiracy. "The proof and logic", they write after three hundred pages, "brings us both to the same conclusion and that is that the crash in the tunnel in Alma was simply an automobile accident."

And here are their reasons. The first is a practical one: the news of a relationship between Dodi and Diana appeared on August 7th and the accident occurred on the night of August 30-31. Who could have organised an attempt on such short notice? The second is cynical: there are more efficient ways to carry out a murder. How would it have been possible to control the succession of events that led to the crash in the Alma underpass? The third reason is institutional: Diana's future choice of husband did not represent a constitutional threat unless she were to convert to Islam, convince her son William to do the same and then, after becoming king, he were to announce his new faith (it had to be afterwards or he would never be allowed to take the throne). At this stage – let's be honest – we are entering the realm of fantasy. Instead one begins to think that her exit was a tragedy, dressed up as a soap opera. And Diana didn't deserve that. No matter what one may think of her.

This then is the mystery. Not a thriller, but a bittersweet memory. Because deep down, we miss you, Princess. You would have become a splendid, tempestuous, cantankerous forty-year-old. Instead we are left watching the ubiquitous bimbos on television grow old. Not the same, really.

(2002)

LONDON

Foreigners who arrive in London make two mistakes. First, they come looking for Londoners, who elude them, and then they try to find a centre, which doesn't exist. There is the West End, but it is an artificial centre. Once, as its name suggests, it was at the extreme western edge of the capital, the last frontier before you reached the village of Kensington. Today, around Piccadilly Circus, it's mostly theatres, cinemas, shops and fast food. And foreigners.

The truth is that London doesn't have a real centre because it is not a real city. It's really a cluster of villages. If you don't understand the one, you won't understand the other. The various villages are well known, diverse and self-sufficient. Islington and Fulham – two names among many – have their own restaurants, often better than those in the so-called centre, their own cinemas where you can see the same films that play in the West End, their own bookstores and cafes, their own parks and pubs. Residents of each village are proud of their neighbourhoods. Hackney residents brag about their terraces of Georgian houses. Residents of Wapping in the new Docklands area will talk to you about modern architecture. In Hammersmith, in the west,

277

on the road to Heathrow, people will show their friends the pleasures of a Sunday lunch along the river.

It's not just the English who live in these villages. Their very Englishness resides there. It is not coincidence that writers find inspiration in these atmospheric places. The place where the protagonists live in George Orwell's magisterial work *Keep the Aspidistra Flying* is more than a neighbourhood. It is a moral environment. Clapham, home of Everyman, "the man on the Clapham omnibus," is a perfect background for Graham Greene's characters in *The End of the Affair* as they pursue each other across the damp green parks. John Le Carré's spies live in more anonymous neighbourhoods. It is there that they perfect the ancient art of dissimulation.

If you want to understand something about English character – and understanding it all is impossible, not even the English manage that – don't wait too long to tear yourself away from Westminster or Knightsbridge. In London the periphery is not an option as it is in most European cities. London is all periphery. It is a collection of small villages each built up around a high street, a park and a few lights. Hampstead, whose vaguely shabby aspect is a statement of ideology, is completely different from equally attractive Holland Park. The air you breathe among the pink houses of Maida Vale is not the same air as Southall's, where there is a whiff of Asia about. Camden Town cultivates a certain non-conformity which Chelsea pays no attention to. In Finchley, Ealing, Acton, Chiswick and Battersea, every evening the lower-middle class gears up behind its white trimmed bay windows and in front of its switched-on televisions.

There is little doubt that London and Britain will remain incomprehensible to anyone who persists in looking for its secrets behind the windows of Mayfair. This is because the key to understanding the greatness and the limitations of this country lies farther away, in the neighbourhoods where characteristics of the Victorian era – competence and determination as well as a cautious attitude towards change – never died out. These places took root in the collective psyche along with the life style they represent. Mail that is always delivered at the same time. Dinner in a local restaurant. Shopping at the corner shop run by an Indian family. A film. Returning home on the night bus.

Soft City is the title of a book that Jonathan Raban wrote about London. An apt title for a city that does not have the monumentality of Paris, the ancient air of Rome or even the vitality of Berlin. The attractions of London, a horizontal city, are scattered among its suburbs, lie hidden in the details of everyday life, and are protected by English reticence. In any case, they are not immediately obvious. And those that are, are buried under commonplaces. In spite of all the films and novels, the many photographs and the vignettes in books for people learning English, the visitor still can't quite believe that the English really do like their Saturday football and Sunday lunches, their green parks where they go to read or relax, their convivial pubs, the front seat upstairs on a red double-decker bus below which the city unfolds like a documentary, the *Daily Mail* and BBC Radio 4, the countryside and flower gardens.

To the British these aspects of London cannot be improved. Is it proof of their wisdom (as the Anglophiles would have it) or a demonstration of their arrogance (as not insubstantial numbers of Anglophobes would claim)? Whichever, this attitude serves to illuminate the rapport between Londoners and their city. Many complain that life in the capital is demanding and are not reluctant to criticise it (dirty streets, chaotic traffic, crime, inefficient police). But they also make it clear that London, though not a paradise, is still the purgatory they love.

They make it clear, but of course they don't admit it openly. That would not be English.

(1993)

DEEP CITY

I've always had this fantasy of taking an Italian who has never been to London on a blindfolded tour of the London Underground. We would go down its dizzyingly steep stairs, buffeted by unexpected gales and wobbling on the wooden steps of the escalators. We would hear strange primitive sounds: groans, sighs, blows. We would smell strong odours and not all pleasant (sawdust and damp, motor oil and fried onions, fake fur and real sweat). On the train itself, my tourist would think he'd been dropped into an electric blender. As he walked through endless corridors in the stations groping his way along the tiles with his hands, he'd think he had ended up in the restrooms of purgatory. When the blindfolds were finally removed, he'd find himself in a cavernous station full of echoes, blind corners and tunnels and he'd beg me, "Put the blindfold back on. I don't want to know".

The subway system in London is called the Underground. This is not only a fact, it is a threat, and at times a punishment. It's not something you take lightly. The Underground is a cross between a painting by Escher and a Sherlock Holmes mistery. It is deep, ancient and mysterious. It is filthy where it ought to be clean and it is clean where you would expect it to find it dirty. It is enormous and unpredictable. Ten years ago at King's Cross station, thirty people were killed in a fire, started by a lit cigarette butt and helped by the questionable wisdom of keeping wooden stairs in a labyrinth of tunnels. From time to time, announcements over the loudspeakers – level six of understanding English. If you can understand them, you are ready to take on the world – inform you that "service has been temporarily suspended". Londoners don't ask if there's been a breakdown, an alarm, a strike or a suicide. They simply turn on their heels, head out and re-emerge into the bright lights of London's streets, vaguely relieved.

Like many British institutions, the Underground provokes strong feelings in foreigners. Claustrophobics, neurotics and hygiene-freaks detest it and one can understand why. The English, however, respect it. They call it *the Tube* and love it the way you love an eccentric old aunt. The London underground is the oldest in the world. The first line, the Metropolitan, was opened in 1863, and it has continued to grow ever since. Today it has 408 kilometres of track, 11 lines, 273 stations, 467 trains and carries 735 million passengers a year.

But by being first, Londoners have paid a price. While Koreans have built rapid, efficient and safe new metro systems, the English have had to adapt, patch, resew, repaint and clean up what they have. Modern stations, like the futuristic Docklands Light Railway, are few and far between. Others are brilliant renovations, like Liverpool Street, and voluntary clean-ups, like Tottenham Court Road, but there are still worryingly large caverns like Covent Garden, Notting Hill Gate, Piccadilly Circus and Holborn.

Trains run from 5:30 am until midnight. London has been divided into six concentric zones. Zone 1 is defined by the Circle Line (the yellow one) that circles the centre of the city. You can either buy a ticket at the ticket booth, giving the name of your destination, or you can avoid standing in a queue by using one of the ticket machines at the entrance. Next, you feed your ticket into the ticket gate and it spits it back. Save it, as you'll need it to get out of the station at your destination. These ticket gates are imperfect inventions. Punks jump over them with impunity, but they often scare tourists because the gates seem to sense when a foreigner is coming through and humiliate them by maliciously closing on them.

In some stations, two different lines run on the same track. To get the right train, you have to look for your destination written on the front. Londoners, of course, know where they are going and will often run to catch their trains. A foreigner on holiday standing in the wrong place in the middle of a crossroads can get swept up by a surge of people. Salvation lies in the Tube map, officially called the Journey Planner. It might seem at first like the scribblings of a madman, but in fact it is a small masterpiece. It was designed in 1933 and the designers chose to ignore topography and actual distances for the sake of clarity. It hasn't changed since and now is part of the collective imagination of Londoners.

Each line on the Underground has a distinct

personality. The black Northern line is called the Misery Line, a reference to its rate of punctuality and level of comfort. The impeccable blue Piccadilly Line is the first one most visitors arriving from Heathrow travel on. The red Central line cutting horizontally across London, is the fastest and serves the City. The grey Jubilee line is new. The green District line brings in suburban passengers from the southwest (Putney, Richmond). The yellow Circle line is in a class of its own. Unlike the other lines it has no destination but as its name suggests, continuously circles the city. The Circle line has played host to parties (guests get on and off as they please), sordid love affairs, furtive sex, and long naps.

Like metros everywhere, all sorts of characters pass through the corridors of the London Tube. Watching people as they change lines, a documentary of urban life develops: sporty types with bicycles, loners with their walkmans, homeless people with shopping bags which they cherish like overnight cases; businessmen in pinstriped suits carrying attaché cases that show more wear than the shopping bags. Often you come across the remnants of earlier musical styles, from punk to rap. Talk to the musicians – many are Italian, behind the times as usual.

With few exceptions, the English don't talk to strangers to pass the time, they read. They read the huge advertisements on the walls of the platform (called cross-track ads). They read poetry that some unknown poet has written on the walls of the corridors and carriages and that London Transport has cruelly framed, killing it. They read cheap paperbacks, office memos, free newspapers given away at the entrance of the station. And regular newspapers.

The strong sales of daily newspapers can be explained by Underground habits. *The Evening Standard*, the only evening newspaper in London, was created for the Tube, spends its life on the Tube, and will die on the Tube. Having leafed through it, many Londoners leave it folded neatly on their seat. It is left like a flower as a homage to their comrades in arms.

(1996)

SIMPLE CITY

When you start reading that a city is the new centre of the universe, take care. Television and magazines are good at creating The Phenomenon of the Century – which usually lasts about one season. London, though, is different. The city has not become famous because of any event nor is it a product of fashion. London has worked hard to be the most interesting city on the plant. It has done its homework. Now, it's exam time and high marks are predicted.

Why London? Is it because it attracts so many intelligent and curious travellers? Or because there's so much to see and do and listen to and read? Maybe. But it's not all. London attracts visitors because it is multi-faceted, a city at once fragmented and homogeneous, revolutionary and traditional, exciting and relaxing (think of all the parks). London also attracts visitors because it is an easy city to visit. For Italians, the ease with which one can make a reservation, buy a ticket, and get around the city is impressive. The straightforwardness of a yes or no is reassuring. London is not far away, but somehow it seems distant, overseas – we still think in terms of the Channel, something no tunnel can change. It's a city that many of us, whether through work, study, or a holiday, have been to. And going back to a place where there is a mixture of déjà vu and surprises, has always been an ambition of travellers.

If I had to name a period when the city started its journey toward its present triumph, I would say the seventies. Back then, Britain was going through a particularly difficult period. The institutions (trade unions, police, local governments and universities) and infrastructure (roads, the Underground, industry, and public building) were irremediably aging. While the Germans and Japanese were building, the English were left to mend and prop up things they had been among the first to develop, a rather unrewarding and humiliating work. Then in 1979 Margaret Thatcher arrived and like a cyclone she began to tear down the old and build new foundations for the future. John Major put the finishing touches on this construction. And Tony Blair gets the honour of taking the city and the country into the new millennium.

This short history lesson is necessary to understand what is happening today. The political whirlwind of the eighties brought down the old London. Only then was it possible to build a new one. Museums were forced to take public taste into consideration; new businesses and restaurants opened. Entire sectors of the city were renovated. Architects were given a free hand. Even the idea of using the lottery to finance art projects shows a practical mind that avoids the rough edges of the Germans or the zeal of the Japanese.

Of course, this alone is not enough. Lausanne is also a well-organised and administered city but it is not London. What the English did was to add an element of fantasy to it which, when you think of it, has always been there. The city has undergone profound changes in recent years and yet has managed to reflect the spirit of the times. Around 1956, after a long post-war period, it was reborn. Those were the years of the underground youth culture, night clubs and Notting Hill. By 1966 the English capital was the youth, music and artistic capital of the world. *Time* magazine immortalised the moment, coining the phrase *Swinging London.* In 1976, a brusque change of style and mood gave birth to punk, which still influences fashions and behaviour today. In 1986, deep into the Thatcher years, yuppies entered the scene along with the myth of a city of businessmen. In 1996, it has all changed again.

Today's London has a new outlook, new hot spots and new fashions, more sophisticated, more conciliatory, but still innovative.

You won't find French artifice or American excess there. What you will find is a combination of ingenuity and simplicity, two qualities inherent every British product, from the Beatles to Norman Foster's architecture, from the dark work of Martin Amis to the sunny works of Nick Hornby, from Andrew Lloyd Webber's musicals to the creations of designers who may have learned their craft in Italy, but remained faithful to the street fashion that makes London a feast for the eyes (especially Italian eyes used to uniform elegance – thousands of women wearing the same shoes, thousands of kids carrying the same backpacks).

Ingenuity and simplicity, originality and accessibility. This is what London offers the world. And, it must be said, it has learned to sell itself. Why do foreigners flock to London's art exhibitions? Because the English know how to explain France to the French and Italy to Italians. Why, elbowed and sweating, do so many of us do battle with shops and museums, concerts and nightspots, restaurants and gardens? Because London, unlike New York, isn't scary. London, while it empties your pocket, reassures you and stimulates your mind.

(1997)

OPEN CITY

London is unique. No other city in the world is like it. Take Paris, its closest rival. Paris has the Arch de Triumph, London, a simple arch made of marble – Marble Arch. Paris has the Champs Elysees; London, Piccadilly Circus, a tribute to the work of lacemakers. One of Paris's great intersections is Etoile; London has a corner (Hyde Park Corner). Paris has the Parc du Champ de Mars next to the Eiffel Tower; London, a simple green park (Green Park) next to Buckingham Palace, and its tallest construction, the towers at Canary Wharf at two hundred and fifty metres, houses banks and offices. The gigantic Millennium Dome, strongly backed by the Labour government in power, is the exception to this list. Let's hope that no one repents of their decision.

It wasn't the British Empire who invented the word "grandeur". If grandeur existed, it was obvious. And we won't mince words: there was and there is. Don't let the understatement of the capital, a city of villages, deceive you. Yesterday's colonial expansion has today become cultural, artistic, musical, linguistic and political ability (think of all

Tony Blair's imitators abroad). The most popular woman on the planet, Princess Diana, was English – in passport, appearance and style. Her funeral was probably the greatest public event of the nineties.

This all goes to prove one thing. Britain's insularity is mainly a result of geography. The United Kingdom has never been truly isolated except during certain periods in history such as the Napoleonic wars or the second world war. Yet, this illusion of "British separateness" has been encouraged by magazines, comic strips and the British themselves, proud to see their distinctness confirmed, even when it doesn't exist, or rather, when this "separateness" is a normal part of the differences you find among any country in Europe, and is one of the things that makes Europe more fascinating than, say, the American Midwest.

Yet there is some truth here. The English are not European. They are ultra-European. Europe for them is not a drawing room but a spring board into the world. They still have empire in the blood. Not the empire of power and domination, but an empire of space. Britain is a country that suffers from claustrophobia. Evelyn Waugh wrote that "the English are half crazy and sometimes they are completely crazy, enough to leave England". Diffidence towards Europe is not so much fear of something too big but a fear of something too restricting (Brussels, rules, protectionism).

Forget Little Englanders, fearful of change. There seems to be a lot of them because they make a lot of noise (though less now than before) but they are in fact a minority: a few aristocrats, a slice of the lower-middle class, two hundred thousand hooligans on leave, a million old-age pensioners in love with their lawns. Everyone else, as Will Hutton writes in *The State We're In*, is preparing for the global market. The capital (London), capital (from the City), airports, workers from soldiers to consultants, culture, music, sport and language – all these are already international. In comparison, the rest of Europe is a quiet backwater.

Are you reading this in London? Walk around and think about the city. Look at the faces of the people, the same ones you saw at Diana's funeral. They come in every race and colour. Once Britain travelled the world. Now the world travels to Britain. And it is welcomed. Not just the tourist, either. In matters of immigration, the British government has not shown the same rush of generosity that we Italians have, but neither have they shown our slap-dash approach. London and other British cities also have their problems with racism. But in few other European countries today are immigrants as well-integrated into society as they are in Britain.

Raise your eyes and look at the temple-like banks in the City or the offices of the large insurance companies. Are you still convinced the English aren't good businessmen? Don't listen to their declarations of love for the pound. The English are not romantics. If the euro works, they will abandon their national currency and jump ship in a flash. What we are witnessing is prudence: the English are simply doing their sums (the best debates about monetary union have come from Britain; the best forecasts have been British).

Take a walk through the West End, go into a music store, buy a copy of the weekly *Time Out*, and go to a concert. For the last forty years the English have been making their pop and rock music an export product. Go to a restaurant. You'll find food from every corner of the world; some of it, starting out in London, has gone on to conquer the West. Buy a book. The authors have faces of every colour. Go to a cinema and see what's showing. Many of the films are American but the English can meet the competition (think of *The Full Monty*). Go to the theatre. Stand in the stalls of the new Globe theatre, a homage to Shakespeare, and ask yourself, was he an English isolationist or a European who set his tragedies in Italy and Denmark and every so often wrote a scene in French?

Look at the traffic in the streets, the telephone boxes, the trains in the stations, and the entrances to museums. They are symbols of a superiority that we tend to forget. The British invented modern privatisation (making a few mistakes along the way as was inevitable). They were the first to open their markets (think about cars – they allowed famous manufacturers with historic roots to be sold to the Japanese and the Germans). A country obsessed with its heritage that risked turning itself into an open air museum was able to transform itself into a dynamic nation where the market may not be god, but it does exist and it does matter. Its museums, symphony orchestras, gentlemen's clubs and universities have been forced to earn their keep to survive, opening their doors to the world and to a changing society.

The British are even beginning to grow tired of the class system that we foreigners find so amusing, but which makes life so difficult and occasionally humiliating for four-fifths of the population. In the past, opponents of this state of affairs protested, but a baleful look – an upper class look, of course – was enough to shut them up. Lately, though, people have stopped protesting. Tony Blair has taught them that the best way to get rid of certain attitudes is simply to ignore them. The lesson of Diana, dead or alive, is also clear: the age of deference is coming to an end. From now on, the ruling class of Britain, from the royal family on down, must be worthy of its privilege, honour and respect. The right accent and the right shoes are no longer enough.

Stay in London. Listen to the language the people speak. The British – fools – still call it the English language but today it is more of a universal code to receive and transmit information. English is no longer theirs alone. They have leased it to the world and are getting a good return back. Everything they produce – a display or a scientific discovery, a film, a book, a newspaper, or an opinion – is immediately available for sale, exportable, consumable on any street corner in the world. Take *The Economist.* It is produced in London, but bought and read in one hundred and seventy countries. The fact that it doesn't have a huge domestic market works to its advantage. *The Economist* has been forced to become international. *Time* and *Newsweek* have only chosen to do so.

It will be interesting to see what the British do with the success they found after the turbulence of the seventies, the necessary tearing down of the eighties and the rebuilding of the nineties, which has made London the centre of the world again. People who believe the British are anti-Europe will have made up their minds already. They believe the country's success will be handed over to the Americans, waiting with sweet transatlantic endearments. Others however, realise that the British have a fundamental task: to open the windows of Europe's house so we can all breathe some fresh air and see outside. Perhaps I delude myself but I think that they will accomplish it.

(1998)

MAD CITY

Ladbroke Road cuts through Ladbroke Grove. It's a part of Notting Hill that was there even before the film. In the mid-eighties I lived in this neighbourhood and often ate lunch at a pub called the Ladbroke Arms (you can't say the English are creative with names). Going back, reliving experiences is something forty-year-olds do. That's why I'm here. I carry a pint of bitter (Directors) and a packet of crisps (Salt & Vinegar flavour) to the first table by the window – it used to be mine, and who knows how many others – I pick up a coaster, draw a line and begin to write. On one side go the things that have changed in London. On the other the things that are still the same.

Here's what's the same. The comforting reassurance of a pub; the beer (not too cold, not too warm); the street lights; the English pound; people who spend their pounds on beer in a pub staring at the street lights. It doesn't matter how modern they are, how many clubs they've been to, how well they dress, how much better they eat, how much they have travelled. Londoners are like actors who find security in the wings of the theatre before a performance. People have not given up this existential backstage in the city. Others things they have.

They have virtually given up using a car during the day, for one. Once they would say "London traffic is crazy". It's not true. Actually, it demonstrates a certain dark logic. The average speed in the city is now 4 miles/6.5 km an hour and falling. There are moments in which London resembles Karachi on a bad day. Private cars are as slow-flowing as lava, impeded by ridiculous rickshaw-like tricycles pedaled by muscular students. Messengers on bikes dart between cars. The privatised buses file along like camels on parade in their designated lanes. Twenty-four thousand black cabs compete for customers with forty thousand unlicensed minicabs. In the streets in the centre there are often traffic jams made up solely of taxis: an immense funeral cortege you never see in Milan, if for no other reason than a shortage of taxis. In some places – for example, between Pall Mall and Trafalgar Square – it's hard just to walk. Road work obstructs the street and blocks the sidewalks. Vans, taxis, cars, bikes, bicycles and pedestrians are all competing for the same space, with a contained fury.

Some would say it's inevitable. A quarter of the British population lives in London and the southeast, one-twelfth of the nation's territory. In short, a full house. While Manchester in the last twenty years has lost 15% of its inhabitants, the population of the capital has grown by 8%. Forty years ago 60% of the big British companies were based in London. Today it's 90%. That's why in London – even though it has a rail-tube link that Rome can only dream about – the average commute to work takes fifty-six minutes. If the price of cars continues to drop, by 2015 it might take as long as an hour and forty minutes (note the preciseness of this pessimism. Only the Americans do it better). Attempts to widen the streets have proven to be useless. The M25 which circles London was no sooner widened than traffic increased proportionately, and clogged it again. Some observers have suggested moving the capital north, to the Yorkshire Moors, something

The Economist proposed forty years ago. They even gave the new city a name: Elizabetha. But this Brasilia without Brazilians or sun is merely an intellectual exercise. Instead what you get is the plan that Ken Livingstone, the mayor – a clever populist – has bet the city's and to some extent his own future on. He is introducing a congestion charge. Anyone entering London beginning on Monday the 17th of February will have to pay 5 pounds/8 euros. Too much, say the drivers. Very little, maintain the experts, who argue that the amount will not be a deterrent. Seven hundred television cameras will record the number plates of commuters to the City, and their accounts will be charged accordingly. We hope they will also show shots of the streets just outside the charging zone, because they promise to be a circus.

The traffic is not the only symptom of the interesting madness of London. There are others. We'll take for granted its complexity (money comes from the central government while projects are dependent on the thirty-two boroughs. Ken the Red is caught in the middle). We'll overlook its violence (you are four times more likely to be attacked in London as in New York). We'll put a veil over public order (the London Metropolitan Police have been rated fortieth out of the forty-two police forces in the United Kingdom). We'll ignore its dwindling prosperity (the city's economy, greater than that of several European countries is at the edge of a recession. From 1993 to 2001 forty-five thousand jobs a year were created. Since then they have lost twenty thousand). Let's talk prices.

We'll start at the beginning. The pound is roughly equivalent to the euro, but the Bank of England has apparently not been informed. Therefore, for those who arrive from other parts of Europe, prices seem obscene. The flat in Notting Hill that I was on the point of buying in 1986 for one hundred forty thousand pounds is now worth a million (a million and a half euros). The wall-eyed estate agent says "Yes, but there's a garden". To inhale "the muskier odours of a sardine-packed train" (*The Economist*, 11 January 2003) costs a minimum of £1.30 (2 euros). On the bus, where the odours are not markedly different but the view is better, a short hop will cost you £1 (1.5 euros) and you can't even get a transfer. As far as shopping in London goes, it's dead. Foreigners can't afford it any more. All we can do is press our nose to the windows, like children in a Dickens novel. In Covent Gardens – phony and excessive – tourist groups are confronted by squads of souvenir hawkers. Around Jermyn Street, pubescent salesmen, uninformed about the products they push, offer what's left of British tradition. Once, the Japanese, at least, fell for it. Now even they are smarter (and poorer).

I don't have the heart to return to the Greek restaurant where at twenty-eight I would have supper in the company of my projects and half a bottle of retsina . It was called Savvas's Kebab House at the top of Ladbroke Road and it was run by a Greek Cypriot who looked like a cousin of Ulysses. Now it's called Aurum, it has long snowy white table-cloths and I don't trust it. Instead I invite a friend to a Lebanese restaurant in Westbourne Grove, a place not many tourists know about. Between the two of us, we spend £70 (more than 100 euros) without wine. At Portobello Road, the same old catatonic salesmen sit perched on the same old stools inside the same old cubicles and demand scandalous prices. If you protest, they give you the offended look of a stuffed owl. Even at the Reform Club where I've been a member since 1986 and talk football with the doorman from Newcastle, there are surprises. I order tea for 8 am and they bring me coffee at seven. I bump into a tipsy American who struggles with the lift (a little tonic, a lot of gin, and a leather armchair are tremendous transatlantic temptations). I discover that the average price for a monastic little room (no bathroom, a sink with rigorously separate taps) is now £60 (90 euros) a night. It's not too much to suffer in style. But it's a lot.

Does it bother me that London is becoming a Mad City? No, of course not. Fifty years ago this strangeness was labeled eccentric and it amused Pierre Daninos (*Les Carnets du Major Thompson*) who, mind you, didn't have to go to a restaurant that looked like a pharmacy and a pharmacy that looked like a grocers shop and a grocers shop that looked like a supermarket. Today, that's the way it is in London. If it seems less eccentric, it's because everything is unexpected and changeable. Manners, places, language, business, dress. There are few rules in the city and this makes life more difficult than it was back in the days when everything was (or seemed to be) regulated. Because of a suitcase packed in too much of a hurry, I arrive at an elegant dinner wearing brown suede shoes. The hostess notices and says "Oh. Brown suede shoes. Even Ken Clarke's wearing them!". Clarke was a brilliant former Conservative minister and the author of a diary which in Elizabethan days would have put him in the tower. I listen and smile. I suspect that in my error I've done the right thing. In spite of myself.

In the late nineties, this marvelous confusion

was given a name: Cool Britannia. Has the novelty worn off? It seems so. The one party-city has become a one style-city, and the fault is not Tony Blair's. My impression is that London is full of new ideas that are on the verge of becoming old. What in 1999 was exciting suddenly seems predictable. The fake French brasseries and the Foster-like constructions, the almost-Rogers buildings and the Millennium Dome, Bibendum and the Conran Shop, all the types like Branson and the girls like Bridget, the minimalism of the white tableclothes and the little black dresses are becoming a bit passé now, stuff for foreign tourists. "Cool Britannia" is warming up.

And yet I'm sure that somewhere, in places I don't know about, London, mad city, is playing with new ideas, creating a new esthetic, inventing new music, perhaps planting the seed for a new political party. That's why thirty years after the first bed-sit, twenty years after the first article, ten years after walking into the Economist for the first time, I'm still here trying to understand it. That's okay. Cities that you love, are like people you care about. If they don't retain a little mystery, it's no good.

(2003)

ACKNOWLEDGEMENTS

I wish to thank Indro Montanelli who sent me to London and brought me back in time; notaio Angelo Severgnini and signora Carla, who didn't complain; and my British friends, tortured for years by my questions and observations. Among them, Melanie Davis (with David Wilson), Peter Grimsdale and Stephanie Calman, Ros Barker, Caroline Stacey (with Richard Beswick), Gabriel Irvin and Liz Bunster from Tufnell Park, Nick Sayers (who believed in *Inglesi*), Claudia Zeff, Kate Blaker from Rudloe Road, Charles Hodgson, Nicky Fox, Ronnie and Cynthia Payne, Gaby Franklin, Max and Stella Taylor, Jim Murdoch, Sebastian O' Kelly, John Lloyd, Catherine and Edward Rossdale. Thanks, of course, to both my translators: Paola Pugsley and Kerry Milis.

Thanks to all my friends at *The Economist*: Daniel Franklin, Xan Smiley, Johnny Grimond, John Parker, Emma Duncan. And to my editors there: Rupert Pennant-Rea and Bill Emmott.

Thanks also to those fellow Italians who helped me to dissect the British: in particular Michele Calcaterra with Francesca, Mino Vignolo with Silvana. And to the following colleagues: Gianni Biazzi Vergani, Sandra Artom, Deda Fezzi Price, Michele Sarcina, Alfredo Pallavisini, Paolo Filo della Torre, Mario Ciriello, Luigi Forni, Carlo Cavicchioli.

I would also like to thank the experts Mauro Tonghini, Giles Watson, Fredrick Schwartz (with Emmanuelle). Some anglophiles, among them Lino Mannocci, Anne Applebaum, Radek Sikorski, Sandro Vaciago, Libby Savill, Massimo e Anna Crovetto, Silvio Marchetti, Ralf Dahrendorf and Gianfranco Zola (both talented players). At least three British Ambassadors to Italy, who put up with me (Patrick Fairweather, Tom Richardson, John Sheperd). And my friends from the British Council: Helena Kennedy, Sharon Memis, Julia Race, Angela Oak-Ashes, Les Dangerfield, Lucia Legnazzi.

My gratitude also goes to some anglophobes, whom I will not name, punished by having the luck of living in London. To the Reform Club, splendid front rows seat on Britain (old and new). And to Mrs Margaret Hilda Thatcher née Roberts, thanks to whom for four years I didn't have the time to be bored for a minute.

(1984-2003)

CONTENTS

ABOUT THE AUTHOR

Beppe Severgnini is a writer and a columnist for *Corriere della Sera*, Italy's leading newspaper. Since 1998, he has moderated Italians (www.corriere.it/severgnini), a popular online forum. He was Italy's correspondent for *The Economist* from 1996 to 2003. In 2004, he was voted «European Journalist of the Year» (www.ev50.com) in Brussels. Since 2007, his articles are syndicated (New York Times Syndicate).

Severgnini's books, all published by Rizzoli, are bestsellers. He has written three «portraits of a nation»: *Inglesi* (1990), *Un italiano in America* (1995) and *La testa degli italiani* (2005); two books about language: *L'inglese. Lezioni semiserie* (1992) and *L'italiano. Lezioni semiserie* (2007); two travel books: *Italiani con valigia* (1993), and *Manuale dell'imperfetto viaggiatore* (2000). He has also written an autobiography he is particularly fond of, *Italiani si diventa* (1998).

Un italiano in America, published under the title *Ciao, America!* (Doubleday 2002), has become a National Bestseller in the USA. *La testa degli italiani*, published as *La Bella Figura* (Doubleday 2006), has been a New York Times Bestseller and is now translated in eight languages.

A soccer expert and fan, Beppe has been writing since 2001 for *La Gazzetta dello Sport*, Italy's leading sport newspaper, and he is the author of a triple declaration of love for his favourite soccer team, Inter: *Interismi* (2002), *Altri interi-*

smi (2003) and *Tripli interismi!* (2007). A collection of all three volumes has been published under the title *Il manuale del perfetto interista* (2007).

Severgnini has written and presented the television programmes *Italians, cioè italiani* (RaiTre, 1997) and *Luoghi Comuni. Un viaggio in Italia* (RaiTre 2001 and 2002). Since 2004 he has been working with Sky Tg24, writing and presenting interview and comment programmes (*Severgnini alle 10, Zona Severgnini, America 2008*). During the 2006 FIFA World Cup, he produced a travel programme across Germany (Sky Sport). Since 2007 he works for RadioMontecarlo.

Beppe was born on 26 December 1956 at Crema, in the province of Cremona, where completed his secondary education, graduating with a classics-oriented school-leaving certificate. He obtained his degree in international law at Pavia, after a training period at the European Community in Brussels. He was London correspondent for Indro Montanelli's *il Giornale* (1984-1988), subsequently becoming special correspondent in Eastern Europe, Russia and China (1988-1992). After a year at *The Economist* in London (1993) he became Washington correspondent for *la Voce* (1993-1995).

Severgnini has taught at Middlebury College Vermont (2006) and at Italian universities in Milan (Bocconi University, 2003 and 2006), Parma (1998) and Pavia (2002); the latter had elected him «Alumnus of the Year» for 1998. He has also lectured at many universities abroad.

In 2001, Beppe Severgnini was made an Officer of the British Empire (OBE) by HRH Queen Elizabeth II.

Since 2008, he is Chairman (Hon.) of Inter Club Kabul.

He is married to Ortensia and they have a son, Antonio.

RCS Libri

ISBN 978-88-17-10043-4